ANCIENT EGYPTIAN FURNITURE

ANCIENT EGYPTIAN FURNITURE
VOLUME III

RAMESSIDE FURNITURE

GEOFFREY KILLEN

 OXBOW | books
Oxford & Philadelphia

Published in the United Kingdom in 2017 by
OXBOW BOOKS
The Old Music Hall, 106–108 Cowley Road, Oxford OX4 1JE

and in the United States by
OXBOW BOOKS
1950 Lawrence Road, Havertown, PA 19083

© Oxbow Books and Geoffrey Killen 2017

Hardcover Edition: ISBN 978-1-78570-489-5
Digital Edition: ISBN 978-1-78570-490-1

A CIP record for this book is available from the British Library

Library of Congress Control Number: 2016961071

Printed in Malta by Gutenberg Press Ltd

For a complete list of Oxbow titles, please contact:

UNITED KINGDOM
Oxbow Books
Telephone (01865) 241249, Fax (01865) 794449
Email: oxbow@oxbowbooks.com
www.oxbowbooks.com

UNITED STATES OF AMERICA
Oxbow Books
Telephone (800) 791-9354, Fax (610) 853-9146
Email: queries@casemateacademic.com
www.casemateacademic.com/oxbow

Oxbow Books is part of the Casemate Group

Front cover: Carpenters building a catafalque. Facsimile of a painted wall scene from the tomb of Ipuy, TT 217, 19th Dynasty, Deir el-Medina. Painted by Norman de Garis Davies (1865-1941). Photograph courtesy of the Metropolitan Museum of Art, Rogers Fund (30.4.116).

All internal figures drawn by the author, unless otherwise stated.

Contents

To my wife Lorraine, and children Sarah, Karen and Caroline and my grandchildren, Ben, Emma, Sophie, Hannah, James, Olivia, Jack and Noah for their patience and the encouragement they have shown during the years this work has taken to materialise.

List of Figures

All the figures were drawn for this book by the Author. Where appropriate they are scaled in millimetres.

List of Plates

Acknowledgements

Firstly, I would like to thank Dr Ian Shaw for his encouragement throughout the preparation of this work; his suggestions regarding its content and presentation have been much appreciated. He must also be thanked for suggesting to Lara Weiss that we should publish a paper that surveyed a small corpus of "furniture ostraca" of Ramesside context that had been discovered at Deir el-Medina. Also, I wish to thank Dr Steven Snape who provided me with advice and allowed access to the Garstang Museum. I am also indebted to Pat Winker who tirelessly provided information regarding the rich collections and archives preserved in the Garstang Museum.

I am indebted to all the museums and curators who have provided information, photographs, research facilities and access to collections much of which were in storage. At the British Museum, I sincerely thank Vivian Davies and Dr Neal Spencer, Keepers, Department of Ancient Egypt and Sudan. They consistently helped with the research undertaken at the museum. Also, I am especially grateful to Dr Neal Spencer, for allowing me access to the database of finds at Amara West.

Professor Stephen Quirke must be thanked for providing access to the Gurob material preserved in the Petrie Museum of Egyptian Archaeology. I also acknowledge the assistance I have received from his colleagues Tonya Nelson and Tracey Golding. I am also indebted to once curator Karen Exell and Dr Campbell Price curator, Egypt and Sudan, of the Manchester Museum, in allowing research facilities at the museum to study the Gurob material that is preserved in that museum.

In Cambridge I am grateful to Sally-Ann Ashton, Senior Assistant Keeper, Fitzwilliam Museum, for providing access to the collections. At the Museum of Archaeology and Anthropology, University of Cambridge. I also wish to express my thanks to Anne Taylor, Curatorial Assistant for Archaeology, in providing access and information regarding the university's collections.

In Oxford, Dr Jaromir Malek and Dr Liam McNamara, Keepers of the Griffith Institute Archive, continued to support my research providing both access to the institute's archives and answering detailed questions regarding Howard Carter's and Walter Segal's papers. I also wish to thank Helen Whitehouse, Curator, Egyptian Collections, Department of Antiquities at the Ashmolean Museum and Dr Michael O'Hanlon, Director of the Pitt Rivers Museum in providing access to these collections.

I must thank Patricia Spencer, Director at the Egypt Exploration Society for information regarding previous work undertaken at Amara West by the EES and Sarah Durant, Research Fellow, Institute of Zoology, Zoological Society of London, for providing information relating to the gross morphology of the cheetah.

I am also sincerely grateful to the following people, who have provided information and given permission to publish photographs in this work:

Dr Ashley Cooke, Head of Antiquities, World Museum, Liverpool; Dr Carolyn Graves-Brown, Curator, Egypt Centre, University of Wales Swansea; Wayne Modest, once, Keeper of Anthropology, Horniman Collection; Bryn Hyacinth, Museum Officer, The Cuming Museum; Carolyn Leder, Curator of the Old Speech Room Gallery, Harrow School; Helen Armstrong, Collections Manager of University Museums, Oriental Museum, University of Durham; Adam Jaffer and Phil Watson, Birmingham Museum and Art Gallery; Morag Clement, Curator, Kendal Museum; Thomas Cadbury, Curator of Antiquities, Royal Albert Memorial Museum, Exeter; Caroline McDonald, Curator of Archaeology (Ipswich), Colchester & Ipswich Museum Service; Lucy Creighton, Curatorial Assistant – Archaeology, Weston Park Museum, Sheffield and Simon Eccles, Senior Curator, The Burrell Collection, Glasgow Museums.

From European museums, collections and university departments I express my thanks to Dr Ben Haring, Lecturer at Leiden University; Dr R.J. Demarée, Affiliated fellow at Leiden University; Dr Maarten Raven, Curator Egyptian Department, National Museum of Antiquities, Leiden; Dr Luc Limme, Keeper of Egyptian Antiquities, Musees Royaux d'Art et d'Histoire, Brussels; Maria Guidotti, Director of Museo Egizio in Florence; Dr Eleni Vassilika, Director of the Museo Egizio in Turin;

Dr Olivia Zorn, Curator, Staatliche Museen zu Berlin – Ägyptisches Museum und Papyrussammlung; Prof. Wildung, Director Naga Project, Staatliche Museen zu Berlin – Ägyptisches Museum und Papyrussammlung; Dr Barbara Magen, Wissenschaftliche Mitarbeiterin, Ägypten-Sammlung, Roemer- und Pelizaeus-Museum Hildesheim; Luis Manuel Gonzálvez, Curator, and Emma González, Egyptian Museum of Barcelona and Gisèle Piérini of the Musée d'Archéologie Méditerranéenne, Marseille. I would also like to thank James D. Beebe who kindly catalogued the furniture preserved in the Field Museum, Chicago.

I am also grateful to Rakesh Chholak, Superintendent, Government Central Museum, Jaipur, and his colleague Dwarka Prasad Gupta, for providing information of a box preserved in this Indian collection. While at the Metropolitan Museum of Art, New York, I wish to thank Dr Catharine Roehrig for her continued support.

I wish to thank my friends who have provided support and encouragement during the research and writing stages of this work. I can't express in words my gratitude to my friend Elizabeth Simpson and once colleague and friend Trevor Porter who has followed this work from conception through to its delivery as a completed manuscript.

I would like to thank my family, my wife Lorraine, and children Sarah, Karen and Caroline and my grandchildren, Ben, Emma, Sophie, Hannah, James, Olivia, Jack and Noah for their patience and the encouragement they have shown during the six years this work has taken to materialise. Finally, I would like to thank Clare Litt, publishing director, and Hannah McAdams, production editor, and the team at Oxbow books who have been instrumental in publishing this third volume.

Geoffrey P. Killen
9th May 2016
St. Ives, Huntingdon.

Abbreviations and Sigla

ASAE Annales du Service des Antiquités de l'Egypte.

BMP British Museum Press.

BSAE British School of Archaeology in Egypt.

CUP Cambridge University Press.

EEF Egypt Exploration Fund.

GM Göttinger Miszellen.

IFAO Institut Français d'Archéologie Orientale.

JEA Journal of Egyptian Archaeology.

JTTHS Journal of the Tool and Trades History Society.

KPI Kegan Paul International.

LÄ Lexikon der Ägyptologie.

OUP Oxford University Press.

RdE Revue d'Egyptologie.

SAE Service des Antiquités de l'Egypte, Cairo.

SARS Sudan Archaeological Research Society.

TATHS Tool and Trades History Society.

ZÄS Zeitschrift für Ägyptische Sprache und Altertumskunde, Leipzig and Berlin.

Theban Tomb Numbers

TT Private Tomb numbers in Western Thebes.

Museum and Society Inventory Abbreviations

ÄM Staatliche Museen zu Berlin, Ägyptisches Museum.

BSI British Standards Institution.

EA Department of Ancient Egypt and Sudan, British Museum.

EES Egypt Exploration Society.

JE Journal de Entrée, Egyptian Museum, Cairo.

MM Medelhavsmuseet, Stockholm, Sweden.

MMA Metropolitan Museum of Art, New York.

UC Petrie Museum of Egyptian Archaeology, University College London.

Sigla

§ Section Sign.

Museum Catalogue Abbreviations

h height.

w width.

l length.

t thickness.

d depth.

dia diameter.

B.H. Beni Hasan.
Badarian Period (5500–4000 B.C.)

EDP Early Dynastic Period (3100–2686 B.C)

OK Old Kingdom (2686–2181 B.C.)

FIP First Intermediate Period (2181–2055 B.C.)

MK Middle Kingdom (2055–1650 B.C.)

SIP Second Intermediate Period (1650–1550 B.C.)

NK New Kingdom (1550–1069 B.C.)

TIP Third Intermediate Period (1069–747 B.C.)

LP Late Period (747–332 B.C.)

PP Ptolemaic Period (332–30 B.C.)

RP Roman Period (30 B.C.–395 A.D.)

Coptic 395A.D.–c.641 A.D.

Meroitic Butana region of Sudan (c.300 B.C.–350 A.D.)

B.C. Before Christ.

A.D. Anno Domini.

Cem. Cemetery.

V.I. Plates and Figures found in Volume I (Killen 1980; Killen 2017A).

V.II. Plates and Figures found in Volume II (Killen 1994; Killen 2017B).

V.III. Plates and Figures found in Volume III (Killen 2017C).

Photographic and Illustration Abbreviations

Burton	Burton Photographic Archive in the Griffith Institute, Oxford.
G.I.P	Griffith Institute Photographs, Oxford.
ORINST	The Oriental Institute of the University of Chicago. Photographs taken during the 1905–1907 Breasted Expeditions to Egypt and the Sudan.
Schott	Schott Photographic Archive in the Griffith Institute, Oxford.
Spie	Spiegelberg Squeezes in the Griffith Institute, Oxford.
T (Number)	Metropolitan Museum of Art Negative Number (Loan copy in Griffith Institute, Oxford).
Wilkinson MSS	Wilkinson MSS in the Bodleian Library, Oxford.
Hay MSS	Hay MSS in the British Library, London.

Tomb Abbreviations

(ur)	upper register.
(lr)	lower register.
(mr)	middle register.
♀	Female occupant.
♂	Male occupant.
NR	Illustrations of furniture not recorded in published material or not present in tomb. Tomb could also be inaccessible or in poor state of preservation.

Chapter 1

Deir el-Medina – A Community of Entrepreneurs?

The Textual Evidence

Deir el-Medina was a remarkable community of craftsmen who together with a small number of state administrators dedicated their lives to hewing stone, plastering and decorating the royal rock cut tombs of the New Kingdom at Thebes. These highly skilled artisans lived with their families in a community, which numbered one hundred or more individuals; in an isolated valley on the western bank of the river Nile close to the tomb complexes they had dedicated their lives to build (Černý 1973).

The archaeological data used to support this chapter comes from textual and non-textual ostraca discovered at Deir el-Medina and artefacts that display similar design characteristics that have been excavated at Deir el-Medina and other Egyptian towns. Together this material provides a detailed record of those wooden products used in people's daily lives. The community at Deir el-Medina were favoured and rewarded by the state, being provided with both provisions and water (McDowell 1999). The value of the whole textual account allows us to obtain the data that enables us to see how the community worked together and where a small group of carpenters collaborated with others to supplement their income by taking private commissions working in wood to manufacture funerary goods and domestic furniture.

Those workmen who toiled to build the royal tombs were a select group of artisans whose efforts were recognised by the state and who were paid a salary of approximately 5½ sacks of grain a month (Janssen 1975: 455–493). However, from the construction, decoration and the procurement of funerary goods deposited in the family tombs at Deir el-Medina it is clear that an individual or even family group from this community could not have afforded the expense of preparing for the afterlife on the state's grain ration alone. Also an internal market within the community based on the economic power of state grain could not have produced the

apparent material wealth these workmen enjoyed. In the building of their tombs and the furnishing of their homes we witness the acquired and impressive material culture of a group of workers who were related neither to the royal family nor to the nobility of Thebes.

The family homes of craftsmen would have been simply furnished and this is shown from an inventory record, on the recto of O. Cairo CG 25670, which lists the contents of an individual craftsman's house.[1] The house contained a significant number of pieces of wooden furniture including two beds, four folding stools, two footstools and several boxes. Also recorded were two pieces of sawn timber and a further two trunks of timber. The anonymous writer, on the verso, notes that some of these items are in the care of *Pȝ-šd* and *Šri.t-Rꜥ*, however, he is concerned about his house and organises *ꜣImn-m-wiȝ* (Amenemwia) to manage the property and protect it.

The seconding of carpenters to other settlements from Deir el-Medina, indicates a degree of workforce mobility, and is recorded on O. DeM 0418.[2] In this document the carpenter (Maanakhtef) writes to his counterpart *Qn-ḥr-ḫpš=f* (Qeniherkhepshef) that he has safely arrived in Hiw, and is being well treated, although he requires not only a wooden door but also his cubit rod to be sent to him by return.[3]

The state employed the Deir el-Medina workmen to labour in one of two gangs of tomb workers to fashion from rock the tombs of their kings (Černý 1973: 101). Although this was their prime function, there appears to be an understanding that the same craftsmen could work collectively and use their skills to manufacture funerary and domestic goods for the middle class (McDowell 1999: 80–81). This enabled the Deir el-Medina workmen themselves to acquire the raw materials to build an acceptable lifestyle as well as to prepare and construct their own family tombs (McDowell 1999: 68). It also provided the ruling class with a mechanism that allowed the middle class to furnish their tombs without the involvement of those craftsmen who worked exclusively for the royal family within the confines of the temple and palace precincts. Yet, those craftsmen of Deir el-Medina could base their furniture designs on the material they had seen being deposited in the royal tombs, although naturally often using inferior materials and methods of embellishment.[4]

Timber Acquisition

The acquisition of wood may have been possible through the procurement of redundant wooden scaffolding used during the preparation of the royal tombs on which they toiled.[5] Another possible method of obtaining wood could have been through the delivery of wood to the village by those called the *šᶜd-ḫt*, whose function was to provide the inhabitants of the village with those services and goods, including wood, which allowed the community to function in this isolated valley. Janssen interprets the role of the *šᶜd-ḫt* as providing the firewood and dung for the village's inhabitants and rejects that they "brought carpenter's wood to the workman" (Janssen *et al.*, 2003: 2). However, even if the wood delivered to the village was of poor quality there is a strong possibility that in the sorting of wood some could have been selected and used in furniture production. Indeed, there is an argument to suggest that some of the smaller personal items of furniture manufactured, including cosmetic and trinket boxes that are made from a patchwork of wooden pieces were made from wood of inferior quality.

Official and Semi-official Carpenters

Fifty-three workmen's tombs have been discovered at Deir el-Medina but only tomb TT361, is that of a carpenter, named Huy; who officially had received the state title "Great Carpenter in the Place of Truth". However, several records show that ordinary workmen also took unofficial carpentry titles when working on private commissions. *Mȝȝ.n=i-nḫt=f* (Maanakhtef) describes himself as "Chief Carpenter of the Lord of the Two Lands" in the opening lines of P. DeM 09,[6] however, in the gang he would have been a normal workman. How these elevated titles were taken or given is uncertain but they must have received semi-official backing from the state as they were linked with the king's position as the ruler of both Upper and Lower Egypt. It may have suited the administration to have a regimented work structure for state projects, where each individual's role could not create the possibility of damaging demarcation disputes. But allowing these talented individuals to work outside the formal state structure on private commissions would provide many of the community's members with the prestige their work deserved.

One method employed by high-ranking officials in commissioning furniture was to give permission for certain workmen to be released from their gang to undertake private carpentry projects. O. Glasgow D.1925.68 suggests that the procedure was officially sanctioned, possibly by the vizier, allowing carpenters to work on a special assignment making beds and boxes.[7] This ostracon amplifies the special significance in the manner in which these men were addressed. On the recto of O. Glasgow D. 1925.68 they are referred to as workmen, working still under the conditions of service determined by the state, while on the verso, they are described as carpenters seen by themselves and others performing a different role. For this particular record we have no evidence as to whether these carpenters were paid for their work. As it was undertaken during the time they had been released from the gang, the work was possibly undertaken as part of their state duties. Naturally, this arrangement would not have been financially beneficial but may have acted as a good marketing tool for other private commissions.

Funerary material required for lower profile commissions appears to have been organised through a scribe, who would bring together a team of craftsmen to undertake the commission. This system of manufacture has been termed the *Informal Workshop* by Cooney (Cooney 2006: 43–56). Each commission would be recorded through a workshop record leading to a receipt that listed the method of payment for the commission. Some receipts also illustrate multiple methods of completing a transaction. Also seen are private letters between the craftsmen involved in the commission, discussing the progress of work and work plans for its completion. Naturally, there were also legal documents to help settle disputes between the parties involved (Cooney 2006: 44–45). One would imagine this structure to be a complex method of delivery, however, Cooney believes it to have been an effective process in regulating the funerary goods output and provided a degree of entrepreneurship within the community (Cooney 2006: 55).

However, how informal was this *Informal Workshop*? The state retained power over the use of those tools used by carpenters. Copper was used as the unit of value to determine the cost of exchanged goods and the weight of a copper *deben* figures in those records issued against the woodwork being manufactured. Therefore, those tools issued to carpenters held a significant exchange value. In O. EA 5631 we see the difficulty experienced by one inhabitant of the village when treasury officials came to reclaim a large set of copper tools.[8] The cache included 50 large copper chisels and 25 copper adzes; his grandfather had apparently hid these tools in pits within in the family home. Although the tools had been registered to his grandfather they were the property of the state. Rather than disposing of them privately for personal gain, his grandson, who had become implicated in this matter, accepted the state's legal ownership of the tools and handed the cache over to the overseer of the treasury, who then released the family's servants (who were being held as collateral).

This clearly indicates that private commissions could

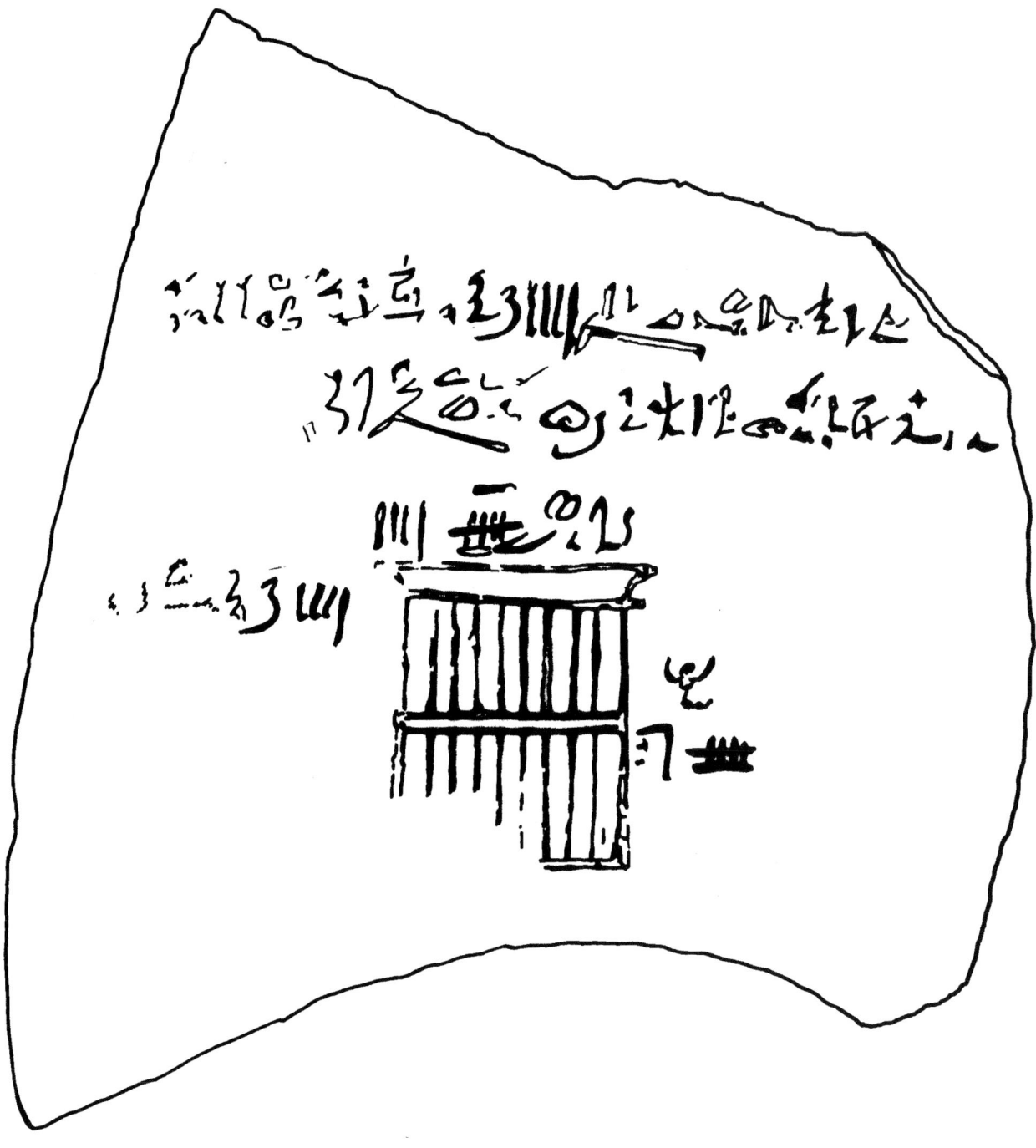

Figure 1. O. Louvre E. 23554.

only be undertaken knowing that the tools were registered to recognised and respected individuals of the village who used them through the patronage of the state. Indeed, when lending tools, carpenters were careful to record the action taken. This is seen in O. Michaelides 006, where a short memorandum records an axe being lent to *Qs* (Qes) for a period of time to manufacture a wooden object for *Mnnꜣ* (Menna).[9]

Therefore, the *Informal Workshop* must be seen as a semi-professional state recognised organisation that was integral to the community's ability to undertake private commissions. It is also likely that those who managed the *Informal Workshop* chose the magistrates and witnesses of the *knb.t*-court or prepared hearings before the oracle. The *Informal Workshop* could not work outside the clearly defined structures of the community imposed by the state.

Nevertheless, accepting that the state was formally involved in the *Informal Workshop*, we can establish from surviving ostraca an account of how wooden funerary goods, architectural elements and furniture were manufactured through the private commissioning service offered by the craftsmen of Deir el-Medina. It would be the community's scribes who would organise the private commissions, distribute work between craftsmen, monitor the progress of work and often complete the transaction. Their role in writing contracts and understanding the judicial process was central to the success of this enterprise. In a letter, P. DeM 18, from the scribe *'Imn-ms* (Amenmose) of the temple of Hathor, he berates *M33.n='I-nht=f* (Maanakhtef) who is given the title "chief carpenter of the Lord of the Two Lands", indicating that he is working on a private commission.[10] *'Imn-ms* (Amenmose) instructs the carpenter to complete the furniture commission, which includes a little bed, and pass the commission onto *Nht-Mnw* (Nakhtmin) as soon as he arrives. In another letter, O. DeM 0419, a client asks the scribe *'Ir* (Hori) to supply a plan for some commission that involves painting.[11] Whether the painting was to decorate a tomb or funerary goods is uncertain.

Working Drawings and Sketches used by Carpenters

Clients would be asked to provide details of the commission, which could involve providing sketches with measurements for the work they wished undertaken. One letter, O. Louvre. E 23554, (Figure 1), provides *Nht-'Imn* with the measurements to make a commission.[12] The unnamed client stresses that he urgently requires four identical frames of four palms in width and five palms and two digits in height.[13] The drawing of the frame is in orthographic format of rectangular form filled with two horizontal rows of eight vertical bars or panels separated by a horizontal rail. The size and form of this commission may indicate that this was either a hinged window shutter or a small door.

The ancient Egyptian carpenter also used full orthographic projection, in that he read accurately drawn front and side elevations of an intended commission to determine the size, layout and proportions of the various wooden elements that would be needed to complete the commission. A fascinating insight into how important commissions were visualised, in their pre-manufacturing stage using full orthographic projection, is seen in the "Gurob shrine papyrus".[14] The intended shrine is drawn from two viewpoints called the front and side elevations. Both views are drawn on a grid of squares that Smith and Stewart determine portray the shrine has been drawn to a scale of 1:3.

Carpenters also made sketches, firstly to provide a visual method to allow potential clients to see the design opportunities that were available for the commission. Secondly, sketches were made to provide information of constructional methods using commonly understood drawing conventions. Thirdly, they were commissioning documents and finally, sketches were made to aid the carpenter to record or tally the furniture he had manufactured and its quality for which he required payment.

In a seminal paper "Towards decoding the necropolis workmen's funny signs", Ben Haring has been able to match some workman's signs by recording daily guard duties to the cycle of duty rosters given for some of the regnal years of both Rameses III and IV (Haring 2000: 45–58). Haring confines his study to the identification of workmen and their marks. He identifies "eleven ostraca bearing 'funny signs' in combination with semi-hieratic calendar dates" (Haring 2000: 48), and provides a suggested list of workmen that can be used to tentatively identify those workmen who were engaged in manufacturing furniture and funerary goods at Deir el-Medina. A number of workmen's signs can be identified in the furniture ostraca described below.

The furniture types illustrated in the following non-textual ostraca can also be identified in wall paintings in private Ramesside Theban Tombs. These have been individually classified by Killen, see Appendices A and B.

The Furniture Ostraca

A total of ten furniture ostraca are known to the author, those preserved in Museo Archeologico, Florence, have been previously studied and published.[15] Not all the signs can be read, however, the thumbnail sketches illustrated in this chapter provide information regarding the quality of some of those pieces of furniture that were manufactured together with those craftsmen involved in the production process. These furniture sketches are cross referenced with similar furniture forms illustrated in Ramesside tombs at Thebes and Memphis (Appendix A) and should be read with the furniture depictions found in Theban (Appendix B) and Memphite (Appendix C) tombs scenes of the Ramesside Period. Where possible reference is made to extant pieces of furniture together with their location and a brief bibliography.

O. TURIN N. 57141 (FIGURE 2)

Technical Description

Material:	Limestone
Condition:	Complete
Dimensions:	160 mm × 110 mm
Provenance:	Deir el-Medina
Date of Acquisition:	1905 (Excavation of Ernesto Schiaparelli)
Contents:	Order for pieces of furniture or a receipt of a sale/manufacture of pieces of furniture.
Date:	19th or 20th Dynasty.
Publication:	Lopez 1978: 22, pl. 62.

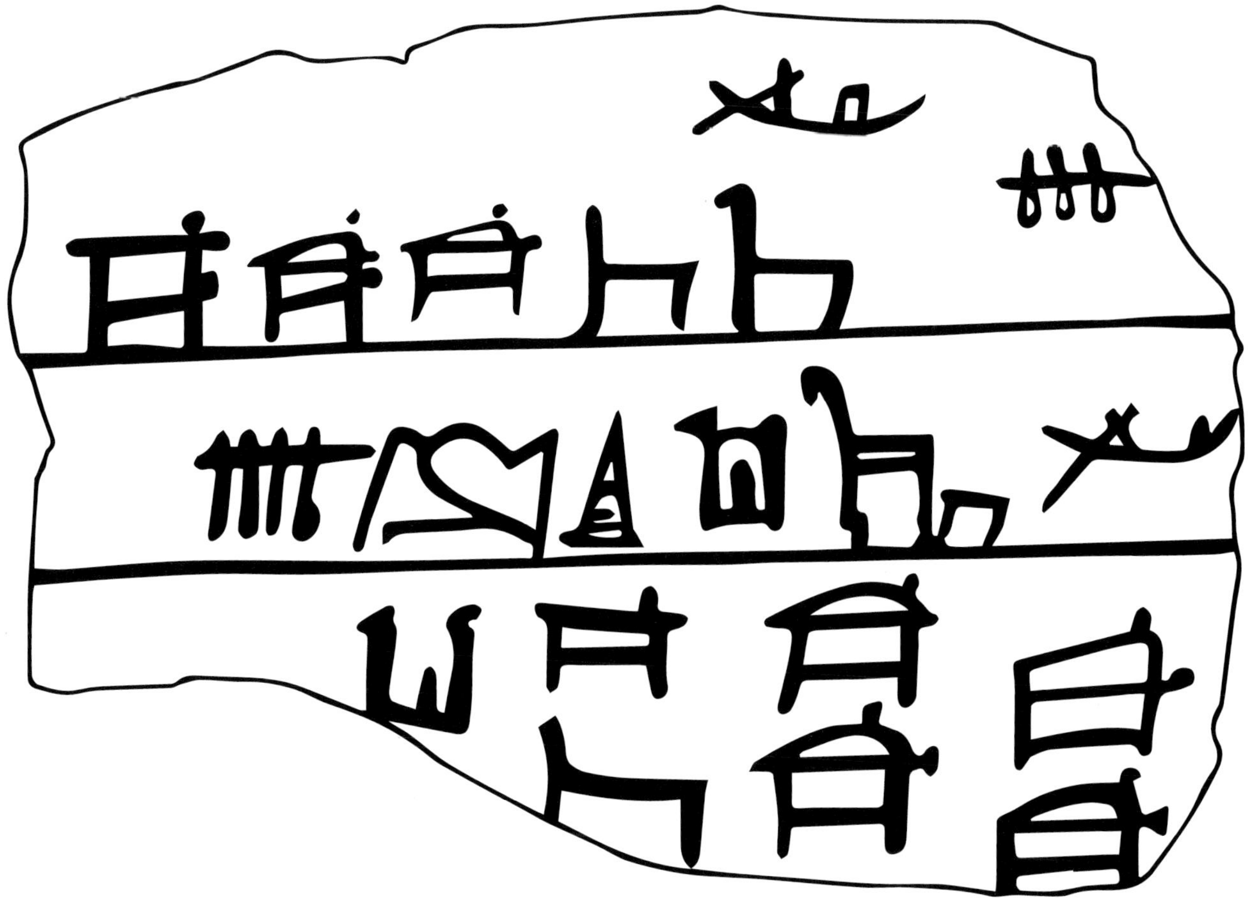

Figure 2. O. Turin N. 57141.

Figure 2.1

Figure 2.1. Three *nfr*-signs. Perhaps used as a quality mark.

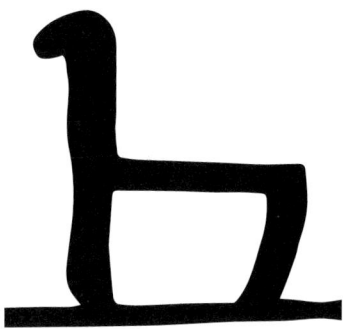

Figure 2.2

Figure 2.2 Chair of simple framework construction. This constructional arrangement, classified by Killen as chair type (Ce), is depicted in Theban Tomb TT111, Amunwahsu.[16] The top rail of the seat back support has been drawn to represent a moulded rail.

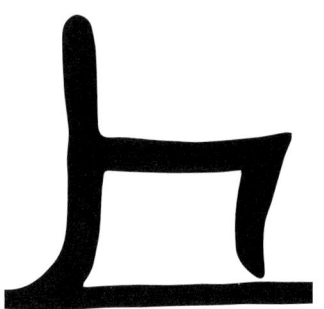

Figure 2.3

Figure 2.3. Simple framework chair. There is no indication that the legs would have been carved in lion form. A fine 18th Dynasty example is preserved in the Staatliche Museen, Berlin, 10748 (Baker 1966: 132, fig. 185). The chair would have been made from straight wood elements with the back legs extending as one element into the upright posts of the backrest.

Figure 2.4

Figure 2.4. Box with a shrine shaped lid. This constructional arrangement, classified by Killen as box type (Bxc), is depicted in Theban Tomb TT51, Userhet (Davies 1927: pl. XIII). A similar box is preserved in the Louvre Museum, Paris. 2915. (Killen 1994: 37, pl. 28; Killen 2017B: 43, pl. 28).

Figure 2.5

Figure 2.5. Box with a shrine shaped lid, type (Bxc). A similar box is preserved in the British Museum, EA 5907, (Figure 25, Plates 63–67).

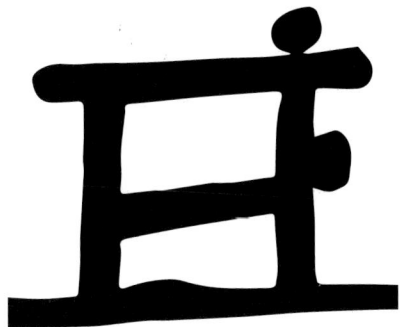

Figure 2.6

Figure 2.6. Rectangular box with a flat lid and button-shaped knobs on the lid and the front of the box. This constructional arrangement is classified by Killen as box type (Bxk); an example of this box type was discovered in Theban Tomb TT339, Huy and Peshedu (Bruyère 1926: pl. 5 [4]).

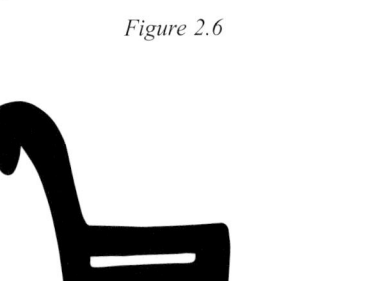

Figure 2.7

Figure 2.7. Footstool with a simple rectangular framework construction. Together with a chair with a single horizontal stretcher below the seat. This constructional arrangement, classified by Killen as chair type (Cg), is depicted in Theban Tomb TT278, Amenemhab (Vandier 1954: pl. XXXII).

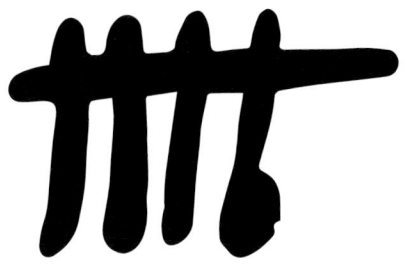

Figure 2.8

Figure 2.8. Four *nfr*-signs. Perhaps used as a quality mark. Also known from O. Florence 2628 (Killen and Weiss 2009: 137–158).

Figure 2.9. Box with a shrine shaped lid, with button-shaped knobs on the lid and the front of the box. This constructional arrangement, classified by Killen as box type (Bxc), is depicted in Theban Tomb TT41, Amememipet Ipy.[17]

Figure 2.9

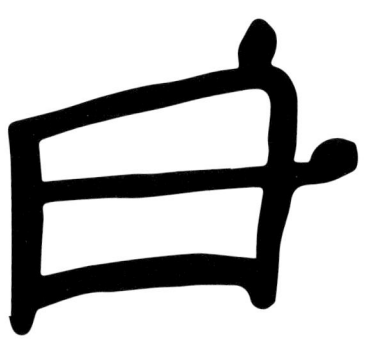

Figure 2.10

Figure 2.10. Box with a shrine shaped lid, with button-shaped knobs on the lid and the front of the box.

Figure 2.11

Figure 2.11. Box with a shrine shaped lid that extends beyond the length of the box. Here a drawing convention is used to show that the top edge of the box would have been fitted with a cavetto type moulding. This constructional arrangement is classified by Killen as box type (Bxc).

Figure 2.12

Figure 2.12. Box with a shrine shaped lid that extends beyond the length of the box. Here a drawing convention is used to show that the top edge of the box would have been fitted with a cavetto type moulding. This constructional arrangement is classified by Killen as box type (Bxc).

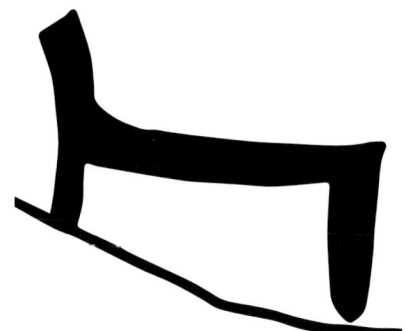

Figure 2.13. A chair.

Figure 2.13

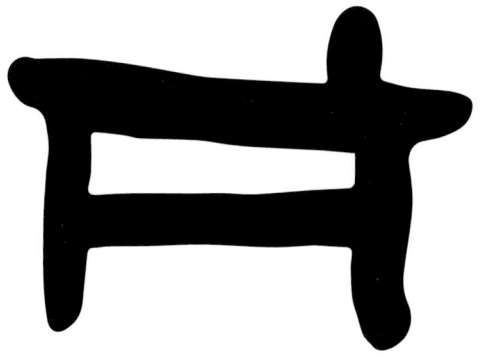

Figure 2.14. Rectangular box with a knob on a flat lid.

Figure 2.14

Figure 2.15. *Ka*-arms; certainly a workman's mark (Gardiner D 28). Known to Haring as referring to Kes and Penaqet. Compare with O. Florence 2630 (Killen and Weiss 2009: 137–158).

Figure 2.15

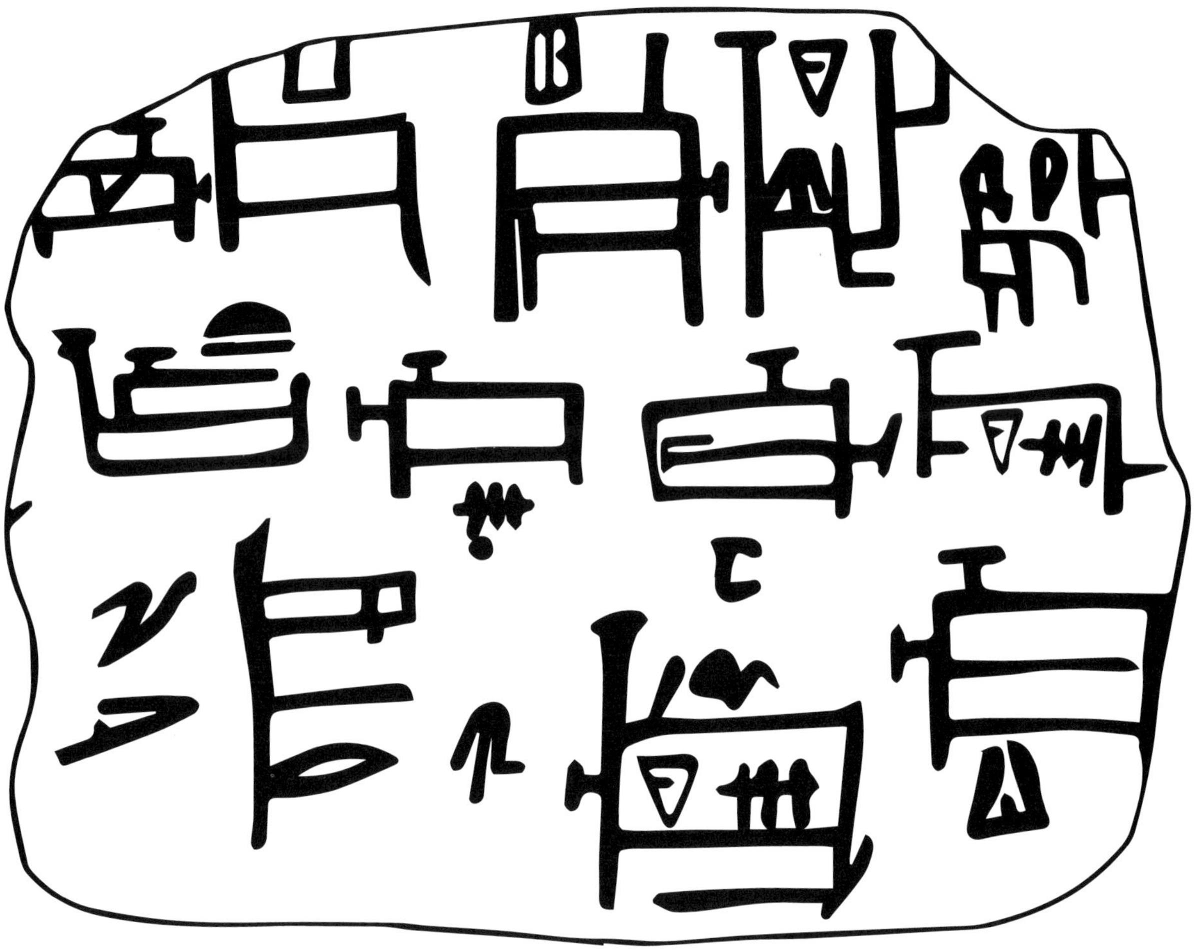

Figure 3. O. EA 5861 recto.

O. EA 5861 RECTO (FIGURE 3)

Technical Description
Material: Limestone
Condition: Complete
Dimensions: 156 mm × 120 mm
Provenance: Deir el-Medina

Date of Acquisition: 1823 (Henry Salt collection)
Contents: Order for pieces of furniture or
                       a receipt of a sale/manufacture
                       of pieces of furniture.
Date: 19th or 20th Dynasty.
Publication: Demarée 2002: 21, pl. 45.

Figure 3.1. Possible vase stand of lattice construction with a single vertical brace and two angled braces. This constructional arrangement, classified by Killen as vase stand type (STb), is depicted in Theban Tomb TT51, Userhet (Davies 1927: pl. XIII). The kite sign is probably an unknown workman's mark seen several times on this ostracon.

Figure 3.1

Figure 3.2

Figure 3.2. A rectangular box. This constructional arrangement is classified by Killen as box type (Bxa). The unusual method of showing one frame within another, possibly suggests that this box was designed to be compartmentalised. The mark above is unknown although could be a plan view of the interior of the box indicating a single partition.

Figure 3.3

Figure 3.3. Simple framework chair. The mark above could be *ka*-arms.

Figure 3.4

Figure 3.4. Rectangular box with large mushroom-shaped knobs on the lid and front of the box. Classified by Killen as box type (Bxa). The mark inside the box is possibly an unknown workman's mark.

Figure 3.5

Figure 3.5. A rectangular frame, with construction marks on both legs indicating bracing stretchers. The top rail is rendered with a horizontal rail. Unknown kite mark and of possible three-times *nfr* quality.

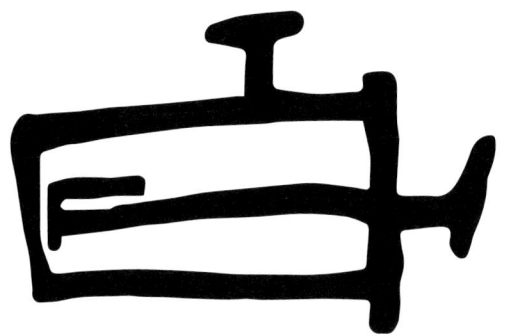

Figure 3.6

Figure 3.6. A rectangular box rendered to suggest the box had been designed with internal compartments is classified by Killen as box type (Bxa).

Figure 3.7

Figure 3.7. Accurately drawn rectangular box with large mushroom-shaped knobs is classified by Killen as box type (Bxa) and is of three-times *nfr* quality. Similar in design to a cosmetic box discovered in the tomb of Sennedjem, Metropolitan Museum of Art, New York, MMA 86.1.8. (Killen 1994: 81, fig. 79; Killen 2017B: 106, fig. 79).

Figure 3.8

Figure 3.8. Rectangular box with mushroom-shaped knobs is classified by Killen as box type (Bxa). *Ka*-arms below the box, certainly a workman's mark (Gardiner D 28). Known to Haring as referring to Kes and Penaqet.

Figure 3.9

Figure 3.9. Rectangular box is classified by Killen as box type (Bxa). Unusual extension of the mushroom-shaped lid knob. Various unknown workman's marks, also of three-times *nfr* quality.

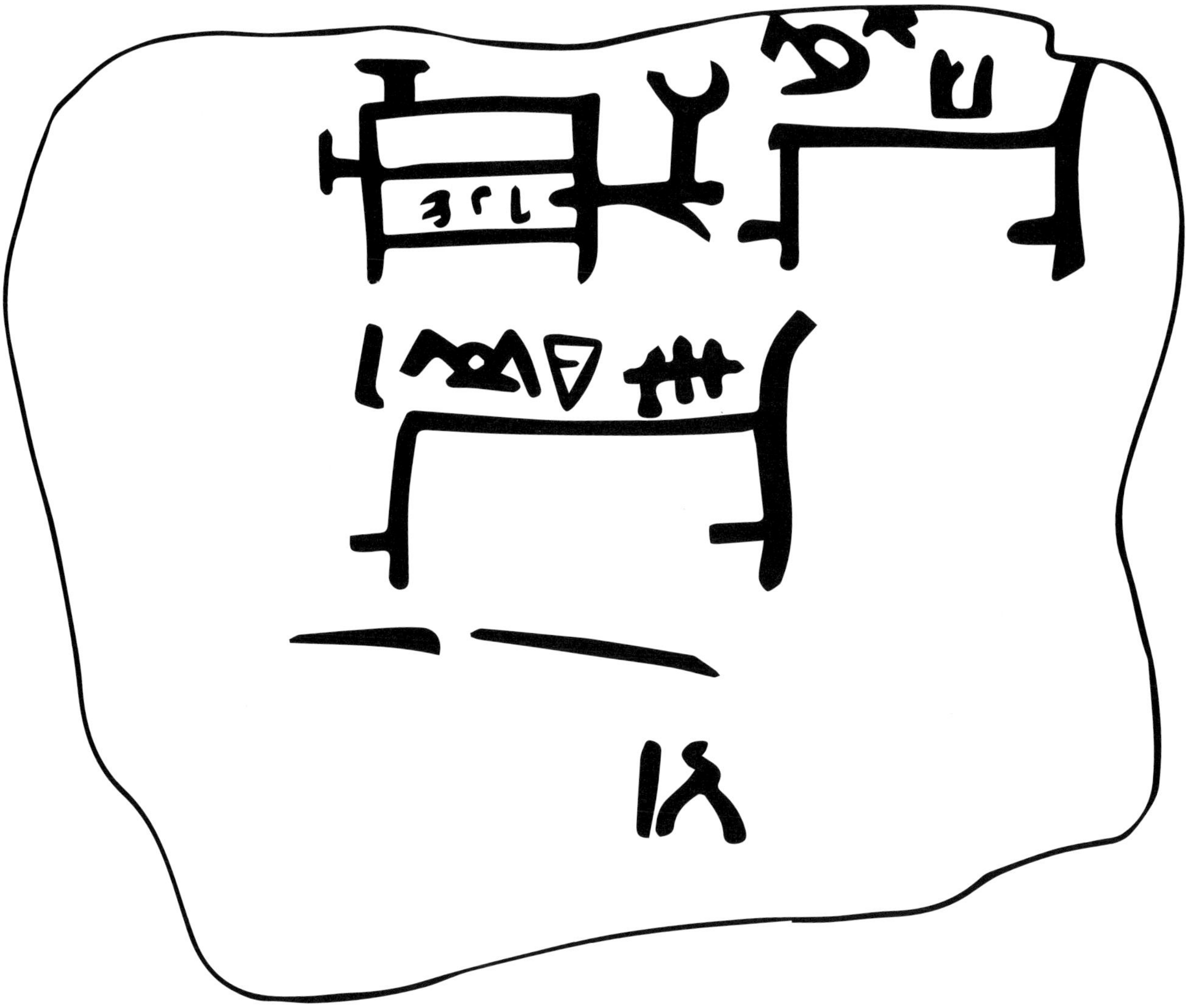

Figure 4. O. EA 5861 verso.

O. EA 5861 verso (Figure 4).

Verso

Figure 4.1. Bedframe with construction marks on both head and foot legs indicating the position of bracing stretchers. The line drawing of the legs indicates that the bed legs were not to be modelled and are made from simple square section elements. *Ka*-arms above the bed, certainly a workman's mark (Gardiner D 28). Known to Haring as referring to Kes and Penaqet.

Figure 4.1

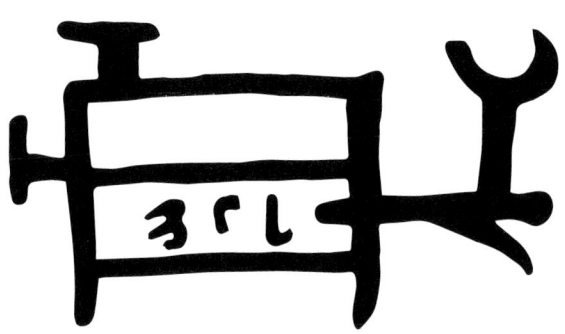

Figure 4.2. A headrest and rectangular box with large mushroom-shaped knobs is classified by Killen as box type (Bxa). Within this box are three unknown maker's marks.

Figure 4.2

Figure 4.3. A bedframe with construction marks indicating the position of bracing stretchers across the head and foot legs of the bedframe. The bedframe was manufactured of three-times *nfr* quality. The other marks are unknown but possibly workman's marks.

Figure 4.3

Figure 5. O. Medelhavsmuseet MM 14129.

O. Medelhavsmuseet MM 14129 (Figure 5)

Technical Description

Material: Limestone
Condition: Complete
Dimensions: 88 mm × 82 mm
Provenance: Deir el-Medina
Contents: Order for pieces of furniture or
                    a receipt of a sale/manufacture
                    of pieces of furniture.

Date: 19th or 20th Dynasty.
Publication: Peterson 1973: 107. pl. 80
                    (149).

Of interest are the three lines of text in red ink written upside down that indicate some type of personal transfer of an armchair associated with *ꜣny-nḫt* Anuynakht (Killen and Weiss 2009: 143–144).

Figure 5.1

Figure 5.1. Rectangular box with large mushroom-shaped knobs is classified by Killen as box type (Bxa).

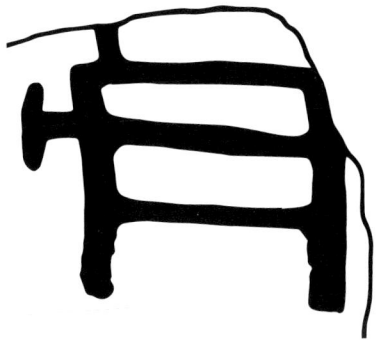

Figure 5.2

Figure 5.2. A framework construction with a simple mushroom-shaped knob.

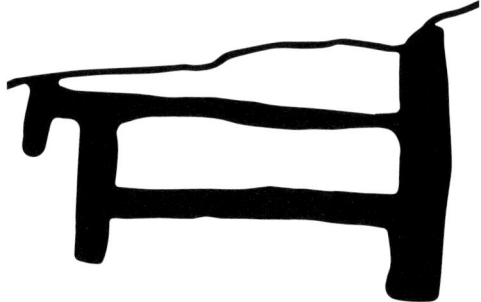

Figure 5.3

Figure 5.3. Rectangular box with large mushroom-shaped knobs is classified by Killen as box type (Bxa).

Figure 5.4

Figure 5.4. Chair frame with a seat supported by a lattice of vertical and angled braces is classified by Killen as chair type (Cmm). Construction marks on the front and back legs indicate the positions of bracing stretchers.

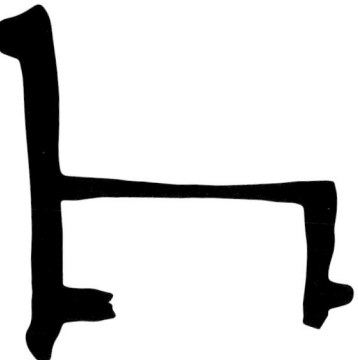

Figure 5.5

Figure 5.5. Badly faded sketch, possibly a bedframe as indicated by the footboard with moulded upper rail. Construction marks on the front and back legs indicate the positions of bracing stretchers.

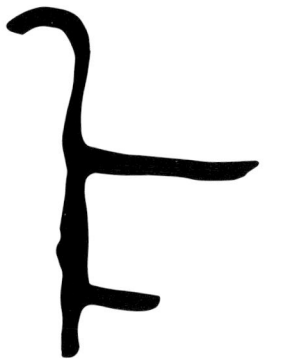

Figure 5.6

Figure 5.6. Chair frame with construction marks on the front legs indicating the position of bracing stretchers.

Figure 5.7

Figure 5.7. Simply sketched chair, the back support is shown with a moulded back rail.

Figure 5.8

Figure 5.8. Rectangular box with mushroom-shaped knobs is classified by Killen as box type (Bxa).

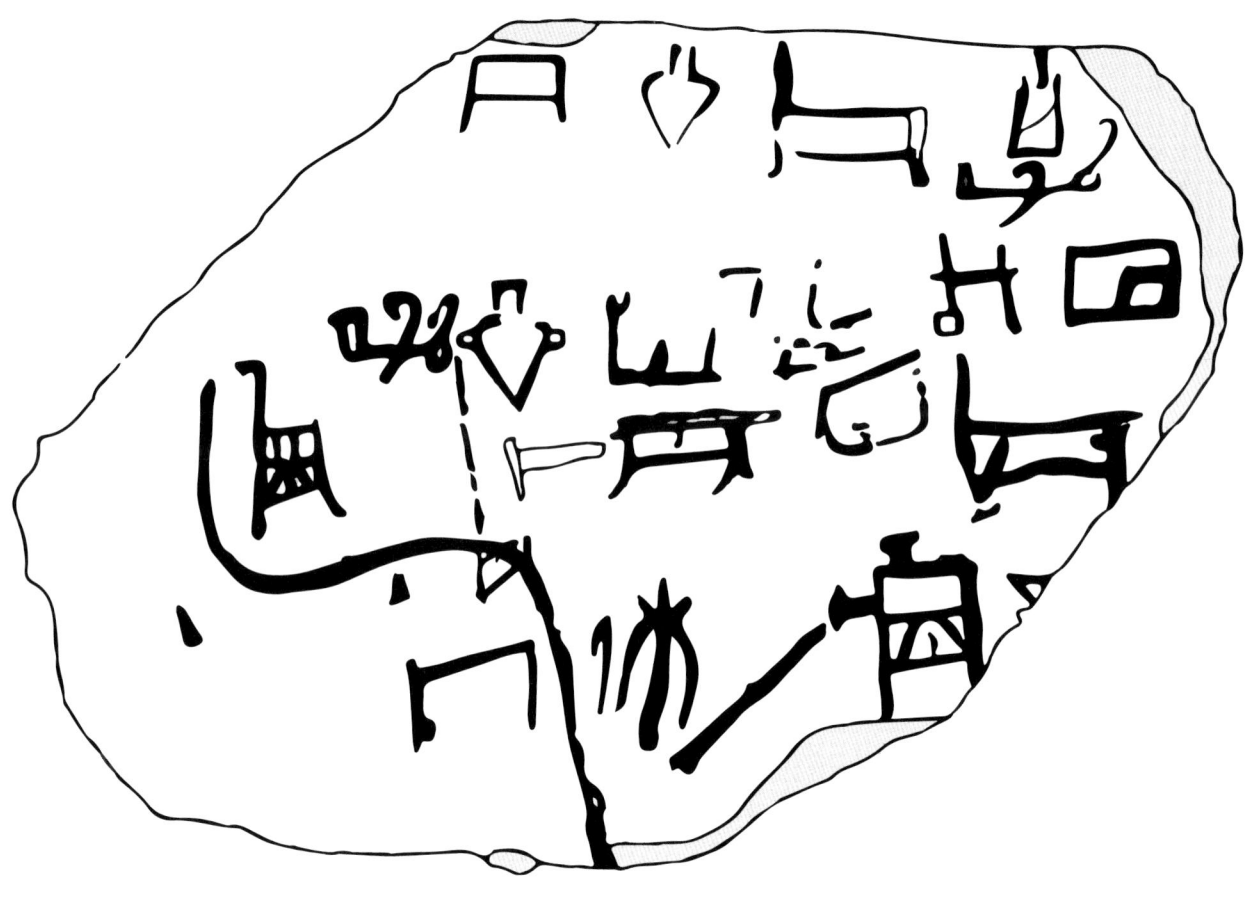

Figure 6. O. Munich 398.

O. Munich 398 (Figure 6)

Technical Description

Material:	Limestone
Condition:	Good with ink faded in some places
Dimensions:	210 mm × 130 mm

Provenance:	Deir el-Medina
Date of Acquisition:	Unknown
Date:	19th or 20th Dynasty.
Publication:	Brunner-Traut 1956: 124, pl. XLIV (153).

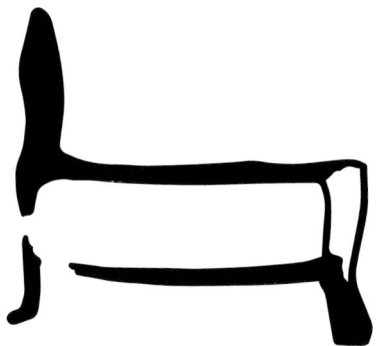

Figure 6.1. A bedframe, the head leg is unusually drawn in outline.

Figure 6.1

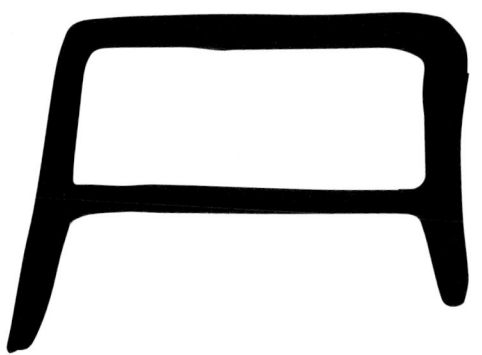

Figure 6.2

Figure 6.2. A table. It is difficult to tell whether the table represents an actual table or a workman's mark. If a workman's mark it could refer to the 20th-Dynasty workmen Mery Re or Amenemope.

Figure 6.3

Figure 6.3. A framework construction with construction marks indicating bracing stretchers across the front and back pairs of legs.

Figure 6.4

Figure 6.4. A chair frame in side elevation with plan elevation of the seat included is classified by Killen as chair type (Cmm).

Figure 6.5

Figure. 6.5. A tall rectangular box with large mushroom-shaped knobs. The base of the box compartment is supported with a lattice of vertical and angled struts. An example of this design was discovered in the tomb of Tutankhamun, Carter No. 56, JE 61448 (Killen 1994: 60, pl. 52, fig. 66; Killen 2017B: 75, pl. 52, fig. 66).

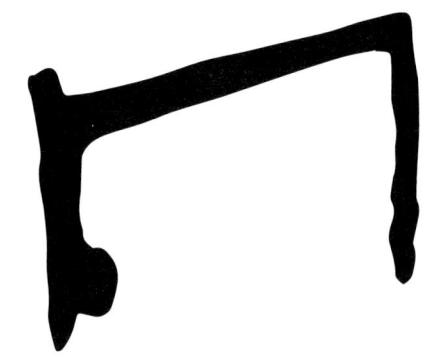

Figure 6.6

Figure 6.6. Simple frame construction, which could represent a bedframe.

Figure 6.7

Figure 6.7. This could represent an unknown carpenter's mark, although it may be a drawing of a simple table.

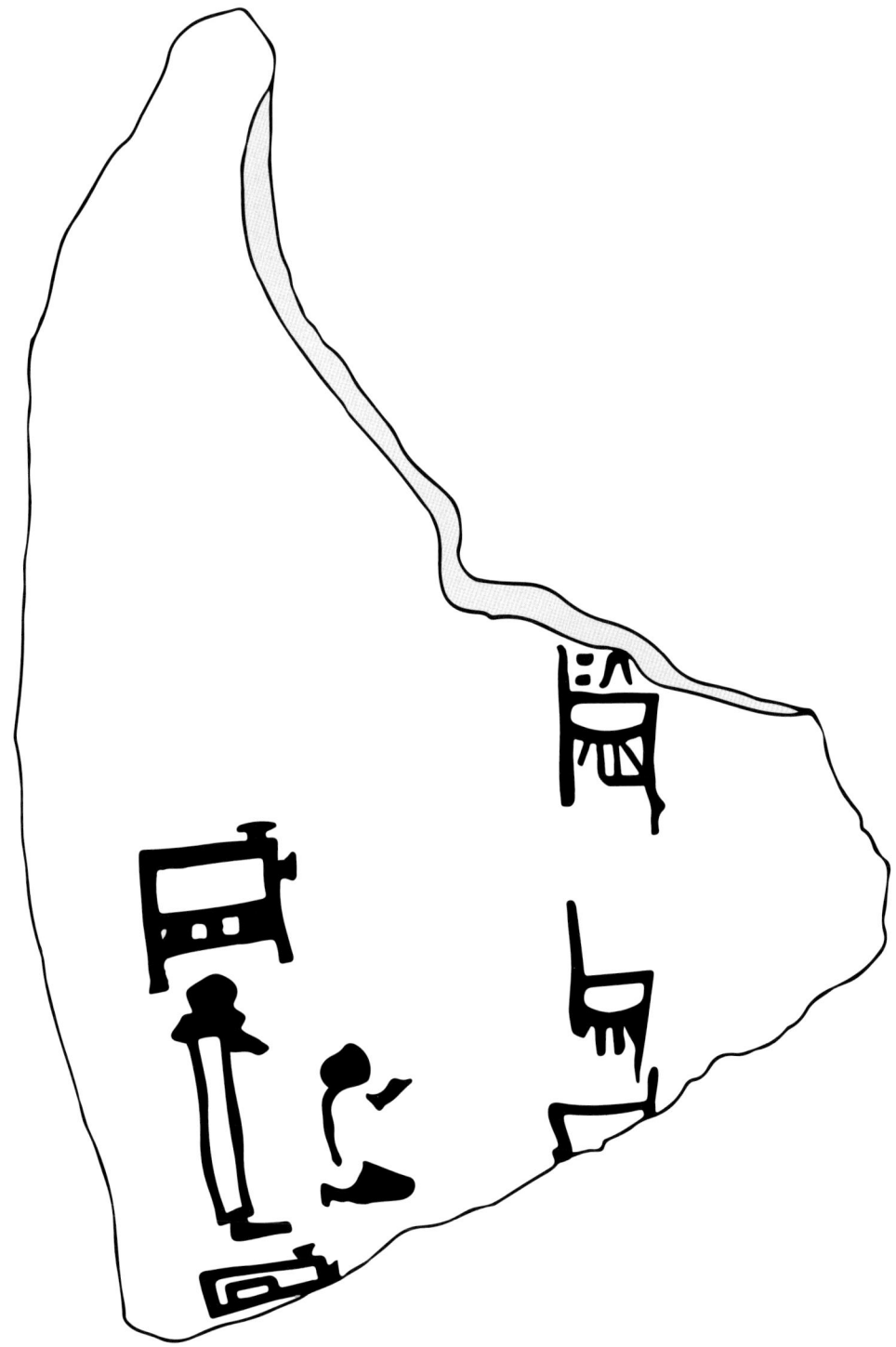

Figure 7. O. University College UC 31992.

O. University College UC 31992 (Figure 7).

Technical Description

Material:	Limestone
Condition:	Complete
Dimensions:	165 mm × 112 mm
Provenance:	Deir el-Medina
Date of Acquisition:	Unknown

Contents:	Order for pieces of furniture or a receipt of a sale/manufacture of pieces of furniture.
Date:	19th or 20th Dynasty.
Publication:	Unpublished

Ink has badly faded; we can establish the outlines of five pieces of furniture.

Figure 7.1

Figure 7.1. An elegant chair frame has been rendered with legs of possible lion form. The bracing below the seat comprises of two vertical struts and two angled struts. This arrangement is classified by Killen as chair type (Co). The seat is drawn to suggest a double curved form.

Figure 7.2

Figure 7.2. An elegant chair frame with a supporting brace of angled and vertical struts below the seat. The seat is drawn to suggest a double curved form.

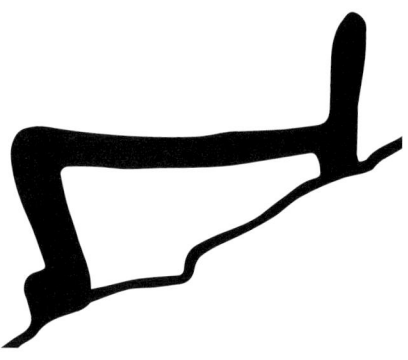

Figure 7.3

Figure 7.3. Either a simple chair or bedframe construction.

Figure 7.4

Figure 7.4. A rectangular box with the base supported on a structural lattice of angled and vertical elements fixed between the legs. A pair of mushroom-shaped knobs are attached to the lid and front of the box. Possibly a toilet box (British Museum EA 24708: Killen 1994: 35, fig. 52, pls. 24–26; Killen 2017B: 41–43, fig. 52, pls. 24–26).

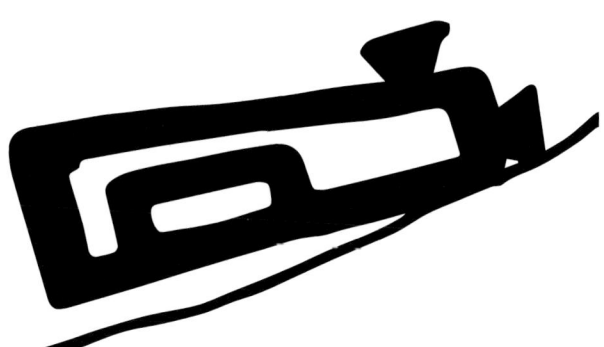

Figure 7.5. A simple low box with a pair of mushroom-shaped knobs. The scribe has rendered this diagram to possibly indicate that the box had to be compartmentalised.

Figure 7.5

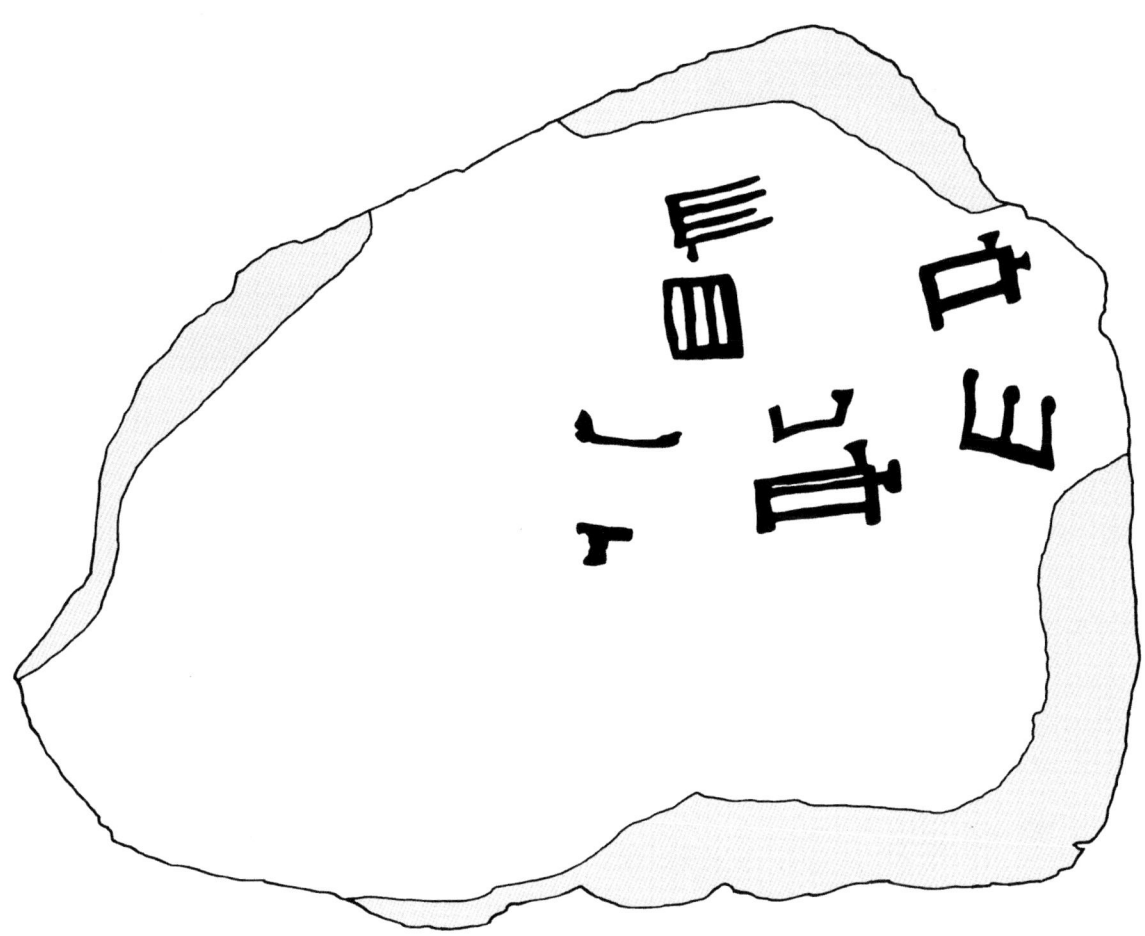

Figure 8. O. Ashmolean Museum HO 1123.

O. Ashmolean Museum HO 1123 (Figure 8).

Technical Description

Material:	Limestone
Condition:	Good with ink faded in some places
Dimensions:	160 mm × 123 mm
Provenance:	Deir el-Medina

Date of Acquisition:	Unknown
Contents:	Order for pieces of furniture or a receipt of a sale/manufacture of pieces of furniture.
Date:	19th or 20th Dynasty.
Publication:	Unpublished

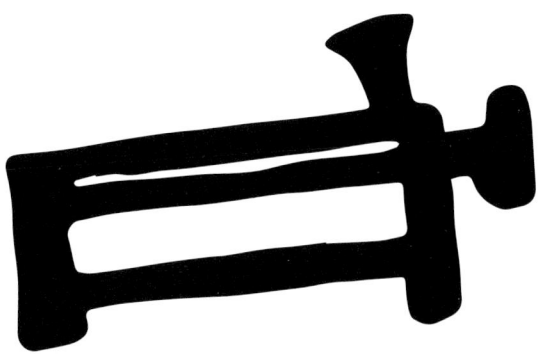

Figure 8.1

Figure 8.1. Rectangular boxes with mushroom-shape knobs, one on the clearly defined lid. Classified by Killen as box type (Bxa).

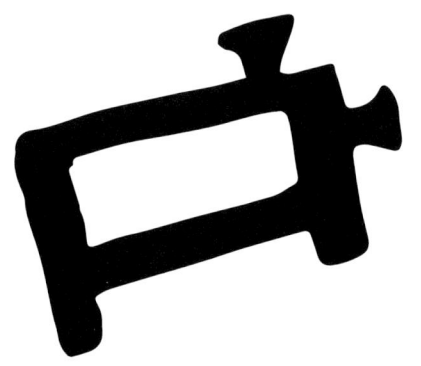

Figure 8.2

Figure 8.2. Rectangular box. Classified by Killen as box type (Bxa). Similar box is now preserved in the Louvre Museum, Paris. N2635. (Killen 1994: 35–36, pl. 27; Killen 2017B: 43, pl. 27).

Figure 9. O. Turin N. 57140.

O. Turin N. 57140 (Figure 9).

Technical Description

Material:	Limestone
Condition:	Good
Dimensions:	275mm × 110 mm
Provenance:	Deir el-Medina, Schiaparelli
Date of Acquisition:	1905

Contents:	Order for pieces of furniture or a receipt of a sale/manufacture of pieces of furniture.
Date:	19th or 20th Dynasty.
Publication:	Lopez 1978: 22, pl. 62a.

This furniture ostracon is possibly an apprentice piece and is poorly draughted.

Figure 9.1

Figure 9.1. Two rectangular table frames. It is difficult to tell whether these tables represent actual tables or are workmen's marks. If workmen's marks, they could refer to the 20th-Dynasty workman Mery Re or Amenemope.

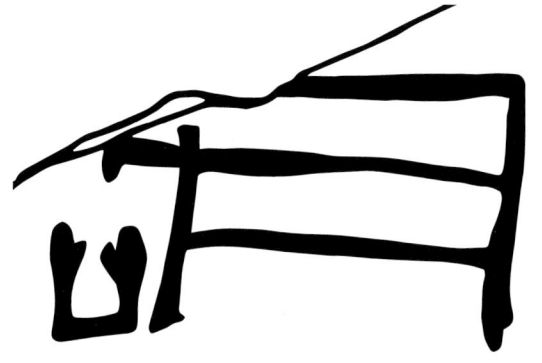

Figure 9.2

Figure 9.2. A rectangular box is classified by Killen as box type (Bxa). *Ka*-arms suggest the work of either Kes or Penaqet.

Figure 9.3

Figure 9.3. A simple rectangular frame construction.

Figure 9.4

Figure 9.4 A possible bed, poorly executed.

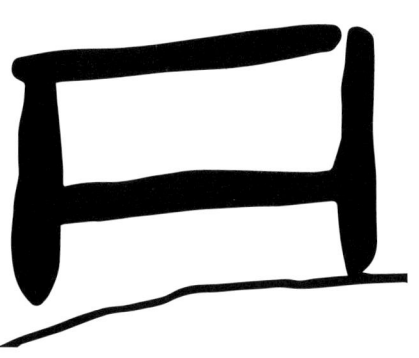

Figure 9.5

Figure 9.5. A box that is classified by Killen as box type (Bxa).

Training and Apprenticeship

Carpenters engaged their sons in the family business; they would work under supervision or on set tasks when their fathers were at work in the royal valleys. O. Ashmolean Museum 119 gives an account of woodwork done for *Ršw-ptr=f* (Reshupeteref) by his son *'Imn-nḫt* Amennakht.[18] This suggests that a boy's apprenticeship to a trade started at a very early age and at first was confined to the family's workshop/courtyard where he would undertake much of the preparation and first fitting for private commissions. Once the training was complete and he could show he was able to produce high quality work he might be considered for gang membership.

However, admission to the gang was not necessarily straightforward and the axles of promotion often needed greasing. On O. Cairo 25800 we see one workman's attempt to gain gang membership for his son.[19] The record shows that he gave a number of pieces of furniture to those who would have influence in obtaining permission for his son to join the gang. Obviously this was the accepted practice and he carefully recorded the gifts together with the expected value of each item. He makes it clear that each item belonged to him and nobody else, which suggests they were made specifically for the purpose of nepotism and they could have been the final apprenticeship pieces of his son. The chief workman *'In-ḥr-ḫˁ* (Inherkhau) receives a wooden chair with a low seat to the value of 30 *deben*; while the scribe *Ḥr-šrì* (Horisheri) is given a large folding-stool with a footstool to the value of 30 *deben*, a wooden chair to the value of 11 *deben* and a wooden container to the value of two *deben*. The significance of the additional furniture that *Ḥr-šrì* (Horisheri) receives probably reflects not only his status as a scribe, as he would correspond with the vizier regarding any potential promotion, but also his importance in managing the outsourcing of private funerary commissions.

The role of the commissioning client

The client or scribe appears to have often been responsible for the supply of raw materials for a commission. On O. Turin N. 57040 the policeman *Pn-iw-m-itr.w* (Peniuemiter) has delivered to *Nfr-ḥtp* (Neferhotep) two large pieces of wood for the manufacture of a coffin.[20] While in P. DeM 03 the workman *Ḥ3y* (Hay) informs the scribe *'Ii-m-sb3* (Imiseba) that he is "engaged in making the bed. It will be beautiful! Send the ebony so that it may not be delayed and also the webbing material." (Wente 1967: 140).[21] These letters do not discuss any exchange mechanism, other than supplying the raw materials, suggesting that these documents were for internal use; clearly in the second letter the scribe *'Ii-m-sb3* (Imiseba) is the go-between the client and carpenter. A further internal document O. DeM 0146 provides evidence of the substantial amount of woodwork a carpenter would produce through the commissioning process and the value

in copper deben he believed the work to be worth.[22] The work was for the deputy *'Imn-nḫt* (Amennakht), who is acting as the agent and managed the commission, and each item is individually priced. Two chairs were valued together at 30 *deben*, a wooden bed at 20 *deben*, a coffin at 25 *deben* and a wooden statue of 15 *deben*. These costs are possibly for labour only and exclude the raw materials, which was supplied by the client. The cost also excludes the fee a draughtsman would ask for decorating and painting these funerary goods and the fee *'Imn-nḫt* (Amennakht) would receive on the completion of this transaction.

There seems to have been a clear demarcation of trade responsibilities between carpenters and painters. In a complex transaction O. Berlin P. 12343 recto, the draughtsman *Ḥr-šrì* (Horsheri) has returned to the workman/carpenter *Bˁk-n-wrnr* (Bakenwerl) a number of painted funerary goods which *Bˁk-m-wrnr* (Bakenwerl) had presumably manufactured.[23] The list of commissioned objects includes "the two doors of the tomb, painted two coffins and this inner coffin of *Bˁk.t-nStì* (Baketenseti) makes 24 deben." (McDowell 1999: 82). However, the verso of this ostracon informs us that *Bˁk-n-wrnr* (Bakenwerl) is also supplying *Ḥr-šrì* (Horsheri) with a number of wooden goods that require decoration. Two boxes; one of which had been prepared with a ground of gesso in preparation for painting while a coffin and two beds had been made from wood that had been supplied by *Ḥr-šrì* (Horsheri). Either *Ḥr-šrì* (Horsheri) was preparing his and his families funerary material for the projected value of 50 *deben*, though this seems unlikely, as he appears to be paying the full price for these goods. Or he was independently commissioning funerary furniture that he could sell on to third parties who either needed an "off the shelf" product or were for some reason excluded from entering the commissioning process.

Trading and the regulation of wooden products

Some carpenters used the open market to sell products that had been privately made and not formally commissioned. It appears that the market-place they frequented was located along the "riverbank". We know that the carpenter *S3-W3ḏ.t* (Sa-Wadjyt) traded at the market-place as he is recorded in O. Brooklyn Museum 37.1880E giving advice to *'Imn-m-'Ip.t* (Amenemope) on the price he paid for a statue in the image of Seth made by the carpenter *Rˁ-mry* (Mery-Re).[24] For this statue *'Imn-m-'Ip.t* (Amenemope) had exchanged "1½ sacks of grain, 3 bundles of vegetables, 1 pair of fowl, 1 basket with lid. Total 2 sacks (of grain) and *meneq*-wood." (McDowell 1999: 85, [no. 55]). The appreciation of the statue given by *S3-W3ḏ.t* (Sa-Wadjyt) was that it was only worth 1 sack of grain. We are uncertain whether *S3-W3ḏ.t* (Sa-Wadjyt) gave an unbiased appraisal, based as an independent trader, on the statue's true market-place value. Whether *'Imn-m-'Ip.t*

(Amenemope) was unhappy with the quality of the statue *Rˁ-mry* (Mery-Re) had made is unknown but in querying what he had paid for the statue may indicate that he may have had it privately commissioned at a set price. This would explain the apparent inflated cost of the statue but could also be the first step to redress the issue of overpriced goods.

Rˁ-mry (Mery-Re) was also involved in another dispute, regarding the materials *rt* (Ruty) exchanged for a similar statue, the dispute was placed before the oracle. In O. Ashmolean Museum 0003 recto we read:

> "What Ruty gave to the carpenter Mery-Re in exchange for the statue:
>
> | | |
> |---|---|
> | 1 tunic | makes 5 *deben* |
> | 5 bundles of vegetables | makes 2½ *deben* |
> | 4 mats | makes 2 *deben* |
> | the statue as wood and also | |
> | its base | makes 1 *oipe* |
>
> And the god gave the statue 8 copper *deben*.
>
> 10 copper *deben*: the excess, 2 *deben*. Likewise the [...]"

(McDowell 1999: 82–83, [no. 53]).

Here we see that the oracle judged the statue to have been overpriced by two *deben*. Also of interest is that Ruty had previously supplied the wood for this commission.

The final transaction between the carpenter and patron is seen on O. DeM 0195 recto.[25] We have an exchange record showing the part payment received by the carpenter *Pn-Tȝ-wr.t* (Pentaweret) for the manufacture of a chair. *Pn-Tȝ-wr.t* (Pentaweret) estimated the value of the commission to be worth 15 *deben*, however, the customer exchanged items for the chair to the value of 10½ copper *deben*. The materials exchanged for this commission:

A quantity of grain	
(possibly 3 sacks)	making 5 *deben*.
2 units of oil	making 1 *deben*.
Fresh fat?	making 1 *oipe*.
2 woven baskets	making 4 *deben*.
Sum 10½ Copper deben.	

(English translation of O. DeM 195 recto from Allam 1973: 103 [No. 74]).

The data provided from the documents show workmen working for state interests and also using their talents privately to maintain a booming funerary and domestic furniture industry that met the needs of local inhabitants. However, the physical material that survived in the family tombs of these Ramesside artisans augments this remarkable corpus of textual and non-textual material.

The marking of wooden funerary material

Those workmen's signs identified in the furniture ostraca can also be found on a large number of artefacts including, pots, headrests, boomerangs and textiles. We find that

they have been written, drawn, carved, embroidered, or produced by a pyrographic process onto the material to be marked (Killen and Weiss 2009: 137–158). These signs serve as either workman's, owner or laundry marks. However, signs appear to have also been employed as location or assembly marks to help carpenters identify the specific matching of cut joints or surface parts of a wooden carcase.

A range of marks can be seen on the wooden coffin of Mariherperi, KV36.[26] Mariherperi's coffin has sides manufactured from boards of wood that are edge-jointed together. These fabricated sides are then fastened down each vertical edge with four dovetail joints. Each sloping surface of the lid is made from three matched boards, edge-jointed together and attached to a central horizontal batten. All seven boards are fastened with pegs to the inside surface of the rectangular end supports. To locate the lid to the coffin, pairs of mortises have been chopped in the edge of the upper end boards of the coffin that match mortises chopped in the bottom edge of the lid's end supports. In these mortises would have been placed loose tenons to locate and possibly lock the assembly.

Once the coffin and lid were sealed the matching surfaces between both components were hidden. On the top surface edges of the coffin, three corner joints have been marked with location and assembly marks, (Figure 10).

In corner A, we have a pair of long V's with a vertical stroke through the middle; the signs have been carved first before being highlighted with black paint.[27] The apex of each sign points to the outer surface of coffin; the black painted decoration is restricted to the outer surface of the box and is not allowed to mask the orientation of these signs. We can also see how the carpenter employed the standard convention that an edge mortise should be one third of the thickness of the rail. Also, the quality of jointing surfaces of the dovetail to socket was very accurately cut.

In corner B, we see of pair of *nb* – signs, both orientated in the same direction, however, associated with each of these signs are four short parallel lines incised into the wood but left unpainted. Including these additional marks suggests these signs were more than just assembly or location marks and may have had a personal tie to the carpenter who carved them.

The third joint, corner C, is incised with a pair of orientated *ka*-signs. They are roughly cut lacking clearly defined hands. Again, whether these signs conveniently indicate the carpenter or enabling those who worked on the coffin to match up parts during the assembly process is difficult to establish. Although the fourth corner joint D, has no assembly signs, this would be expected if the function of the signs were principally for location. A further incised sign has been carved in the edge between corners C and D. Its purpose is unknown, although, it may have aided the correct orientation of the lid to the coffin.[28]

Figure 10. Range of carpentry marks on the wooden coffin of Mariherperi. KV36. Egyptian Museum, Cairo. JE 33833, CG 24001.

The textual evidence provided by ostraca at Deir el-Medina shows a thriving private woodworking industry, where furniture was manufactured using a clear design canon set by the standards of work seen in the royal and private Ramesside tombs. These men worked in a semi-official capacity using tools provided by the state and calling themselves carpenters although in official eyes they were tomb workers. The amount of wood they had to work with may have been greater than previously thought and it appears that for many commissions it was the client who provided the wood and occasionally a drawing with measurements to illustrate the type of product that was required.

The "furniture ostraca" from Deir el-Medina provide evidence that firstly, the design of furniture manufactured by the men of the village closely relates to extant material discovered in the village, and it was based on known generic forms of furniture used by those who inhabited the village. Secondly, they record that the quality of work produced for the client may have been a result of the wood provided for the commission. Finally, the "furniture ostraca" provide evidence of the working practices of men who teamed together to provide a service for their community and others beyond the village. This entrepreneurial enterprise collectively provided them with wealth that enabled them to plan for their own burial and that of their families.

We see that this enterprise also involved the sons of the village learning their father's trade and were able on completion of their apprenticeship pieces to either join those who worked in the royal valleys, or move to other communities. There they practiced their trade using the skills they had mastered and employing the design canon they had learnt at Deir el-Medina.

These skilled individuals worked for not only commissioning clients but also bartered their work in the market. Whether those people who entered into the exchange mechanism when buying wooden products in the market were excluded from the commissioning process is uncertain. However, there were judicial mechanisms that enabled those who had purchased wooden products, who thought later they had either overpaid or it was not of the quality expected, to seek compensation using the opinions of other carpenters before putting a case to the *knb.t*-court.

Those who manufactured goods within the village were keen to leave their mark on all types of products partly as an aid to promote their work, while other marks were placed on goods as ownership marks and some were simply aids to help establish how products were constructed. Those working at Deir el-Medina were keen to privately promote themselves and the services they provided in textual, non-textual and physical forms.

Chapter 2

An Analysis of Ramesside Furniture Used in Gurob and Memphis

At Deir el-Medina there is detailed evidence from ostraca, tomb paintings and a small corpus of excavated wooden material from the tomb of Sennedjem (TT1) that displays the way workmen were employed by the state but worked privately manufacturing wooden products. The tomb of the sculptor, Ipuy (TT 217), at Deir el-Medina provides us an insight into the range of wooden products used in this settlement.[1] Whereas, at Medinet el-Gurob, the excavated material presents us with a range of wooden products that would have been used in a Ramesside town whose occupants were closely related to the state and its royal family. Indeed, close parallels between both settlements is recognised by Kemp in that both have small temples which are similar in design, size and construction using both mud brick and rough-stone masonry and apparently date to the Ramesside Period.[2]

Parts of the cemetery at Gurob were originally excavated under the direction of Petrie, although much of the work was undertaken by his assistant W.O. Hughes-Hughes during the 1888 and 1889 seasons. Much of the material discussed in this chapter originates from these seasons of excavation or were purchased by Petrie from the local inhabitants. Later work on this site continued to excavate parts of the town and its cemeteries and located what was thought to be a temple. A re-evaluation of this temple site has suggested that this complex was a *harim*-town being occupied from the early 18th Dynasty until the reign of Rameses V.[3] Kemp recognised the unique nature of a *harim*-town, where possibly hundreds of women would be quartered, with many focussing on "carrying on industries such as weaving" (Kemp 1978: 132). The surviving archaeological record shows that the types of wooden products excavated at Gurob indicate that the women of the town were indeed engaged in the manufacture of fine linen, however, whether these activities were undertaken as a commercial enterprise or simply to produce linen

to service the *harim*-town is uncertain. In contrast, we have indisputable evidence that the wooden products manufactured in Deir el-Medina were designed for a domestic and funerary context with much of it destined to service a commercial market.

Petrie was to state that at Gurob "of furniture there is none" (Petrie 1890: 33). This certainly was an underestimate; though apart from the headrests and in particular one important folding example; no complete pieces of furniture were discovered. Nevertheless, the fragmentary material discovered provides us with complementary evidence of the use of a single design canon used across Egypt when manufacturing furniture products.

Headrests

In simple practical terms a headrest consists of a curved upper section or platform that supports the skull at a position above the ear. Various methods were designed to elevate this curved upper section. Apart from providing a relatively comfortable sleeping posture and the ability to protect elaborate head-dresses; another advantage was that it enabled air to circulate around the head, this being a major advantage over the use of pillows.

In purely practical terms, ancient Egyptians discovered that the headrest was, as we would say, "fit for purpose". However, the adoption of the headrest was made on more than purely practical needs – there was also a religious and symbolic dimension to its use. We find headrests formed an essential part of the funerary equipment deposited in the tombs, pit shafts and graves of ancient Egyptians. The deceased was considered as a sleeper who was travelling to the afterlife and this analogy is recorded in Spell 166 in the *Ancient Egyptian Book of Coming Forth by Day*, better known as the *Book of the Dead*; and illustrates that ancient

Egyptians considered the headrest elevated the head of the deceased allowing for the deceased's resurrection. The spell instructs the deceased to "raise yourself, so that you may be triumphant over what was done against you" (Faulkner 1985: 161). The ancient Egyptian also seems to have believed that the headrest prevented the head being decapitated, a realistic concern as tomb robbers often destroyed mummies, discarding the head, in their attempts to steal jewellery. Spell 166 finishes with an assurance that for the deceased. "Your head shall not be taken from you afterwards, your head shall not be taken from you for ever." (Faulkner 1985: 161). The headrest is therefore a common feature in interments, being placed near the head in the sarcophagus, or on the head of the coffin.

The use of the headrest is seen from the beginning of Egyptian history, made from shaped blocks of pottery or wood. Its profile clearly emphasises another feature in its symbolic relationship with the sun, which like the head was lowered in the evening and rises in the morning, the headrest also represents the hieroglyph *akhet* sign, denoting the horizon. With the introduction of copper tooling technology, headrests made from a number of fabricated parts, the base, the central support or column and abacus, the square block that is attached to a curved head platform, are seen from an Old Kingdom context. Often the decoration is limited to fluting on the sides of the vertical column.

Headrests of the New Kingdom (1550–1069 B.C.) and Third Intermediate Period (1069–747 B.C.) were very finely executed and more elaborate, many have the lower surface of the curved head support carved with a pair of open hands, the fingers being carefully delineated that symbolically would have supported the head. Other headrests have the underside of the head support carved with face of the god Bes. Bes appears giving additional protection for the head as he was associated with protection of the home and family. Bes was seen to protect the user from evil at a period of time when he or she could not defend themselves. Ancient Egyptians felt that they were vulnerable to demons that could cause illness and create nightmares; supernatural forces that could attack the unsuspecting person as they slept. It is not surprising that sometimes figures or heads of Bes were carved on headrests to fend off these chaotic forces.

HEADREST (PLATE 1).

Gurob.
Manchester Museum, University of Manchester.
Accession Number 3722.
Width 294 mm, depth 87 mm, height 185 mm.

This two-part headrest, (Plate 1), from Petrie's excavations at Gurob is held together with a rectangular pillar that is fastened into the stopped mortise in the base and penetrates

into the curved head support element. The shoulder of the joint between the top and bottom sections is octagonal in cross section. Above this joint the top part has broken through a knot during manufacture and was reinforced with another 3 mm diameter dowel to secure the pieces together. The wooden pegs that lock the two parts of this headrest to the inner vertical pillar have been intentionally tapered from 6 mm to 3 mm in diameter. The curved top head support has been neatly carved and sanded smooth. In the centre of the curved head support is an imitation plaque of wood surrounded by 2 mm thick ivory stringing that has been mitred at the corners. The plaque of wood measures 12 mm × 18 mm and the exposed side grain of this plaque illustrates that it is used as a small piece of veneer to cover the end grain of the central pillar, creating the illusion that the grain of the head support runs continuously in one direction. A separate round-headed dowel with a core of ivory is implanted into the top part of the headrest but does not fully penetrate the stem; its use appears to be a decorative feature.

FOLDING HEADREST (PLATES 2, 4–7).

Gurob.
Petrie Museum of Egyptian Archaeology, University College London. UC 16756.
Height 280 mm.

Discovered at Gurob and dated by Petrie of being from an 18th or 19th Dynasty context, (Petrie 1890: 35, pl. XVIII [17]), the form of this headrest, (Plate 2), structurally parallels the example deposited in Tutankhamun's tomb.[4] Between the two spade shaped head supports a strip of leather was glued to support the head. Fragments of this leather sling and glue remain on both the inner and outer surfaces of the spade shaped head supports indicating they were totally enclosed in a leather sheath, providing a permanent and non-slip fixing when the leather sling was under maximum loading.

The author has manufactured a replica of this folding headrest, (Plate 3); it performs well under loading, either when the side or the back of the sleeping head is in contact with the sling. The replica has been finished with a fitted fabric sling that can be washed for the sake of hygiene.

However, its performance parallels the original, illustrating that the tension in the sling creates the correct geometrical alignment for the headrest and provides both a rigid and stable construction where the head is elevated at a comfortable height above the bed and does not come into contact with the crossing spindles.

The folding headrest is made from two interlocking frames that are held together with bronze pivots. The diagonal spindles are round in cross section and are reduced in diameter at the head end to form a pair of short pegs that locate in holes bored in the spade shaped head supports, (Plate 4).

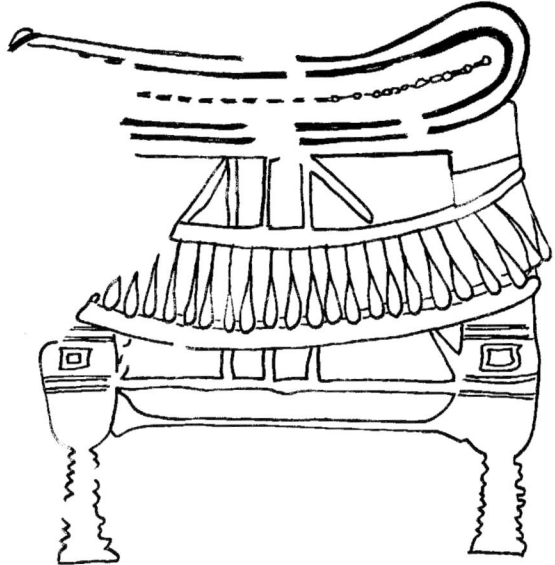

Figure 11. Stool of type Sm illustrated in the tomb of Nakhtamum, (TT341). After Davies and Gardiner 1948: pl. XXIX.

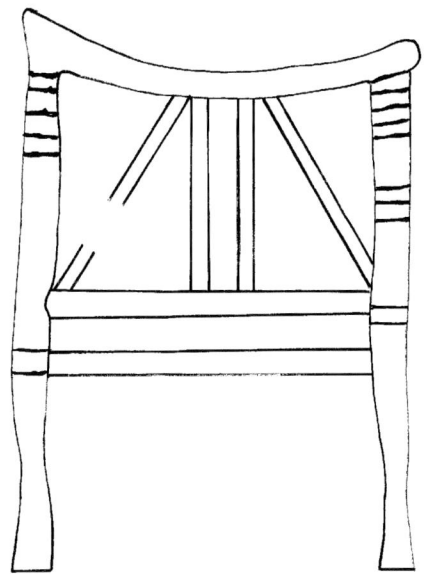

Figure 12. Stool of type Sj, illustrated in the tomb of Ramosi, (TT250). After Bruyère 1927: pl. VII.

The diagonal spindles are jointed to the floor rails with scribed shouldered tenons that locate into through mortises in the floor rail, (Plate 5). Only one of the four joints has been secured through the face of the joint with a dowel. It appears that this joint needed additional reinforcement because of the poor fit of the joint.

The side elevation of the headrest, (Plate 6), illustrates how the concave shaped profile of the head supports and leather sling would raise the head above the crossing spindles, as seen in the replica headrest (Plate 3), allowing the desired posture for the user when sleeping. The ends of each of the horizontal rails, (Plate 7) (shows one end), have impressions in the end grain that are associated with the manufacture of round section elements.

ROUND STOOL LEG (PLATES 8, 9 [TOP]).

Gurob.
Petrie Museum of Egyptian Archaeology. University College London. UC 58988.
Height: 310 mm, diameter 40 mm.

The extant wooden material includes a single hand-rounded leg from a stool, (Plate 8), an analysis of this furniture type at Thebes (Appendix D) shows that such stools were exclusively used by women during the Ramesside Period and therefore could have originated from the *harim* buildings that Petrie confused with a temple structure. What is apparent is that there were two distinct types of round stool leg being manufactured during the Ramesside period.

The first type, as seen in this example from Gurob (Plate 9, top), has one pair of crossing mortises for the bracing rails, and a spike that protrudes from the top of the leg that located in a hole on the underside of the corner joint of the seat rails. This type of stool leg (classified by Killen as type Sm), is similar to that seen in the tomb of Nakhtamun, TT 341, (Figure 11).[5] The second type has a longer leg with crossing mortises in the centre for the bracing rails and again at the top of the leg for the seat rails to join to the leg (Plate 9, bottom). This stool leg (classified by Killen as type Sj), is best illustrated, (Figure 12), in the tomb of Ramosi, TT 250.[6] A fine extant example of stool, that uses this form of leg, is preserved in the British Museum, London, EA 2474 (Plates 23–24)

CHAIR OR STOOL LEG (PLATE 10).

Gurob.
Manchester Museum, University of Manchester.
Accession Number 540.
Height 280 mm.

As at Deir el-Medina, the carved lion leg was used as a sculpted form for the legs of chairs, stools and bedframes at Gurob, (Plate 10). The length of this leg indicates that it was designed to support a stool or a chair. It has been badly burnt leaving only three intact toes at the foot. However, the shape of the leg, the angle of the shoulder of the seat rail tenon, the position of the mortise on the inside of the leg and the two holes above this in which fastened a right angled strengthening bracket, fix this leg as being the right front leg of a stool or chair. The tenon at the top of the leg is well preserved being 48 mm in width, 23 mm in height and 7 mm thick and is pierced with a single peg hole of 6 mm in diameter. The leg stands on its integral drum and, although badly burnt, is incised with two horizontal lines that give three bands. This leg formed part of a seat used by a person of status.

CHAIR OR STOOL LEG (PLATE 11).

Gurob.
Petrie Museum of Egyptian Archaeology, University
College London. UC 7918.
Height 285 mm.

Similar evidence of high status chair or stool use at
Gurob can be seen with another elegant leg, (Plate 10).[7]
This leg forms the back right leg of a chair or stool; it
has been very accurately worked with fine anatomical
toe and tendon detail. Chopped into the knee of the leg
is the stretcher mortise that once connected this leg to
the chair's or stool's front leg. Down the inside of the
leg's thigh are two peg holes for the right angled bracket
that once connected this leg to the back seat rail. A tenon
is cut on the top of the leg and would have located in a
mortise cut on the underside of the side seat rail. This leg
joint would have been secured with a single peg; its hole
is seen in the tenon.

Memphis

The necropolis of Memphis also provides interesting
evidence of carpentry and its associated woodworking
trades in Lower Egypt. The monumental building projects
of the earliest dynasties at Memphis would have consumed
large quantities of timber and its position, together with the
later city of Pi-Ri´amsese would have been in a location
to exploit the import of coniferous timbers from the more
temperate areas north of Egypt. How far this source of
timber influenced furniture design is difficult to establish
as little organic material has survived from these more
northern sites. Paradoxically, did this closer source of
coniferous timber reduce the need for hardwoods that
could be found in areas to the south of Thebes?

The working of wood in Memphis was well-established
by the Early Dynastic Period, with the finds of both
tools and furniture made by W.B. Emery in the royal
cenotaph tombs of that period.[8] Later, with the extant but
decomposed furniture of Queen Hetepheres I at Giza, we
see the importance wood imports had during the reign of

*Figure 13. Scene from a lost tomb of a "hereditary prince" from Memphis. Rijksmuseum van Oudheden, Leiden. AP 40 [K. 17].
After Martin 1987: pl. 25.*

her husband Snofru which permitted his architects and builders to plan and execute those larger building projects of the Old Kingdom.[9]

The extent of commonality of woodworking techniques in both Ramesside Upper and Lower Egypt is first recognised in the furniture illustrated in those wall reliefs found in a small number of Ramesside tombs in the Memphite necropolis, (Appendix C). The canon of furniture design used in Memphis parallels those examples seen in either painted or relief forms in the Theban necropolis (Appendix B) and the wooden material discovered at Gurob. This indicates that the timber procured, whether from areas north or south of Egypt's borders, did little to influence furniture design.

Additional evidence of furniture types and the carpentry workshops in which these products were manufactured is seen in two limestone tomb fragments that date to either the end of the 18th or early 19th Dynasty. Along the top register of the first limestone fragment we see (Figure 13, from left to right), a carpenter using a pull-saw.

His left hand holds the integral metal handle of the saw while his right hand is placed firmly on the saw's back. This technique was used to prevent the thin blade from twisting and gave him a firmer grip on the saw as he drew it through the log. The next two carpenters are planing the sides of a sawn plank with adzes; both sit on three-legged stools, commonly employed by carpenters to overcome the unevenness of the workshop floor, these stools are classified by Killen as a Si type of stool. The next carpenter is using a mortise chisel and mallet to chop holes through a squared wooden plank but the register breaks before we can properly establish what process the next carpenter is engaged upon, though his body posture indicates he may also be using a pull-saw.

In the register below, a scribe is seen instructing an overseer, discussing the finishing of a large wooden funerary shrine. Two carpenters are seen with adzes, perhaps completing the second fitting of the shrine before the remaining two men, who are painters, begin its elaborate decoration. Between the scribe and overseer is a shrine shaped box.

Figure 14. Scene of carpenters working at Memphis. Staatliche Museem zu Berlin, Ägyptisches Museum, Berlin. ÄM. 19782. After Martin 1987: pl. 23.

Another carpentry scene dating from the same period is found on two adjoining blocks of limestone (Figure 14). Of interest is the right hand block, which is divided into three registers; the lowest shows the top part of a scene which has a number of carpenters engaged in planing and shaping wood. One is seen shaping the wooden body of a small statue; the other is planing the sides of a long staff. Another carpenter is shown using a pull-saw, sawing at an angle through a trunk of wood that has been tied to an upright post. Interestingly, two of the products manufactured by this team of carpenters are also to be found in the scene. A chair, (classified by Killen as a Cpp type), is uniquely rendered as both front legs of the chair are shown, behind this chair has been placed a headrest.

The middle register shows two craftsmen stretching a skin or fabric sheet across a rectangular frame. One man is pulling and attaching the sheet to the frame and is shown sitting on a three-legged stool (classified by Killen as a Si type). The other craftsman is supporting and holding the frame rigid. In the top register two further craftsmen, are seen engraving the side of vessels, both sit on similar three-legged stools.

Furniture used in Gurob show clear parallels in design to those seen in Thebes and Memphis, illustrating the wide spread use and acceptance of an established generic design canon. Wooden furniture had been developed and refined over hundreds of years to provide efficient and effective products that standardised Egyptian society and harmonised the lives of these ancient people. However, subtle changes in product use can be seen at a local level determined by the social characteristics of those people who lived or worked in each town.

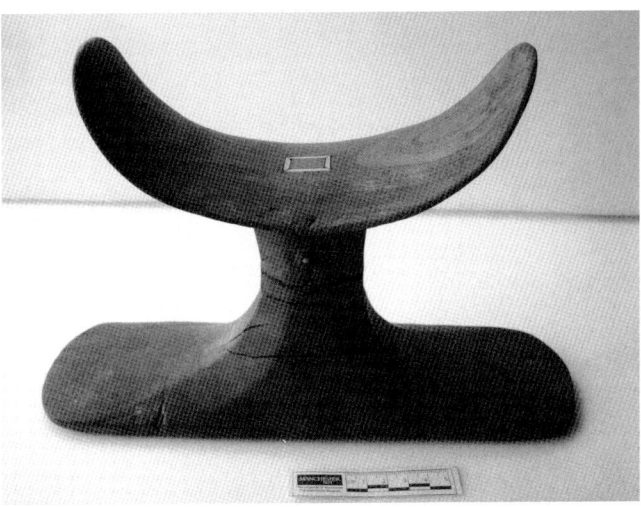

Plate 1. Headrest. Gurob. The Manchester Museum, University of Manchester, Accession Number 3722. *Photographic credit: G. Killen.*

Plate 2. Folding headrest. Gurob. Petrie Museum of Egyptian Archaeology, UCL. UC 16756. Petrie Museum, University College London. *Photographic credit: G. Killen. See also colour plates section.*

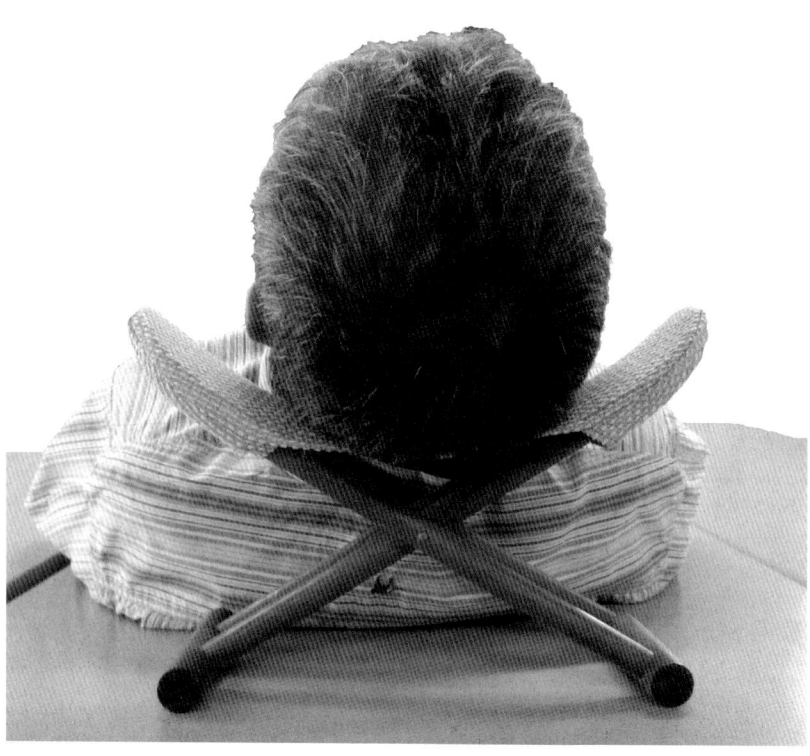

Plate 3. Replica folding headrest, made by the author. Based on folding headrest, Petrie Museum of Egyptian Archaeology, UCL. UC 16756. © *G. Killen.*

Plate 4. Folding headrest. Gurob. Petrie Museum of Egyptian Archaeology, UCL. UC 16756. Petrie Museum, University College London. *Photographic credit: G. Killen.*

Plate 5. Folding headrest. Gurob. Petrie Museum of Egyptian Archaeology, UCL. UC 16756. Petrie Museum, University College London. *Photographic credit: G. Killen.*

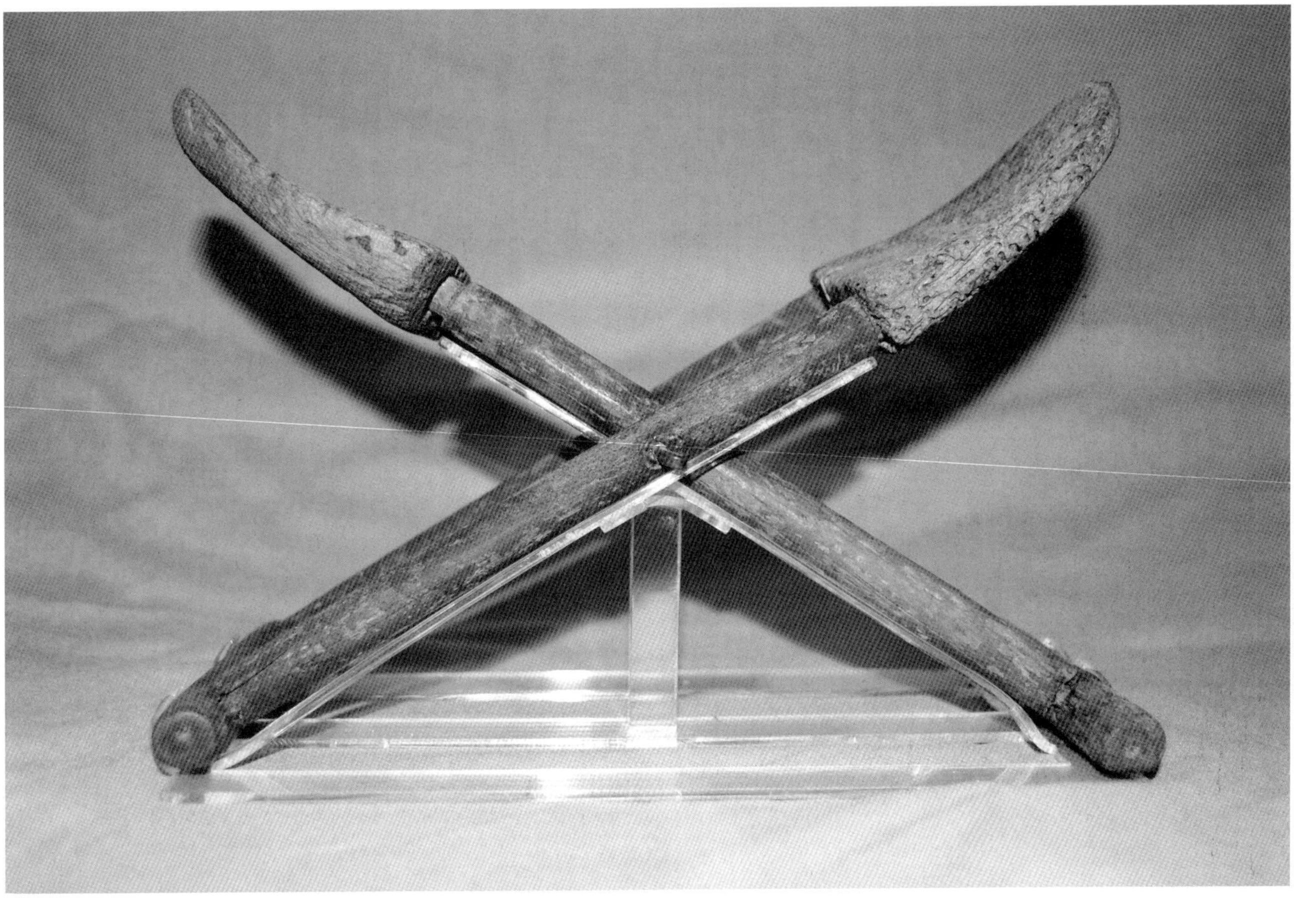

Plate 6. Folding headrest. Gurob. Petrie Museum of Egyptian Archaeology, UCL. UC 16756. Petrie Museum of Egyptian Archaeology, UCL. *Photographic credit: G. Killen.*

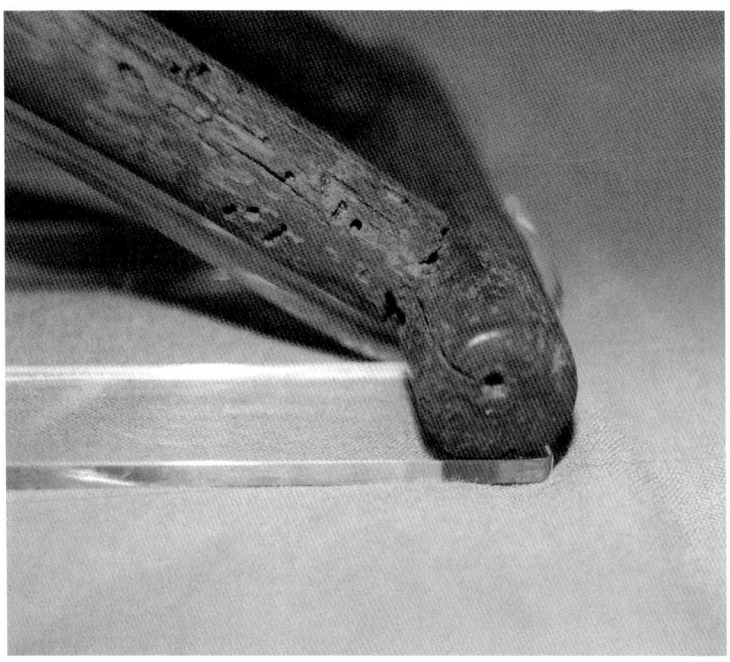

Plate 7. Folding headrest. Gurob. Petrie Museum of Egyptian Archaeology, UCL. UC 16756. Petrie Museum, University College London. *Photographic credit: G. Killen.*

Plate 8. Stool leg. Gurob. Petrie Museum of Egyptian Archaeology, UCL. UC 58988. Petrie Museum, University College London. *Photographic credit: G. Killen.*

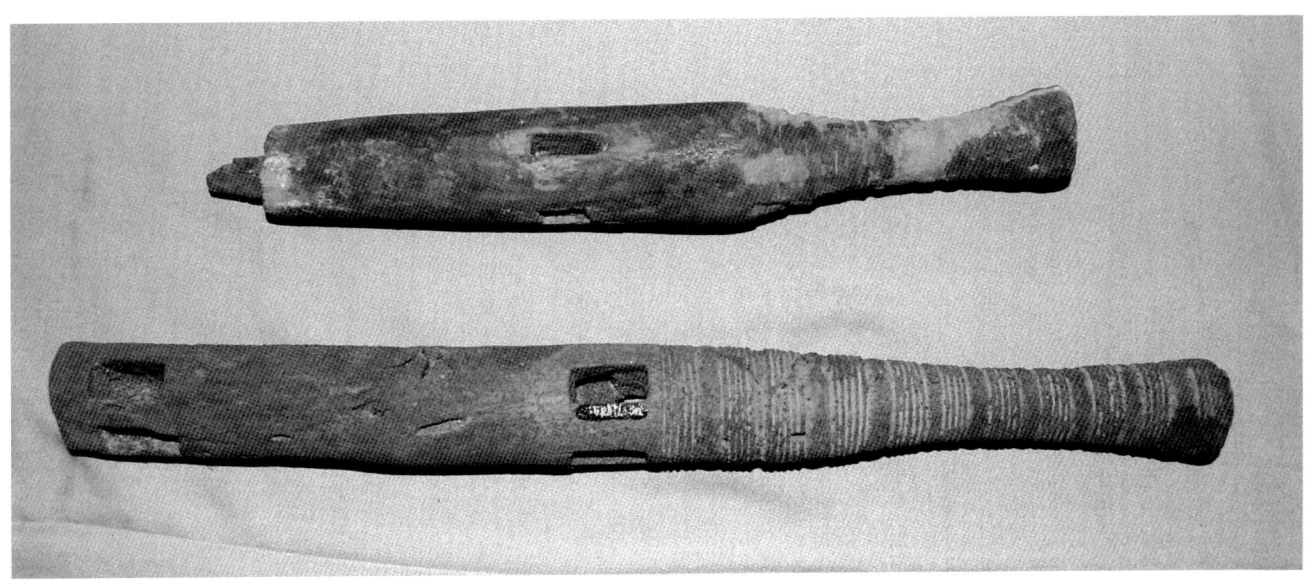

Plate 9. Two round stool legs. Top (Gurob) UC 58988, bottom UC 71984. Petrie Museum of Egyptian Archaeology, UCL. Petrie Museum, University College London. *Photographic credit: G. Killen.*

Plate 10. Chair or stool leg. Gurob. The Manchester Museum, University of Manchester, Accession Number 540.
Photographic credit: G. Killen.

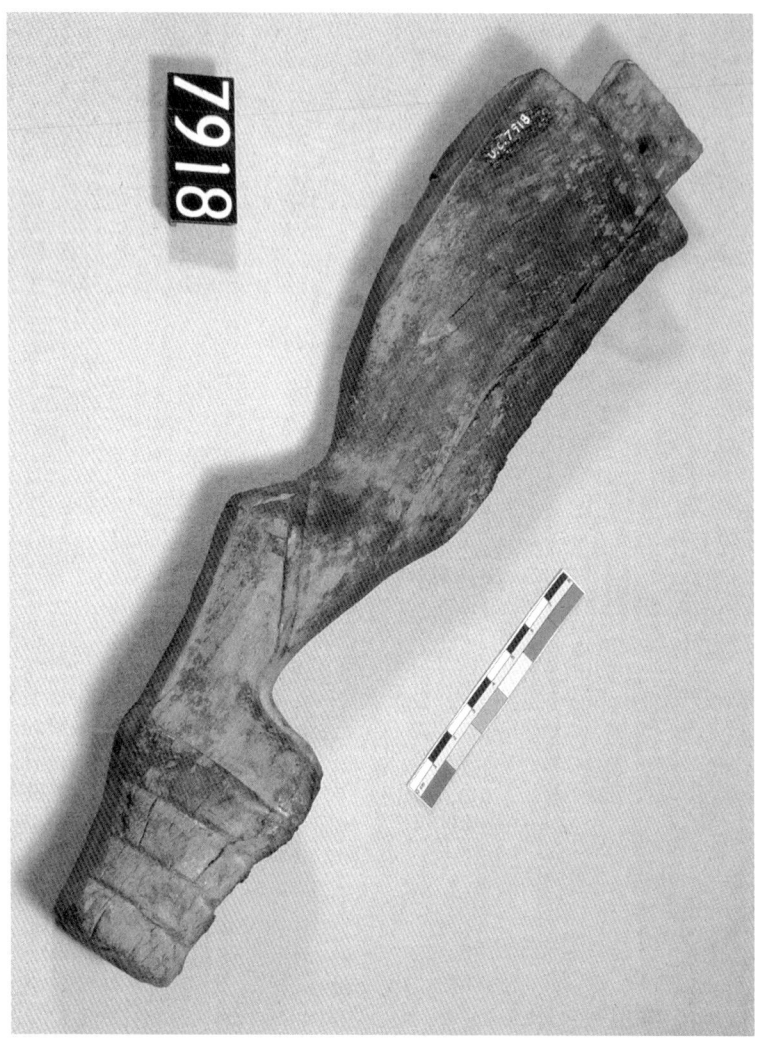

Plate 11. Chair or stool leg. Gurob. Petrie Museum of Egyptian Archaeology, UCL. UC 7918. © *Petrie Museum, University College London.*

Chapter 3

Ramesside Furniture Forms

A pictorial survey of Ramesside furniture forms depicted in tomb wall paintings or reliefs, stela and blocks can be found in Appendix A. Listings of individual tombs and the types of furniture illustrated in them can be found in Appendix B (Theban tombs) and Appendix C (Memphite tombs). Depictions of furniture forms found elsewhere are cited at the beginning of each sub-section in this chapter.

Chairs

Leonine Forms

Ramesside chair forms (Ca–Cjj, see Appendix A) depicted in private tombs at Thebes and Memphis follow a clearly understood anthropometric design canon based upon accurate measurements taken from the human body.[1] Earlier chairs often had lower seat heights created by the use of very short chair legs. Indeed, 18th Dynasty tomb scenes occasionally show that low chairs were used by women, and that some young women knelt on low chairs usually with one knee raised.[2] This method of seating is not seen during the Ramesside Period as chair legs are taller allowing the user, both male and female, to sit upon the chair without having to elevate the knees above the horizontal plane of the seat; this provides a more comfortable sitting posture. The modelling of late 18th Dynasty and Ramesside chair legs, although still based upon a leonine form, is often stylised, being less anatomically correct with some being elongated.

The artistic convention of apparently placing a husband and wife on a bench or double type of seat (classified by Killen as a Cy and Caa type) where there is no indication of a third leg under the seat or a second backrest, rarely appears in painted wall scenes in Ramesside tombs.[3] This form of seating is also depicted in three usurped tombs that originally date to the 18th Dynasty.[4] However, there is no archaeological evidence to support the use of bench or double type seats.

New Kingdom chairs were manufactured with a range of seat heights, the lowest range typically having a leg height of between 280–300 mm. An example preserved in the Garstang Museum, (Figure 15 and Plate 12), has a leg height of 300 mm and is well modelled from an open grain wood, finished with a thick layer of gesso. From the positions of the mortises, on the side and back of the leg, we can establish that it is a front chair leg. The size of the mortises (25 mm × 15 mm) indicate that the ends of the stretchers were not tenoned with cut shoulders, but connected with a joint known as a barefaced tenon. From the top of the leg projects a tenon, onto which the seat's side rail would have fitted. This joint would have been secured with a pair of dowels.

Two distinctive forms of leg can be observed when examining examples of a Ramesside context, firstly, (Form A) a longer leg, and secondly, (Form B), a shorter leg. The Form A example (Figure 16 and Plates 13–14), is 470 mm in height excluding the tenon, and is manufactured from a dense and fine grained wood, this property allowed the carpenter to reduce the cross sectional area of leg throughout its length without compromising the structural strength of the leg. The positions of the mortises confirm that it is a back leg. The widths of the mortises are narrower indicating that the tenon on the end of the stretcher would have been cut with shoulders. Due to the increased height of the leg the carpenter had to dowel a supporting bracket down the inside of this leg and across the underside of the seat rail. The top of the leg has been cut with a tenon, which locates in a mortise on the underside of the side seat rail. A fragment of seat rail remains attached to this joint providing evidence its strength and is again secured by a pair of through dowels. The Form B example (Figures 17 and Plate 15), is 340 mm in height, has graceful lines

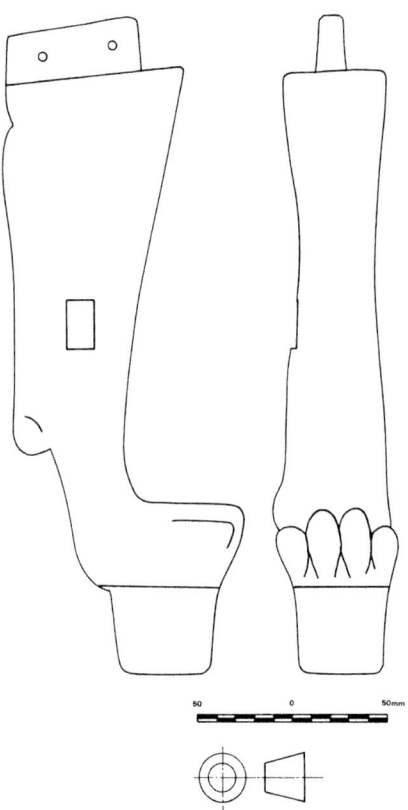

Figure 15. Chair leg. Garstang Museum, University of Liverpool, E 7161

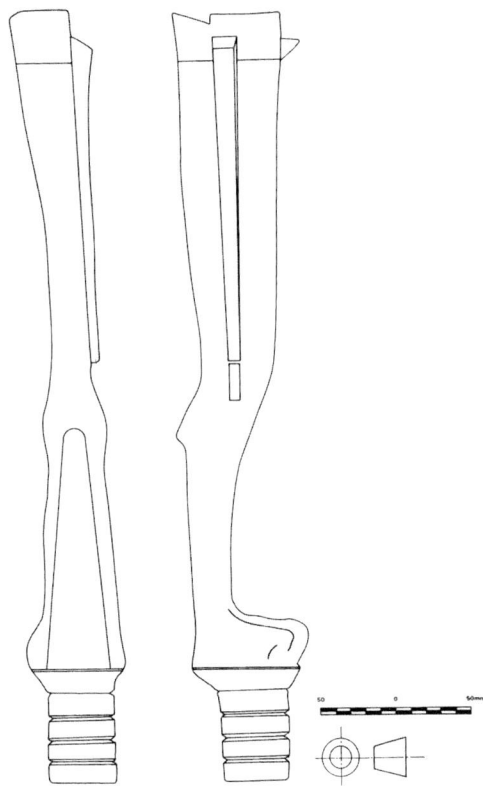

Figure 16. Chair leg (Form A). Petrie Museum of Egyptian Archaeology, University College London. UC. 36478

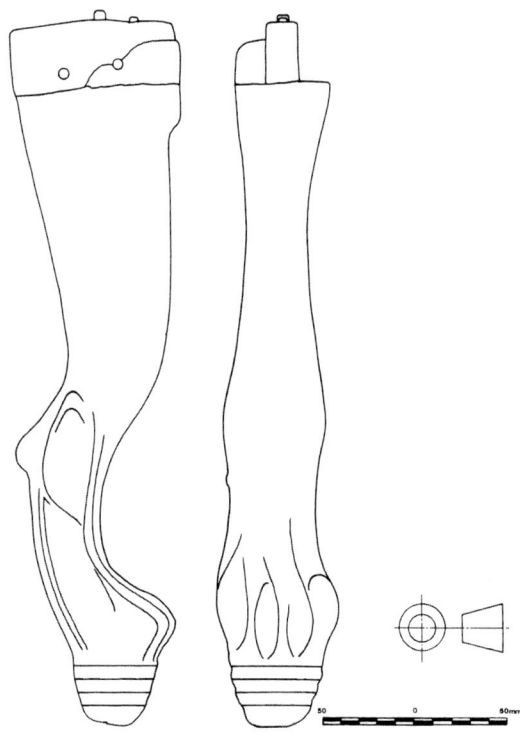

Figure 17. Chair leg (Form B). British Museum, London. EA. 49123.

and relies more on its stylised form than anatomical detail to indicate its feline characteristics.

Both forms of chair leg (Forms A and B) were carved on three-dimensional stone pair statues of the late 18th and 19th Dynasties. The first, (Plate 16), depicts an official and his wife seated on a Cf type chair, that employs a Form A leg. Whilst (Plate 17) depicts Yuny and his wife, Renenutet seated on a Cp type chair that employs a Form B leg.

CHAIR (PLATES 18–19).

Louvre Museum, Paris. N2950.
Height 874 mm, width 584 mm.

The Louvre Museum possesses a remarkably well-preserved chair of unknown provenance, (Plate 18), (classified by Killen as Cf type) purchased from the Salt Collection in 1826. The quality of its construction and use of different woods and inlays of ivory and African Blackwood indicate that it was made by carpenters in the royal or temple workshops. Strikingly the legs are painted blue - the paintwork may have been restored during the 19th century, but parallels exist in now lost wall paintings, once seen in the tomb of Rameses III (KV11) (see *Chapter Four: Royal and Temple Furniture*).[5] Also, there has been no attempt to conceal either the chair's construction or the materials from which it was manufactured. The quality of the carpentry is remarkable with emphasis being placed on accuracy and attention to detail.

The finely worked feline legs (Type B) are tenoned into stopped mortises in the seat rails. Each joint has been secured with a pair of dowels. The front and back seat rails are mortised and tenoned into the side seat rails. All the elements that make the seat frame are straight and not curved; holes are drilled through the inner edges of each seat rail and a webbing of leather has been laced across, as a modern restoration, to form the seat.

The chair's shaped back support is made with a panelled construction; the top rail is curved and the top edge is rolled over. The interior space has been filled with vertical panels and strips of wood of different colour, two darker boards have been inlaid with ivory plaques cut to the profile of an opened Egyptian lily. As a finishing feature caps of ivory have been used to highlight the constructional technique being employed to fasten the outer back support frame together. A band of lozenge shaped pieces in African Blackwood are set against triangles of ivory. This is a common Ramesside applied decorative technique either inlaid or imitated in paint, has been placed as a ribbon below the moulded top back support rail.

To connect the shaped back support to the seat, a pair of angled supports, made from two parts and covered with a thin layer of veneer, has been dowelled to the edge of each side seat rail and the sloping side rail of the back support. The method of holding the curved back support rigid is illustrated clearly on this chair frame, (Plate 19). Three vertical wooden pillars are fixed with right-angled brackets behind the shaped back support and mortised and tenoned into the top curved back support rail, providing a triangulated construction that gave sufficient rigidity to the frame.

Stools

Evidence from the private Ramesside tomb scenes show the wide use of different forms of stool that can be classified into seven generic forms (Appendix A) – round legged stools (types Sa, Sb, Sc, Sj, Sk, Sl, Sm, Sn, So, Sp, St, Su, Sw, Sx); folding stools (types Sd, Se); lattice stools (types Sf, Sq, Sr, Ss, Sv); three-legged stools (types Sg, Sh, Si); animal leg stools (type Saa); shaped legged stools (type Sz) and rectangular frame stools (type Sy). See Appendix D for the distribution of stool type by gender as illustrated in private Ramesside Theban tombs.

Round Legged Stools

There is a striking change in the gender usage of round legged stools during the three dynasties that constitute the New Kingdom. During the 18th Dynasty round legged stools were used by both genders.[6] However, data of gender stool usage drawn from wall paintings in the Theban Ramesside tombs, show that stools fashioned with a wide range of rounded legs were exclusively used by Theban women during the 19th and 20th Dynasties (Appendix D), although paradoxically a number of Ramesside kings would use stools and chairs fashioned with round legs (see Chapter Four: Royal and Temple Furniture).

The trend for women to use round legged stools in the Ramesside Period is also seen in a number of statues of seated couples, where the woman is seated on a stool fashioned with rounded legs.[7] A notable wooden statue of this genera of 19th Dynasty provenance is preserved in the Ägyptisches Museum, Berlin. ÄM 6910.[8] It portrays Amenemopet seated on a chair of a Cp type, while his wife Hathor, sits upon a Sl type round legged stool. Amenemopet is the owner of tomb TT265 at Deir el-Medina and Hathor displays the use that women made of round legged stools. The carving of this wooden statue is particularly fine. The stool is well-modelled and the surfaces of the legs have been incised with rings and bands of lily petal decoration. A thick linen cushion has been placed on the seat on which Hathor sits.

The round stool leg fashioned on the stool on which Hathor sits is similar to the example discovered at Gurob (Plate 8), it has one pair of crossing mortises, for the bracing rails, and a spike that protrudes from the top of the leg that located in a hole on the underside of the corner joint of the seat rails. This type of stool leg (classified by Killen as type Sm), is similar to that illustrated in the tomb of Nakhtamun (TT341) (Figure 11).

A second type of stool leg is longer with crossing mortises in the centre for the bracing rails and again at the top of the leg for the seat rails to join to the leg. This stool leg (classified by Killen as type Sj), is best illustrated (Figure 12) in the tomb of Ramosi (TT250). Both types of leg are found on two stools now preserved in the British Museum and described below.

ROUND LEGGED STOOL (PLATE 20).

British Museum, London. EA. 2473.
Length 395 mm, width 395 mm, height 265 mm.

The legs of this stool, (Plate 20), have been worked to shape in poor quality wood. The upper section has been finished to a cylindrical form while below the stretcher joint each leg had been gracefully shaped to form a narrow waist. The surface of the waist has been incised with a series of deep rings, a decorative technique also clearly visible on the stool illustrated in the tomb of Nakhtamun, TT 341, (Figure 11). The round section stretcher below the seat locates in a round hole bored in the leg. Plaster has been used to disguise the joint to give the appearance of an ivory ferrule in the shape of a papyrus flower.

Each of the seat rails has been shaped to provide a curved profile to the seat. The seat rails are mortised and tenoned together; a hole bored in the underside of each joint at each corner of the seat frame was designed to retain the spike that extends from the top of the stool's leg.

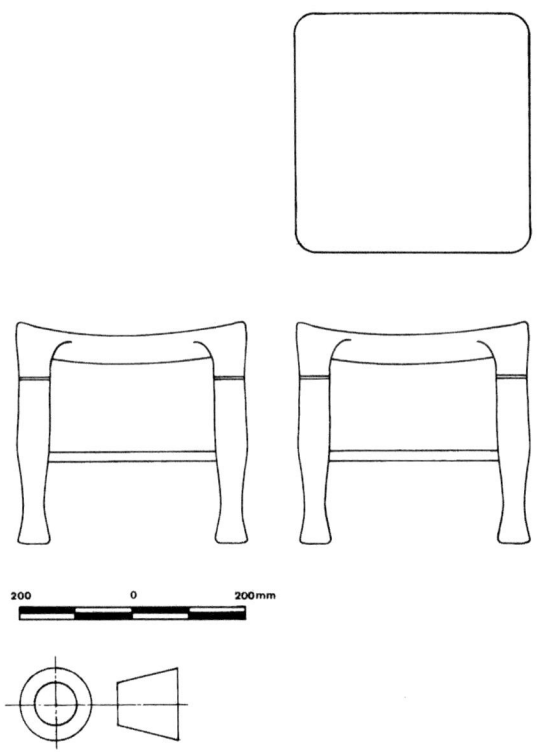

Figure 18. Round legged stool, Tomb of Sennedjem. Egyptian Museum, Cairo. JE 27255A.

The legs and stretchers have been painted black to imitate the harder African Blackwood. Around the top of each leg a band of white lily petals has been left from the original gesso foundation. Interestingly, this band of decoration is only rendered on the outer visible surfaces of each leg. Painted rectangles outlined with a stringing of gesso have been applied to each leg to give the appearance of mortises. The seat rails are painted with a red pigment over a gesso foundation. As there are no fragments of an animal hide seat it suggests that a linen cushion, filled with duck or goose feathers, would have been placed on the seat. The small central opening enclosed by the seat rails would support this view as the majority of force applied to this stool would be absorbed by the stool's seat rails.

ROUND LEGGED STOOL (FIGURE 18).

Tomb of Sennedjem (TT1). Egyptian Museum, Cairo. JE. 27255A.
Height 248 mm, width 356 mm, depth 370 mm.

The quality of both the construction and decoration of furniture manufactured at Deir el-Medina, and possibly made exclusively for funerary use, is seen in this stool made for Sennedjem's wife Iyneferti (Figure 18). It repeats the established formula of having black painted legs to simulate African Blackwood, with imitation

painted white line work to suggest the position where the through mortise holes would have been capped with plugs of ivory and ebony veneer. The seat was made from a fabric, consistent with canvas or a similar coarse material, which had been applied with gesso to the seat rails, and then painted red. The edges of the fabric seat have been carefully bound and moulded in a wet condition around the seat rails to conceal the leg and seat rail joints. The condition of the seat is surprisingly good; there is only one small hole, while some of the gesso has peeled away from the seat rails. The centre of the seat has been painted with two rectangular frames lined in yellow and black paint. A single line of hieroglyphic text on the seat shows that this stool belonged to Iyneferti.

The second round legged stool Egyptian Museum, Cairo, JE 27255B, which also belonged to Iyneferti, is of better constructional quality and has taller legs.[9] Having painted legs that replicate better quality wood, each leg has been painted to simulate incised rings and petals with chequered and rosette patterns of ivory and African Blackwood veneer.

SEAT FROM A ROUND LEG STOOL (PLATES 21–22).

British Museum, London. EA 2517.
Width 432 mm, depth 430 mm.

This complete seat, (Plate 21), allows us a unique opportunity to examine one form of seat construction used in the manufacture of round legged stools.[10] The wooden curved frame of the seat is constructed from four shaped rails, two long and two short. Each corner of the seat frame is mortised and tenoned together. In the edges of the long rails are chopped the mortises that hold the tenons which spring from both ends of the short rails. This jointing arrangement provides a solid section of wood in which to bore a hole where the spike that extends from the top of the hand-rounded leg locates.

These leg holes, two of which still retain a broken spike, were bored completely through the rail, seen in (Plate 21) bottom right corner, before the gesso surface was applied. A series of holes was then drilled along the inner edge of the seat frame through which a webbing made from four strands of rush cord was threaded and then woven across the frame to produce the seat, (Plate 22).

This form of seat construction is typical; however, the embellishing process was taken further. Once the round legs were fixed into the frame, a large amount of gesso has been applied to the wooden seat frame and the woven rush seat, which was additionally reinforced with a linen sheet. On the underside of the woven seat can be seen evidence of the leakage of gesso from the seat's top surface through the fine woven linen sheet used to reinforce the top surface of the seat, (Plate 22). Once the gesso had set, ochre coloured paint was applied to the outer wooden frame, top and bottom, then a decorative arrangement of ruled square boxes in ochre and blue paint together with lozenges and circles was applied directly to the gessoed surface in the centre of the seat.

Round Legged Stool (Plates 23–24).

British Museum, London. EA 2474.
Length 380 mm, width 380 mm, height 320 mm.

This stool, (Plate 23), is of a much finer construction and would once have been covered with a hide skin that was glued to the top curved surfaces of the seat rails. The legs have been worked with a decorative spindle effect and have pairs of crossing mortises chopped through the top and centre of each leg to accept the tenons that have been cut on the ends of both the curved seat rails and stretchers. Small ivory plugs have been used to conceal the end grain of the crossing stretcher tenons (Plate 24).

Round Legged Stool Fragments (Plates 25–29).

Petrie Museum of Egyptian Archaeology, University College London.
Legs UC 71984, Stretchers UC 71985.
UC 71984 Length 420 mm. UC 71985. Length 430 mm, 440 mm.

The method used to construct a round legged type stool is clearly seen in these fragmentary remains. The top pairs of mortises in the legs are aligned to accept the tenons on the end of the seat rails (Plate 25). Both these mortises are of the stopped variety, i.e. they have not been chopped completely through the leg. The tenons on the opposing seat rails would have been finished with mitred surfaces enabling them to meet at right angles in the mortise. The shoulders of each tenon have been scribed to allow them to seat and match the circular section of the leg.

The mortises in the centre of each leg (Plate 26), have been offset to accept the tenons that have been cut on the ends of stretchers (Plate 27). These tenons have been haunched and halved (Plate 28), allowing the stretcher rails to lie in the same plane which provides strength of the joint.

As with EA 2474, (Plate 24), the ends of the stretchers are shaped to imitate a papyrus flower and the shoulders of the tenon have been scribed. The tenon does not completely penetrate the mortise, (Plate 29), indicating that a small plug of some resistant type material, probably ivory, would have been used to cap this joint.

Folding Stools

Folding Stools Fashioned with Bird Legs
The folding stool made with two pairs of crossing legs whose terminals are carved with duck headed terminals, classified by Killen as stool type Se, continued to be manufactured during the Ramesside Period and were

used exclusively by men.[11] From the reign of Rameses II we have evidence of its use in scenes found in the tomb of Ipuy (TT217), (Davies 1927: pls. XXVIII, XXXVI). Fischer identified the folding stools earliest use in Egypt on a stele dated to Year 8 of Amenenhet IV, (Egyptian Museum, Cairo, JE 38547). He also re-evaluated the folding stool (Metropolitan Museum of Art, New York, MMA 12.182.58) that had been assigned the provenance Meir, establishing that it came from Rifa and probably should be dated as New Kingdom rather than Middle Kingdom (Fischer 1986: 99. n 53).

In the Ramesside tomb of Huy and Peshedu, TT339, a complete folding stool was discovered by Bruyère that belonged to Peshedu. This folding stool shows those typical constructional and decorative characteristics of this form of furniture (Bruyère 1926: pl. V [3]). A similar stool that had been deposited in the tomb of Sennedjem, had been inscribed to him along the front edge of the seat cover.[12] Sennedjem's stool has plainly finished ends to the crossing legs, similar in construction to (MMA 12.182.58). Whereas the example that belonged to Peshedu has crossing legs finished with duck headed terminals that grip the floor rails.

Folding Stools Fashioned with Animal Legs
Folding stools were also manufactured during the Ramesside period with animal shaped legs, classified by Killen as stool type Sd. In the tomb of Userhet, TT51, we have a wall painting depicting the use of this type of folding stool (Davies 1927: pl. XV). While another scene in the tomb of Hatiay, TT324 shows two folding stools whose legs are fashioned in a feline form (Davies and Gardiner 1948: pl. XXXII).

On one of these stools, (Figure 19), the upper part of each leg has a decorative pattern applied suggesting that bands of inlaid material have been added to each leg.

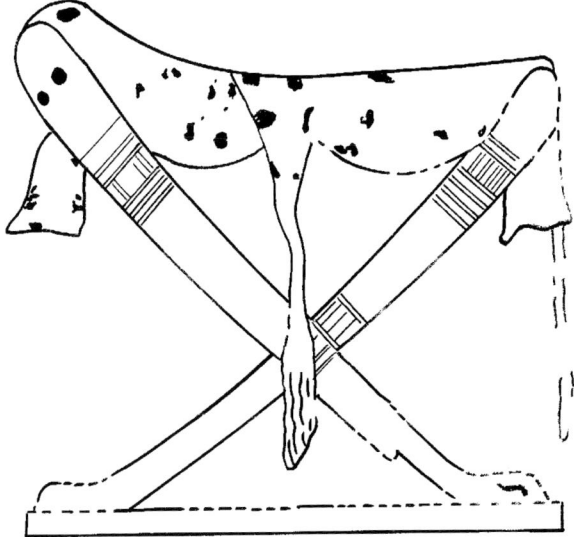

Plate 19. Folding stool from a scene in the tomb of Hatiay, (TT324). After: Davies and Gardiner 1948: pl. XXXII.

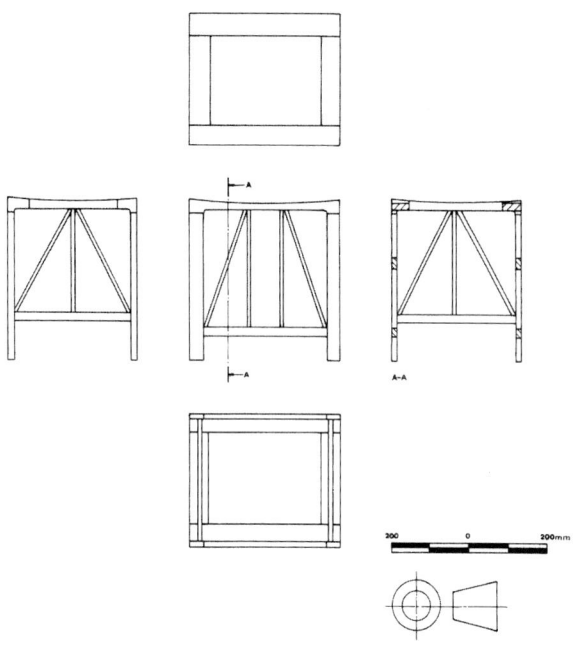

Figure 20. Lattice stool, Tomb of Sennedjem, (TT1). Egyptian Museum, Cairo. JE27291.

The seat of this stool is rendered to give the appearance of being made from a cheetah skin, with its tail hanging from the side of the seat and its skin draping over the corners. It is uncertain whether this seat was made from actual skin or fabricated from curved boards and attached elements of wood then painted to simulate an animal skin. A stool with a rigid fabricated seat and crossing legs terminating with ducks' heads was deposited in the tomb of Tutankhamun (Killen 1980: 42–43, pl. 64; Killen 2017A: 63–64, pl. 64).

FOLDING STOOL LEG FRAGMENT (PLATE 30).

British Museum, London. EA 2496
Length 110 mm.

This folding stool leg fragment, (Plate 30), shows how the leg illustrated in (Figure 19) was jointed to its floor rail. A tenon extends from below the sole of the flat paw and would have located in a mortise chopped at an angle into the floor rail.

FOLDING STOOL (PLATES 31–32, 35).

British Museum, London. EA 37406.
Height 470 mm, width 485 mm.

Another folding stool variant has four paws that most likely are modelled on the cheetah, an animal that was indigenous to Egypt until recently.[13] The modelling and carving of these legs has been precisely executed, particularly the

carpel complex of bones. The carpenter's knowledge of the gross morphology of the cheetah is displayed by his carving that replicates the little pad of flesh, the carpal pad, which covers the pisiform bone.

The paw, (Plate 32), is finely carved with four claws and a dewclaw. Cheetahs are unable to retract their claws whereas lions can (Plates 33 and 34). Extending from below the paw, a tenon locates into a through mortise, with a transverse dowel fastening the joint. The floor rails have been worked to a circular shape by hand and there is no indication that they were made on a simple machine.

The top of each leg, (Plate 35), is again mortised and tenoned into the underside of a slightly curved seat rail. Moulded bosses have been carved below the seat rail to provide a flat surface for the shoulder of the tenon to match against. The seat was made by gluing an animal hide across the seat rails, fragments of this hide survive in a now cracked and brittle state of preservation on both the top and bottom surfaces of both seat rails.

Lattice Stools

Illustrations of lattice type stools can be found in a small number of Theban tombs (see Appendix B). Their use was mainly reserved for males although a female is shown seated on a Sr type lattice stool in the tomb of Paser.[14] Those variants (types Sf, Sq, Sr, Ss and Sv) of lattice stool are simply differentiated by the number of vertical and horizontal rails that are used to strengthen the stool's frame, while on each plane surface of this type of stool, two angled braces are included in the design to triangulate and give the rigidity expected of this structure. The lattice stool efficiently uses material and is often finished with a fine layer of gesso.

LATTICE STOOL (FIGURE 20).

Tomb of Sennedjem (TT1).
Egyptian Museum, Cairo. JE. 27291.
Height 340 mm, length 480 mm, width 300 mm.

One of the lattice type stools deposited in the tomb of Sennedjem, (Figure 20), conforms to the Sf type. The seat rails are slightly curved with the tenons on the ends of the shorter rails locating in stopped mortises chopped in the inner surfaces of the longer rails. The top of each rectangular cross section leg has been cut with a stub tenon that locates in a mortise below each corner of the seat.

As the legs are rectangular in cross section the bottom stretcher rails have been deliberately offset allowing the stub tenons of the stretcher to penetrate deeply into the leg without breaking through the outer surfaces. On the wider faces of the stool, two vertical and two angled struts have been included in the structure, while on the ends it has only been possible to have a single vertical strut enclosed by a pair of angled struts.

The second stool deposited in Sennedjem's tomb has a single vertical support and two angled braces placed between the seat rails and the horizontal stretchers on each side of the stool. This arrangement is not seen in those depictions of lattice type stools in the private Ramesside tombs in the Theban necropolis. The front and back seat rails are curved while both side seat rails are straight. Holes have been drilled through the inner edges of the seat frame through which has been woven cord that forms the seat. A separate horizontal rail has been attached below each of the side seat rails into which locate, using mortise and tenon joints, a single vertical and two angled braces.

LATTICE STOOL SEAT (PLATE 36).

Musées Royaux D'Art et D'Histoire, Brussels. Inv. No. 2411.
Depth 102 mm, length 440 mm, width 405 mm.

Some stool seats, (Plate 36), were manufactured from shaped boards that were joined together to form a double curved seat. The front and back rails of this seat were carved from carefully selected boards; mortises were chopped on the underside of these front and back rails at each end and into these mortises fitted the tenons sawn on the top of each leg. Along the inner edges of both front rails were chopped a series of mortises into which fitted tenons cut on the ends of each curved seat board. These joints were fastened by a dowel that passed through the inner edge of each front rail. The two outer rails were manufactured from wider boards to give the appearance the seat frame was made from similar cross section boards.

Three-Legged Stools

The three-legged stool (variants classified by Killen as types Sg, Sh, Si) were the preferred choice of stool for Egyptian craftsman, particularly those who were working in a workshop environment. It was a functional piece of furniture, its three legs allowing it to rest on an uneven floor surface. The use of this type of stool is seen in the 18th Dynasty, an example being discovered by Bernard Bruyère in pit tomb 1352 at Deir el-Medina.[15] In the Ramesside Period its use continues to be exclusively used by craftsmen as seen in the tomb of Neferrenpet (TT178 – Hofmann 1995: pl. XXXIX, pl. XL), and with carpenters seen using them in the tomb of Ipuy (TT217 – Davies 1927: pl. XXX, pl. XXXVI, pl. XL), where we have scenes of woodworkers engaged in manufacturing a range funerary goods. This type of stool is also seen being used in the carpentry workshops found at Memphis, (Figures 13 and 14).

THREE-LEGGED STOOL (PLATE 37).

British Museum, London. EA 2482.
Height 262 mm, width 455 mm, depth 355 mm.

The seat of this three-legged stool, (Plate 37), (classified

by Killen as a Si type) is made from a solid slab of wood that resembles a modern saddle type stool seat, being semi-circular in shape with a straight front edge. The top surface of the stool is slightly dished with its edges rounded.

Tenons on the ends of three splayed legs locate in stopped mortises in the underside of the seat. These legs have been made from pieces of wood whose grain intentionally follows the curved line of each leg, indicating the carpenter selected the wood from a curved branch knowing that this would give the constructional performance he desired. Each leg has been carefully worked to shape and the edges have been chamfered, the completed stool being finished with a fine gesso ground. This stool was manufactured without horizontal bracing stretchers set between its three legs, but others do appear to have been designed with this additional feature as depicted in the tomb of Ipuy (TT217) where seven workmen are showed seated on Sg and Sh type stools (Davies 1927: pl. XXX, XXXVI; see Appendix B).

Animal Leg Stools

An example of an animal leg stool (classified by Killen as a Saa type stool) is depicted in the Memphite tomb of Khay, south chapel, north wall. (Martin 2001: pl. 11). We do have evidence of their earlier use with an example discovered in the 18th-Dynasty tomb of Kha.[16]

Three interesting examples of stool with their side seat rails carved to represent the body and head of an animal are preserved in British Museum, London [EA 66652] (Plates 38–41, Figure 21); Musées Royaux D'Art et D'Histoire, Brussels [Inv. E 2409] and the Burrell Collection, Glasgow [Inv. 13/91]. The inclusion of animal heads, even though simplistically modelled, would possibly suggest furniture designed for royal use. Parallels with the generic form of these stools can be seen on a chair that once was painted in side chamber Cg: right wall (lower part) in the tomb of Rameses III, KV11.[17] (This example with other forms of royal furniture will be discussed in Chapter Four: Royal and Temple furniture). However, the modelling of the heads on the three stools described below cannot be confirmed as being based on the head of a lion.

STOOL (PLATE 38–41, FIGURE 21).

British Museum, London. EA 66652
Depth 355 mm, width 390 mm, height 345 mm.

The modelling of each of the legs of this stool is particularly fine (Plate 38 and Figure 21). There is no pronounced dewclaw on the fore leg although the claws are shown, suggesting these are a decorative feature rather than an accurate anatomical detail. The stretchers that brace the frame are modern; the pair that span the front and back legs are unusually low, as the mortises have been chopped into the side of the paws. This constructional detail is not seen on the other two stools described below and could

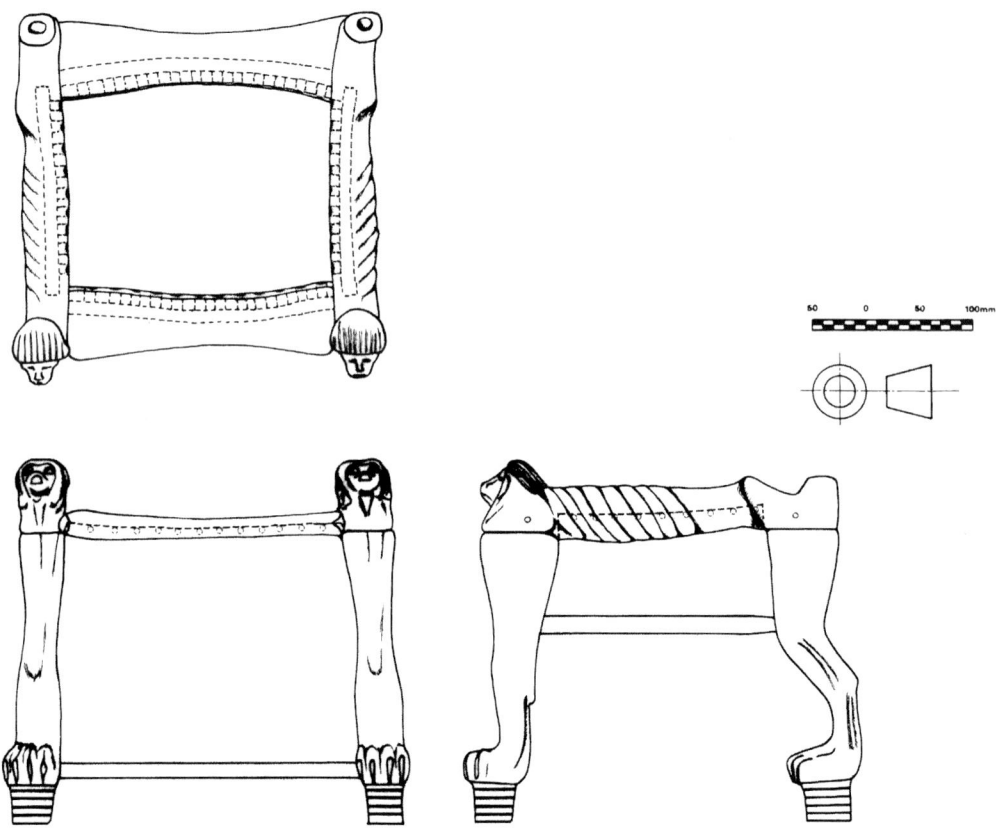

Figure 21. Stool, British Museum, London. EA 66652

indicate that the stool has been reworked at some period.

The carving of the side seat rails is rendered to suggest the body of the animal; the ridges of the rib cage are accurately modelled, whilst the animal's head, (Plate 39), is much stylised and cannot be conclusively identified as feline in form. The back of each side rail has been bored with a socket. It is unlikely that these sockets were part of the joint for the uprights of an attached backrest.

Typical elements that form a chair's backrest were deeply mortised in the chair's seat rails and were not fitted into shallow sockets. The sockets, (Plate 40), that have been set over the back legs of this stool have been bored into a protruding platform that is modelled above the animal's hindquarters.

This feature eliminates the sockets were part of a backrest; however, they may once have held a short curved tail, a decorative feature that was used on bier and couch construction. Illustrations in the Theban tombs provide evidence that the side rails of biers were also modelled with animal heads and bodies, with curved tails that sprung from the animal's hindquarters.[18] We also see that two of Tutankhamun's couches were manufactured with wooden curved tails.[19]

The use of cord to form the seat is indicated by a series of holes that have been drilled through the inside edges

of each seat rail, (Plate 41), and a deep groove, that has been chiselled along the underside of each element to meet these holes. Cord would have been fed through each hole into the groove before being woven across the seat opening to form the finished seat. The method employed to string this stool allows the modelling of the animal body side rails to be fully appreciated.

The stool preserved in the Musées Royaux D'Art et D'Histoire, Brussels. Inv. E 2409 is in general construction similar to EA 66652. Again the use of modern stretchers has been included, however, the pair that brace the front and back legs have been raised and lie in the same horizontal plane as the side stretchers. Also the front and back seat rails are modern replicas, whereas, the side seat rails have been accurately carved replicating an animal's body and including in the design the position for a short curved tail that would have located in a socket over each back leg.

Each of the animal head capitals are different, one is similar to the British Museum stool but the other represents a completely different animal. This suggests that this stool is a composite construction of stool fragments, and not an original structure although in the context of this study is worthy of examination.

The stool preserved in the Burrell Collection, Glasgow. Inv. 13/91 follows the design principles established by the previous examples. The side rails of the stool are finished with well-modelled animal bodies, while above the front legs both side rails are capped with a capital carved with an animal head. Sockets are carved into the rear of each side rail to accept a short curved wooden tail. Where this stool differs is that there are no supporting stretchers, the bracing of the legs to the seat rails is achieved by triangular brackets. This reinforces the view that the generic form of side seat rail, modelled upon an animal's torso, was a design feature of Egyptian furniture although it is difficult to establish the true nature of the frame and its reinforcement.

Shaped Leg Stools

Stools had been manufactured with either shaped legs or straight legs since the Middle Kingdom. At the Beni Hasan necropolis, John Garstang excavated several stools and bedframes that had legs fashioned with square legs that tapered to a narrow waist and had rush type seats (Garstang 1907). These features of stool design can also be seen on some stools manufactured during the 18th Dynasty. Bernard Bruyère's excavations of the 18th Dynasty pit tombs at Deir el-Medina provides evidence that simple stools with shaped legs were commonly used in the New Kingdom (Bruyère 1937B). However, their use during the Ramesside Period, through taking evidence from tomb paintings in the Theban necropolis is particularly weak. Only one type of stool, classified by Killen as stool type Sz, and seen in the tomb of Ipuy, TT217 (Davies 1927: pl. XXXVI), can be considered to be a stool with shaped legs and is being used by a carpenter who works at a typical block bench, carving a large *djed* pillar with a chisel.

The lack of pictorial representations of simple utilitarian stools in Theban and Memphite tombs of the Ramesside period is not surprising as the furniture depicted in these tombs was generally designed for those Egyptians who had status and wealth or who were artisans where their trade determined the type of stool they used. The much larger corpus of simple furniture that would have been used can only be surveyed from the archaeological record.

Ramesside Settlements in Nubia

Material excavated at Aniba that dates to the end of the New Kingdom, shows that those Egyptians and Nubians living in Nubian Ramesside settlements south of Thebes were using Egyptianised stools, chairs and bedframes. Some with lion shaped legs, similar to those used in Thebes, but also a range of more utilitarian stools and chairs. The excavation of furniture from Egyptian cemetery S at Aniba during Steindorff's excavations of the site, support the view that those living in Nubia still desired sophisticated high status furniture and those of lesser social status retained expectations of using simple furniture forms.

The high status leonine form legs found at Aniba are typical of those forms found in Thebes and other Ramesside sites in Egypt.[20] However, four plain straight stool legs discovered at Aniba in (Tomb S 91, 29), display strong technical and design parallels with stools discovered at Deir el-Medina.[21]

Having established that simple plain legs with rounded tops and crossing mortises for the seat rails to engage in were present at Aniba it is surprising that the cemetery excavation of Amara West by the EES during the 1938 –1939 season did not record any similar wooden material.[22] However, Neal Spencer's recent excavations at Amara West have shown fragmentary evidence of simple stool and bedframe construction.[23] Spencer's work at Amara West has also uncovered coffin and bier fragments.[24]

Bedframes

A range of biers and bedframes (types BDa–BDg) are depicted in Ramesside Theban tomb scenes, (see Appendix B). Some are clearly funerary in character (types BDa, BDd, BDf) being manufactured with lion heads and curved tails that spring from the bier's back legs and arch over the body of the deceased. Others are domestic forms (BDb, BDc, BDe, BDg) that would have been found in the home to be finally placed with the deceased within the tomb. Evidence also exists that specially commissioned bedframes were manufactured for women for use during their confinement and childbirth.

Birth and Women's Bedframes

To protect women during childbirth the image of the hippopotamus goddess Taweret and the dwarf god Bes were used to embellish a bedframe with either painted representations of the deity or carved as a pierced wooden panel that was incorporated into the footboard of the bedframe. We also find these deities shaped from wood to form the supporting bedframe legs.

These bed legs are significantly different in both character and purpose to typical domestic type bedframes. These differences are illustrated on an ostracon, (Figure 22), preserved in the Medelhavsmuseet, Stockholm, MM 14 005. It presents a typical maternity scene, where the use of a bedframe with Bes shaped legs played a significant part in the act of labour and gave protection to both the mother and baby.[25]

The setting illustrated in MM 14 005 reflects the private nature of childbirth and nursing, possibly occurring within an outdoor sanctuary protected by drapes, where a woman could withdraw with a few personal items; some toiletry materials, her jewellery, birth amulets and cosmetics. The dangers of childbirth, to both the mother and baby, are reflected in the need for this specially commissioned bedframe being used at the time of confinement. Being more elaborate and covered with a thickly decorated mattress, the image of the god Bes stands at the corners and in the centre of the bedframes side rail, providing the woman with a protective elevation and a reassuring place to give birth.

Figure 22. Ostracon, Medelhavsmuseet, Stockholm, MM 14 005.

Janssen records the transactions of only two "women's beds" from (O. Ashmolean Museum 0009 [O. Gardiner 0009; HO. 24, 4]) and (O. Ashmolean Museum 0105, [O. Gardiner 0105; HO. 53, 1]), (Janssen 1975: table XVIII, 181, 184), indicating only small numbers of birthing beds were manufactured, perhaps reflecting the nature of its usage. Indeed, this type of bedframe may have been used by women of the extended family or even passed on through successive generations. With the limited space within a family home at Deir el-Medina it is also possible that the birthing bed could have been designed to be disassembled when not required.

After birth, women returned to using single bedframes and evidence shows that infants and often an older child shared the bed. Preserved in the British Museum, is a figure of a naked woman with a child beside her sleeping together on a single bedframe.[26] This bedframe is shown to be made from wooden rails including a cross rail

that supports the lumbar region of the woman's body whilst her feet lie against a vertical raised footboard. The woman wears only a large wig and a collar, but her sexual identity is clearly established by the carved emphasis given to her large hips, breasts and pubic area. Such limestone models acted as amulets being intended to increase the fertility, or at least give witness to the wife's sexuality.

BED LEGS CARVED IN THE FORM OF THE GOD BES (PLATES 42–43).

Rijksmuseum van Oudheden, Leiden. Inv. No. F 1964/1.4 and F 1964/1.3.

These two finely carved bed legs, (Plates 42–43) are similar to those seen on ostracon MM 14 005, (Figure 22). Each deity is standing on a furniture drum that makes the foot of the bed leg. Their plumed head-dresses which form the bed leg's tenons would have located in mortises chopped in the underside of the bedframe's side rails. Unfortunately, these tenons have been sawn through, making it impossible to establish whether the frame could have been easily dismantled. The angle of the saw cut indicate that they were the foot and head legs jointed to the curved side rail of a bedframe, similar in form to the constructional arrangement seen in ostracon MM 14 005, (Figure 22).

Both Bes figures are grotesque in appearance, having large ears and protruding tongues. Each has a lion's mane or a cape made of lion skin. The bodies of both have been painted black and they wear kilts that are painted to represent an animal skin. One is seen playing a pair of pipes (Plate 42), while the other holds his hands to his chin, (Plate 43).[27]

LION LEGS WITH THE PAINTED DEPICTION OF TAWERET AND BES (PLATES 44–51).

Egypt Centre, Swansea.
Inv. No. W 2052b (Plates 44–47).
Inv. No. W 2052a (Plates 48–51).

One leg (Plates 44–47) is from a pair that probably came from the same bedframe, and is modelled on the foreleg of a lion. Although the tenon on the top of the leg has been broken, the inclined angle of the shoulder indicates that it was the head leg of a bedframe as classified by Killen as type BDg.

The other leg, (Plates 48–51) still retains its tenon, which is pierced with a single peg hole. Formed in the shape of a lion's rear leg it originally would have been the bedframe's foot leg.

Both legs were lightly gessoed, providing the ground for the painted representations of Taweret and Bes. The outer surface of the head leg, (Plate 44), is painted with the figure of Taweret seen standing on a *sa* sign, at her right foot lays a knife. Chopped into the inner surface of the leg, (Plate 46), is a stopped mortise into which would have fitted a supporting stretcher that braced both head legs. The front edge of the leg has been applied with a painted snake design, (Plate 45). This snake decoration is also seen on the outer edge of the foot leg, (Plate 47), strongly suggesting that the painted snake decoration was also applied to both of the bedframe's side rails, paralleling the snake decoration seen on Sennedjem's bier (Mahmoud 2011: 186). We can also see a stopped mortise on the inner surface of the foot leg, (Plate 48), however, the position of both mortises being on opposite faces of both legs reinforce that these legs came from opposite corners of the bedframe. The outer surface of the foot leg, (Plate 50), has the figure of the god Bes drawn in black ink and filled with blue paint. In the depiction of the birth bed seen in (Figure 22), we see that both the head and foot legs were rendered with the

image of the god Bes which is also supported by the carved Bes legs (Plates 42–43). Perhaps, we can see from the Swansea bed legs that pairs of legs attached to each common side rail were either decorated with images of either Bes or Taweret. The construction of this bedframe does not suggest that it was designed to be dismantled. The purchase of a "decorated (painted) women's bed" (Toivari-Viitala, J. 2001: 178), recorded in (O. Ashmolean Museum 0009 [O. Gardiner 0009; HO. 24, 4]) is possibly indicative of these bed legs.

Sir Henry Wellcome purchased these legs in 1906 from the collection of Robert de Rustafjaell. The place name "Akhmim" is written on one leg indicating a possible provenance.

PAINTED SLAT FROM BEDFRAME FOOTBOARD (PLATE 52).

Fitzwilliam Museum, Cambridge. Inv. No E.236.1932. Height 203 mm.

The footboards of some bedframes would have also been embellished with the figure of the god Bes. This example, (Plate 52), illustrates one thin vertical slat that with others would have formed the panel of a bedframe's footboard. Tenons at the top and bottom of the slat would have located in mortises chopped in the inner horizontal surfaces of the footboard frame. The profile of the god Bes has been carefully carved onto the slat's front surface with details outlined in black ink and the skin tones of the god rendered in red and yellow paint. The small hole in the front surface of the slat indicates how thin the slat is; unfortunately, at some earlier period the slat had been glued to cardboard to preserve it, making it now impossible to examine the slat's back surface.

WOODEN ELEMENT CARVED IN THE FORM OF THE GOD BES, PART OF A BEDFRAME. FOOTBOARD (PLATE 53).

Fitzwilliam Museum, Cambridge. Inv. No. E.GA.2681.1943.
Height 201 mm.

We also have examples of slats that have been carved in the form of the god Bes. Again they have tenons at the top and bottom of the figure allowing for their fixing into the bedframe's footboard. This example, (Plate 53), is delicately carved with the exaggerated, grotesque feature associated with the god Bes. He is shown wearing a kilt and shaped head-dress. The painting is particularly fine on the front surface; the god's body is painted green and his mane red, while his kilt is rendered to indicate that it has been pleated. The back surface of the slat has a smooth finish, indicating that this elevation had little significance to the bedframe's overall appearance.[28]

Domestic Bedframes

Those bedframes, which can be identified as domestic in character, in the Ramesside Theban tombs scenes, have been classified by Killen as bedframe types BDb, BDc BDe and BDg. As these examples are illustrated in a funerary context we must assume that they had a dual purpose, being finally intended as funerary pieces to be placed in the tomb. We also have evidence from O.EA 5861 verso (Figure 4.1) that carpenters were still manufacturing bedframes similar to those that were deposited in the 18th-Dynasty tomb of the architect Kha and his wife Merit.[29] Unfortunately, little material evidence has survived and two bedframe footboards that are preserved in the Archeologica Museum, Florence, are erroneously displayed and referenced as window shutters.[30]

Whether the use of single bedframes was determined by cultural practices or the result that larger double bedframes were difficult to construct is uncertain. However, the concept of using a double bedframe is seen in a stone funerary statue that shows the royal scribe Paser and his wife reclining together. The statue dates to the 18th Dynasty, the bedframe is clearly seen to have a wide footboard and the frame is supported on lion shaped legs.[31]

Simple bedframes constructed from square section or tapered legs with the bedframe rails being attached to the leg with through mortise and tenon joints are known from at least the Middle Kingdom, with examples discovered at Beni Hasan (Killen 2002: 655, pl. 1A), through to similar bedframes discovered in the 18th Dynasty pit tombs by Bruyère at Deir el-Medina (Bruyère 1937B: 45, fig. 19). Indeed, the design and construction of such simple furniture is still seen in rural parts of Egypt. The lack of physical evidence is surprising; for example in the tomb of Sennedjem, where neither his nor his wife's bedframe had been deposited.

Janssen records that the prices of Ramesside bedframes "fluctuate between 12 and 15 *deben*, with only one instance of 10 *deben*....Whether this fluctuation is a result of quality remains uncertain" (Janssen 1975: 184). Quality would have been a factor in price as indicated by the quality mark attributed to a bedframe depicted in O. EA 5861 verso (Figure 4.3).[32]

Bedframes with Round Legs

There is also evidence that during the Ramesside Period bedframes were manufactured with round or turned legs. Depicted in the tomb of Ipuy, TT217, we see a bedframe which has been manufactured with round legs (Davies 1927: pls. XXXVII, XXXVIII – classified by Killen as type BDc bedframe).

This unique bedframe, (Plate 54), has curved side rails and a footboard that is either covered with a fabric sheet or supported with moulded wooden brackets. At the other end of the bedframe is placed a headrest. The legs of this bedframe are carefully drafted in red paint and filled in with white paint that imitates a gesso foundation. They are rendered to graphically communicate that they would have been made in a clear rounded form with bands of incised decoration around the lower part of each leg.

Boxes

A limited range of box types are depicted in Ramesside Theban tomb scenes (types Bxa–Bxj). This range can be classified into three types – rectangular boxes with flat lids (types Bxa, Bxb, Bxg); Boxes with shrine shaped lids (types Bxc, Bxd, Bxe, Bxf, Bxh, Bxi) and a box with barrel shaped lid (type Bxj); see Appendix B for those types depicted in Ramesside Theban tombs. Type Bxk completes this series being included in Appendix A to illustrate the form of a box discovered in TT339, Huy and Peshedu. (Bruyère 1928: pl.V [4]).

Sennedjem's tomb contained ten small rectangular cosmetic type boxes. Six boxes were designed with double lids and four with single lids.[33] Although their form was not depicted in any Ramesside Theban tomb, it was recorded in a number of previously discussed furniture ostraca (Chapter One: Deir el-Medina: A Community of Entrepreneurs?). In studying simple sketches of boxes made by carpenters on flakes of limestone and comparing them with the products they represent allows an insight into how Egyptian carpenters developed apparently rough diagrams into tangible and imaginative products.

Box with Double Lid, Belonging to Iyneferti (Figure 23).

Government Central Museum, Albert Hall, Jaipur, Inv. No. 10719
Length 259 mm, width 260 mm, height 120 mm.

Unfortunately, this box, (Figure 23), has no actual provenance to the tomb of Sennedjem, even though the inscription in black ink, ruled between two red lines on both leaves of the lid, reads "*Osiris the Mistress of the House Ij-nfrt (Ij-Nfr.t) justified*" (Silvano, in Bresciani and Betró 2004: 104), indicating that it belonged to a woman whose name was the same as Sennedjem's wife. This box formed part of a collection of important artefacts privately acquired by Émile Brugsch in Egypt between 1883 and 1894 that were deposited in Jaipur. Brugsch worked as assistant conservator at the Bulaq Museum, a position that he held under Maspero at the time of the opening of Sennedjem's tomb, and would have had access to the finds. It appears he was an impatient individual who had been severely reprimanded by Maspero in 1881 for unwrapping the mummy of Thutmose III before Maspero had returned from France. As there was no definitive catalogue of finds, it is plausible that the box has a provenance to Sennedjem's tomb.

This box, as with another with a confirmed Sennedjem provenance, has a double lid and is constructed from four

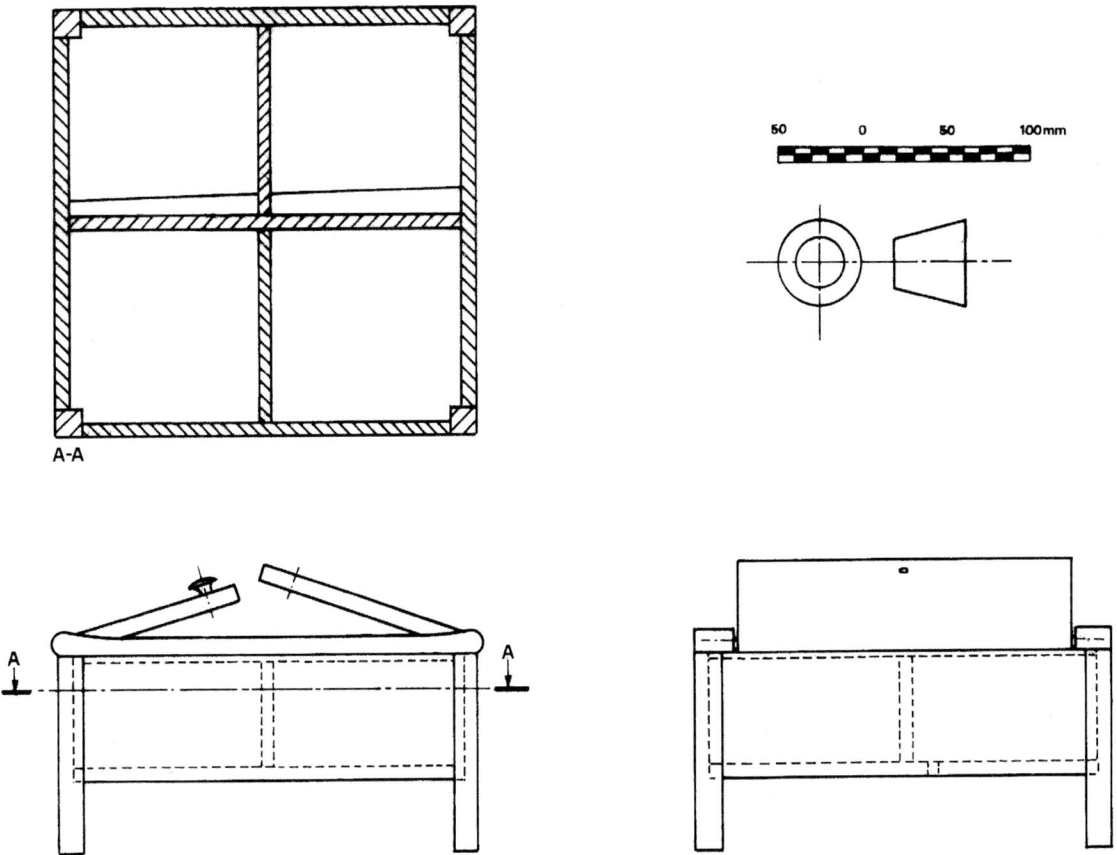

Figure 23. Box with double lid, belonging to Iyneferti. Government Central Museum, Albert Hall, Jaipur, Inv. No. 10719.

square legs onto which are dowelled the side panels of the box.[34] Opposite side panels are painted ochre or yellow and are enclosed by a painted stringing of black painted lines on a white gesso ground. The bottom is fitted inside the box and dowelled into position; and is made from boards; the gaps are heavily filled with gesso.

Two battens on two opposing edges of both boxes are moulded at the ends to hold the carved pivots that protrude from each lid. Both moulded battens have been painted with a lozenge decoration. Each lid is bordered with white lily petals, created on a gesso ground, outlined with black paint. The interior of the box is divided into four compartments using two boards that are connected by a cross-halving joint. Each lid is fabricated from two edge-jointed boards; the outer boards are intentionally longer allowing them to be carved with shaped pairs of round pivots.

Sennedjem's boxes were not the only examples of this form of box discovered at Deir el-Medina. A similar box was discovered by Bernard Bruyère in the tomb of Huy, TT 361, whose title was "Great Carpenter in the Place of Truth". Huy lived during the reign of Seti I, and was a significant figure, in being the only recognised state carpenter working at Deir el-Medina.[35] The box discovered in Huy's tomb has similar constructional characteristics to those discovered in the tomb of Sennedjem and is similarly

decorated. An inscription written on both leaves of this box shows that it once belonged to Huy's wife Tanehesi.

Deposited in the tomb of Sennedjem were an additional three boxes, each of which were covered with a single lid. One example is preserved in the Metropolitan Museum of Art, New York (Killen 1994: 81, fig. 79; Killen 2017B: 105–106, fig. 79). This type of box construction can be seen in O. Florence 2628 (Killen and Weiss 2009: (Figure 2) [11]). Another fine example of this type of box construction is preserved in the British Museum, London. EA 21818.

BOX WITH SINGLE LID (PLATES **55–62**, FIGURE **24**).

British Museum, London, EA 21818.
Length 270 mm, width 275 mm, height 140 mm.
Purchased from: Rev. Greville John Chester.
Acquired: 1887.

The acquisition date of this box, (Plate 55, Figure 24), and its decoration suggests it draws on material designed and manufactured to standards set at Deir el-Medina by those carpenters who worked on Sennedjem's and his family's commissions.[36] Unfortunately it is not inscribed, yet decoratively it is similar to Metropolitan Museum of Art, New York. MMA. 86.1.8 (Killen 1994: 81, fig. 79; Killen

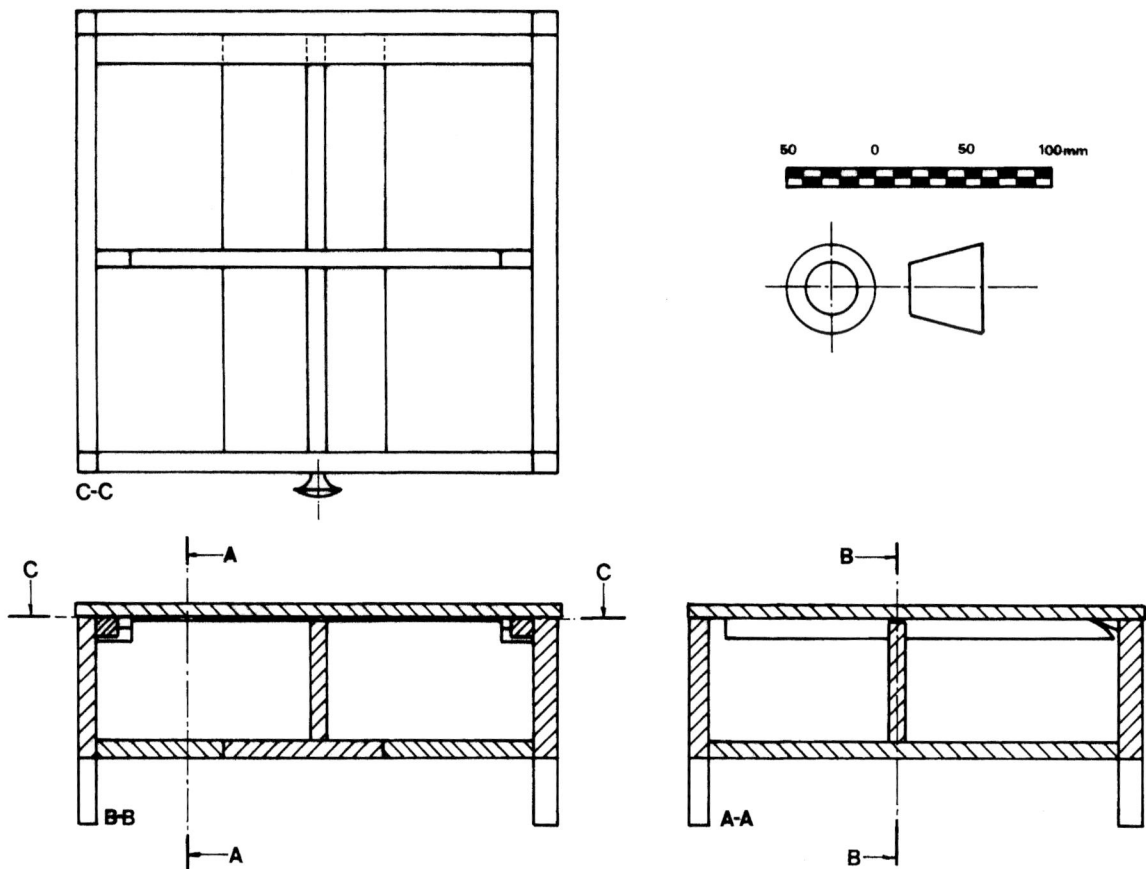

Figure 24. Box with single lid, Ramesside Period. British Museum, London, EA 21818.

2017B: 105–106, fig. 79). Closer examination shows that artist who decorated this box also knew of MMA 86.1.8 (indeed the same artist may even have applied decoration to both). Although the paintwork that imitates a frame and panel construction on both boxes is similar, it has perceptively been reversed by the artist. On this box the lily petals are left from the white ground and the background painted black, whereas, the opposite is seen on the box discovered in Sennedjem's tomb, Metropolitan Museum of Art, New York. MMA. 86.1.8.

Constructionally, the carcase of this box, (Plate 56), is similar to (MMA. 86.1.8.). Each of the four side panels are made from a single piece of wood that are butt jointed to the square legs with dowels. The bottom is similarly fitted with dowels that pass through the bottom edge of each side panel. Some of the dowels are now exposed, either where the wood has broken away or where the gesso has flaked from the end grain of the dowel, allowing us to see the box's construction in more detail.

As the legs are dimensionally the same in cross section as the thickness of each panel, it was possible to fit the box's bottom in the square opening without any adjustment to the corners, (Plate 57). The bottom is made from three pieces of sawn wood, edge-jointed together and dowelled along the bottom edge of each side panel. The

quality of the wood is quite poor and the entire surface of the box's bottom was heavily gessoed.

The interior of the box has been divided into four compartments (Plate 58), used for the storage of cosmetics, judging from the fact that two small linen bags were found inside it on discovery. Two pieces of sawn wood have been used to form the partitions for the compartments. They have been connected together with a typical cross-halving joint. Where this box differs from others previously examined is the method by which the lid is attached.

The lid is not hinged; the box is designed to allow the lid to lock into position. The lid is made from two pieces of wood that are edge-jointed and held together by two edge battens, which are deliberately set in the width of each of the box's side panels (Plate 59). This allows the battens on the underside of the lid to drop into previously sawn steps on the opposing partition (Plate 60).

To accommodate the lid, a tapered wooden strip has been attached to the back of the box; the partition has been modified, by cutting away a step, to accept this attachment (Plate 61). The ends of the battens on the underside of the lid have been similarly tapered allowing them to slide and lock into position (Plate 62). The lid would have been slid into position and secured to the box with cord, which would have been bound around both of the small

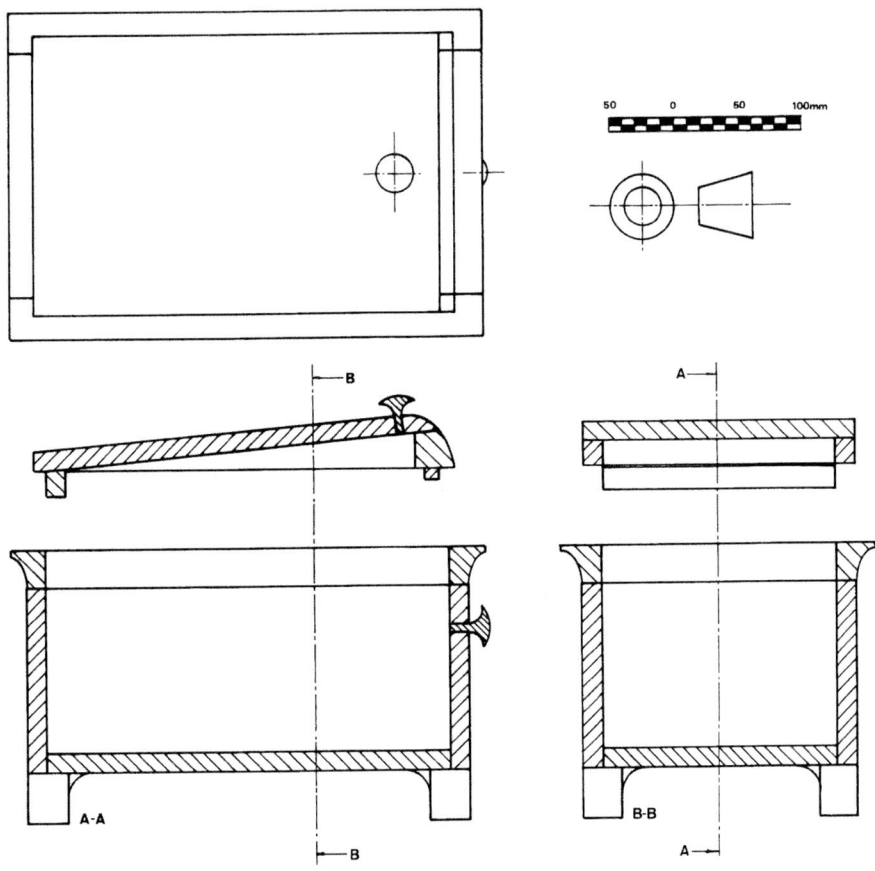

Figure 25. Box with shrine shaped lid, Ramesside Period. British Museum, London, EA 5907

delicately carved knobs. These have been attached to the box and lid with small dowels.

BOX WITH SHRINE SHAPED LID (PLATES 63–67, FIGURE 25).

British Museum, London. EA 5907.
Purchased at Sotheby's 1835 (Salt Collection).
Length 338 mm, width 247 mm, height 250 mm.

The form of this box, with its shrine shaped lid, (Plate 63, Figure 25), (classified by Killen as box type Bxc) is depicted in Theban Tombs TT41, TT51, TT106, TT193, TT217 and TT341 (see Appendix B). These tombs date from the reigns of Seti I and Rameses II. Its form is also recognised in O. Turin N 57141 (Figure 2.5). It is manufactured from sycomore fig and is in good condition; the side boards are painted with an ochre coloured paint on a gesso foundation to give the impression of cedar panels that are edged with painted stringing, imitating strips of African Blackwood and ivory.

The main carcase of the box is manufactured from four planks of roughly sawn wood that have been butt jointed together and fastened with dowels. The bottom of the box, (Plate 64), is again made from a single board

of wood, which was fitted and fixed with dowels to the lower interior edge of the box. The carpenter then glued four separate cube shaped blocks of wood to the corners of the carcase to provide four short legs. These have been heavily gessoed to conceal the joint between the legs and the bottom of the box. These short legs were painted black, this paintwork being extended up the edges of the box to give the impression that the box had been made from an African Blackwood framework construction.

The top edge of the box has been fitted with a moulded cavetto cornice. The corners of the two longer mouldings have been worked to allow the curved profile of the moulding to match the shorter end pieces. This technique eliminated the need to mitre the joint, for the cutting of the mitre would not have been accurate. The technique seen here of butting the moulding together, at right angles, provides a sharp corner to the apparently intersecting curved surfaces of the cavetto cornice (Plate 65, Figure 25). The black painted vertical stripes applied to the white gesso ground of the curved surfaces of the cavetto cornice moulding gives the impression that the moulding has been rendered to give a ribbed effect.

The lid, (Plate 66), is made from a single board; the shrine shaped profile is formed by two tapered battens being attached to the long sides of the lid with a thicker

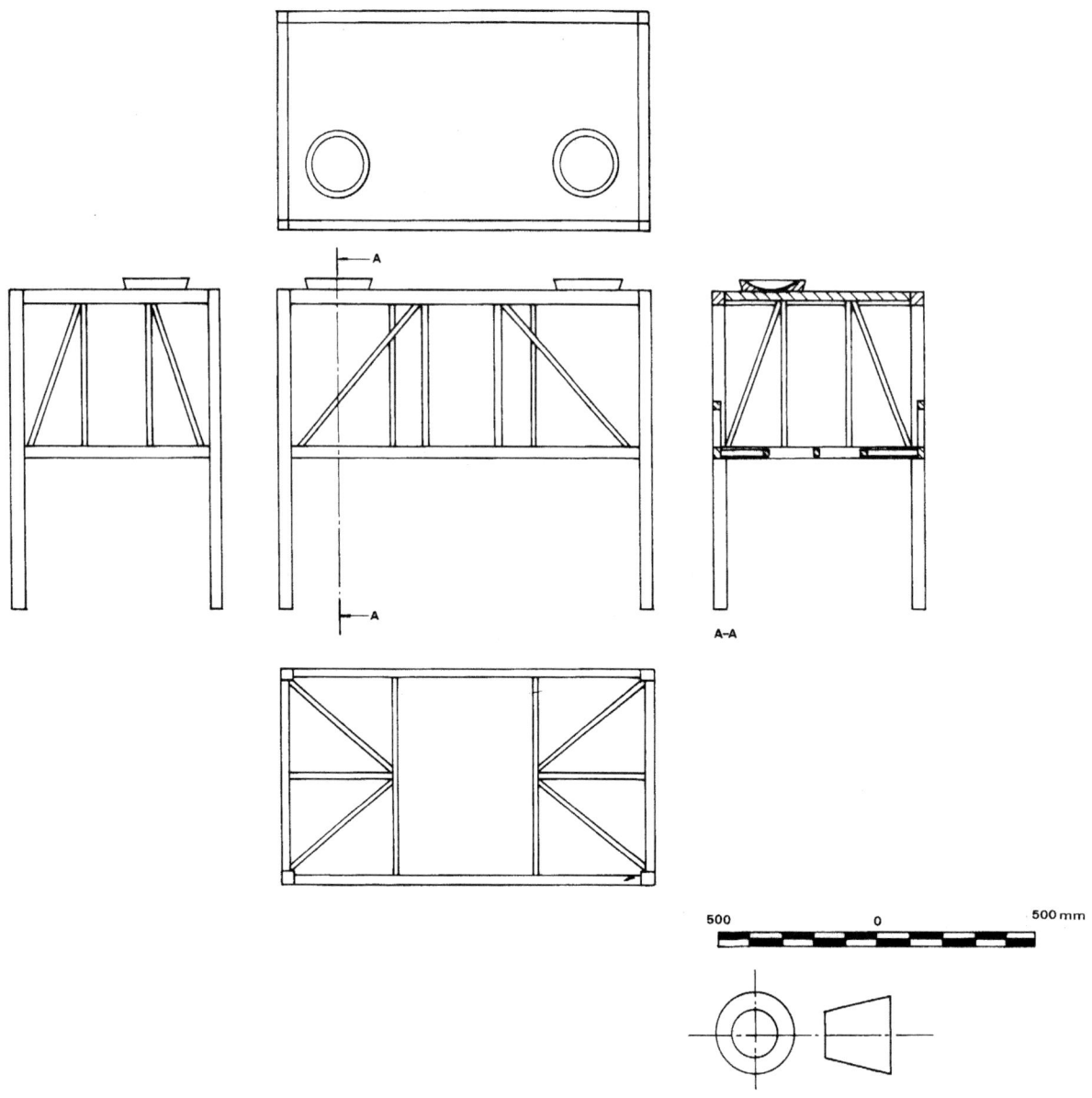

Figure 26. Offering table. Tomb of Sennedjem, (TT1). Egyptian Museum, Cairo. JE 27257.

batten across the front of the lid. The front has been worked to a curved profile and two additional battens, which have been attached across the underside of the front and back of the lid, provide the method that prevents it from moving when placed on the box.

The lid has been painted with a light gesso foundation, (Plate 67) and outlined with three black lines to imitate African Blackwood and ivory stringing. The central panel is painted with an ochre colour and the inscription in black paint dedicates this box to the sailor Denreg.[37]

Boxes with gable lids

Boxes with gable lids, where one leaf swings open and the other is fixed, continued to be manufactured during the Ramesside Period. A box dedicated to Khataouy, now

in the Louvre Museum, N. 2918, is painted to imitate a frame and panel construction with the edges of the box and gable painted with a ribbon of black lozenges placed between black and white lines. The carcase of the box is manufactured from horizontal boards; the legs that extend from below the box are blocks of wood glued to the underside of the box.

Petrie was to discover a gable lid box at Sedment in grave 1962 (Petrie and Brunton 1924: pl. LV[20]), its construction shows that the horizontal boards that make the side panels of this box were jointed to separate legs. Both triangular gables were also fitted separately and were of thinner section wood. To these were attached rails into which one lid was permanently fixed and the other opened on a pair of pivots.

Tables, Stands, Offering Tables and Gaming Tables

Depictions of furniture forms found in the Ramesside tombs at Thebes show a wide range of table and stand forms (table types classified by Killen, Ta–Tp; stand types classified by Killen STa–STp, see Appendix A). Although none are shown being used to eat from, we see that Egyptians used tables and stands for specific purposes, either to display goods that were being presented as a form of tribute, or to hold pots, while some were designed as meat preparation tables and others as gaming tables.[38] Tables were also commissioned to be used in a religious context to hold and present offerings.

A number of tables and stands depicted in the Ramesside Theban tombs (Appendix A) are to be found as extant forms. Table and stand designs were used throughout the New Kingdom; two tables that have their tops edged with cavetto cornices and torus mouldings that conform to the table classified by Killen as type To, are preserved in two New York museums.[39] We also find depictions of three-legged tables, classified by Killen as type Tc in the tomb of Userhet, TT51.[40] Whilst in the British Museum, London, a vase stand with splayed legs and supporting lattice can be classified as type STb.[41]

TABLE (FIGURE 26).

Tomb of Sennedjem, TT1.
Egyptian Museum, Cairo. JE 27257.
Length 590 mm, height 330 mm, depth 490 mm

This rectangular table has been manufactured to the form classified by Killen as Type Ta (Figure 26).[42] The frame is constructed from a sophisticated lattice of rectangular strips of wood, and its structural arrangement would suggest that it was designed to hold a significant load. The table top is made from three sections; the two outer sections are panels while the inner section is made from eighteen strips of wood. The loading would have been in the form of two round bottom vases placed in a pair of wooden collars on the outer sections of the table top. On some tables these collars are hollow allowing tapered or wider round based vases to be seated more firmly on the table, preventing them from toppling over or becoming unstable. This arrangement is seen in a depiction of a table in the tomb of Ipuy, TT217.[43]

The four faces of the table have been braced using horizontal stretchers across each pair of legs, with two vertical struts set between these stretchers and the rails that are connected to the table top. On each table face a further two diagonal struts are then placed from corner to corner of the outer spaces to triangulate the structure. However, the interior space was also filled with an elaborate lattice arrangement, that is not seen in the two dimensional Theban tomb depictions (Appendix A). This interior space is divided into three cells using an arrangement of two additional sets of horizontal stretchers combined with vertical and diagonal struts that replicate the lattice arrangement found on both ends of the table. An additional fan of three wooden struts fills the two outer spaces created by the external and internal horizontal stretchers. This complex lattice arrangement provides an elegant solution, creating a piece of furniture that is able to support heavy loads yet uses a minimum of material. Egyptian carpenters can be seen here to have knowledge of the physical properties of wood exploiting both its tensile and compressive strength.

Three-Legged Tables

The use of three-legged tables continues to be seen in the Ramesside Period, following the constructional form of a three-legged table that was made for Perpawty and is preserved in the British Museum.[44] Three similar tables, laid with offerings, are seen in the tomb of Userhet, TT51 (Davies 1927: pl. XVI). These tables, classified by Killen as table type Tc, are rendered to suggest a three-legged design with curved legs and braces between the legs.

Other variants of this table design seen in the Theban private tombs depict examples with only two curved legs in side elevation, although in reality they were probably manufactured with three legs. In the tomb of Ipuy TT217, can be seen a pair of meat preparation tables (classified by Killen as table type Tf).[45] The curved legs of these tables are strengthened with a single horizontal brace, whilst a similar table, classified by Killen as table type Tn, seen in the tomb of Neferhotep, TT216 has no horizontal brace below the table top.[46]

VASE STAND (PLATE 68).

Louvre Museum, Paris. Inv. No. N 1391.
Height 430 mm, depth 198 mm, width 205 mm.

The method of supporting a round bottomed vase in a wooden collar seating is illustrated with this vase stand, (Plate 68). The collar is attached to a wooden platform that has been heavily gessoed to conceal the line of fixture. The edges of the platform have been painted with red and black lines imitating a stringing of cedar and African Blackwood. The edge of the platform has been moulded with a cavetto cornice, below which is a torus moulding, seen on tables classified by Killen as types Tk and To.

The legs of this stand are square in section and are slightly splayed; gesso has been applied, and painted in parts with lines of red and black stringing or a repeating black lozenge pattern. Four stretchers have been mortised and tenoned into the legs and are similarly treated with gesso and applied with a painted stringing or black rectangular decoration. The spaces that fill the open sides have been filled with roughly carved hieroglyphic signs including a crudely worked "*ankh*" similarly painted red and black, together with other flower shaped wooden

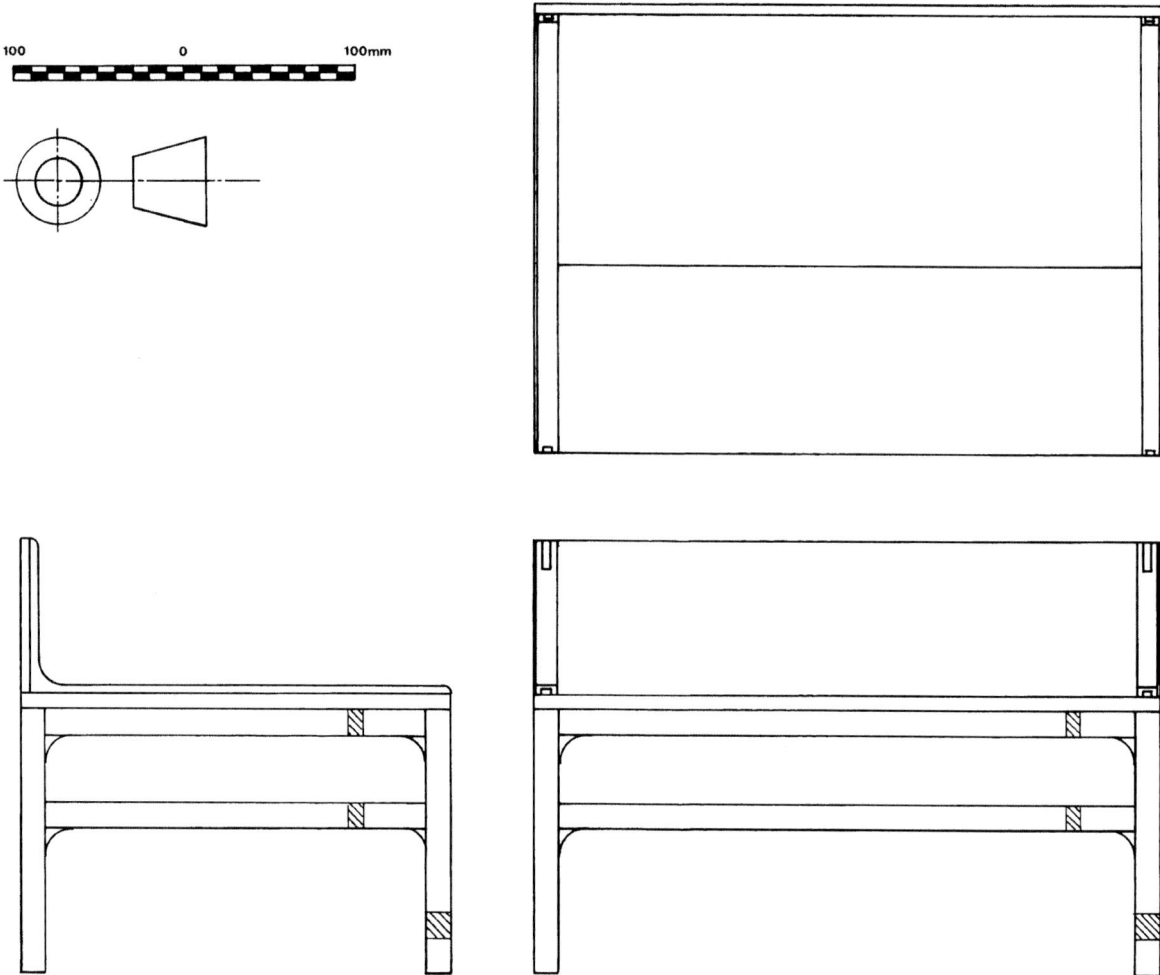

Figure 27. Offering table. Tomb of Tutankhamun. Carter No. 33. Egyptian Museum, Cairo. JE 62057.

elements. Similar elements were found in house S.O. IV at Deir el-Medina (broken in two fragments 30–35 cm): (Bruyère 1939: 23–24, fig. 193). It is debatable whether these carved flower and plant forms were used as substitutes for real flower bouquets used during offering ceremonies or are really furniture elements.

Offering Tables

A major function of Egyptian tables was for the display of offerings, however, we also see a generic form of table that had an integral backboard that in appearance can be confused with a chair. This type of offering table is classified by Killen as types (OT a, b, c, d and e). This generic form can be divided into two sub-sets, firstly, those that are similar in construction to a chair (Types OT b, c and e). Types OT b and OT c, have a sub-frame that was made from thin strips of wood. However, each type has a vertical backboard that is attached by brackets to the table top. The right-angled corners of the exterior frame of type OT b are reinforced by small blocks of shaped wood that have been apparently glued into position.

One of a pair of offering tables, (classified by Killen as an OT b type) are seen as part of the funerary furniture painted in Ani's Book of the Dead, that had been deposited in his 19th-Dynasty tomb.[47] These offering tables show that their frames and back boards were finished with gesso that parallels the finish applied to Sennedjem's table, (Figure 26).

The second form of offering table is designed with a box type structure (OT a and d) that encloses the table top; its function being more like a crate that prevents loose offerings falling from the table and gives additional stability to tall vases and pots. An example of this type of offering table, (classified by Killen as an OTa type) can be seen in a stele fragment belonging to Neferabet.[48] Whether this stele came from his tomb, TT5 at Deir el-Medina, is uncertain. We can see that the inclusion of wooden walls around the table surface prevented the offerings from falling during its transportation to the tomb. These wooden walls are made from vertical panels of wood placed within a frame, which on the sides are triangular in shape. The lightness of the wooden lattice construction, together with the offerings on the table, still allowed one man to carry the table by apparently standing inside the frame and carrying it above his head whilst holding a pair of legs.

Offering table designs, that are more elaborately decorated, are also seen in either painted or relief forms rendered on the temple walls of Ramesside kings and will be discussed further in Chapter Four: Royal and Temple furniture.

Offering Table or Stand (Plate 69, Figure 27).

Tomb of Tutankhamun, KV62
Egyptian Museum, Cairo. Carter No. 033, JE 62057.
Length 362 mm, width 253 mm, height 244 mm.

This small stand, (Plate 69; Figure 27), was correctly identified by Carter and his assistants and catalogued as a wooden stand.[49] Recently, it has been referenced by Marianne Eaton-Krauss as a plain low chair made for a child.[50] The design and constructional characteristics of this piece of furniture could lead one to believe that it is a utilitarian form of child's chair that would have been found in areas of the temple associated with the royal apartments. However, there are a number of features of this piece of furniture that define it as a stand or small offering table.

To test this hypothesis a full size replica chair/offering table was made by the author, (Plate 69). Anthropometrically, it could not function as a child's chair; with a seat height of 164 mm and a seat width of 253 mm it is too low. Children are generally able to sit safely on a chair once they can walk without falling. This occurs as early as eighteen months with all children able to sit unaided by the age of two. The smallest modern chair manufactured to British and European Standards (BS EN 1729-1:2006) is designed to allow a child with a popliteal height range between 200 mm and 250 mm to comfortably sit on a chair with a seat height of 210 mm.[51] This form of chair is used by children in the foundation stage of pre-school and aged between eighteen months and three years. Also, if it were designed as a chair the seat depth is too great and the vertical backboard is not of sufficient height to support a child's back and would be of no practical use.

Extant examples of chairs specifically designed for the children of elite Egyptians are found as smaller examples of adult forms, having seat heights considerably greater than this small stand.[52] They exhibit those characteristics associated with chairs, having seat rails manufactured in a double curve shape, legs that are carved in feline form

and back supports that are proportionally correct in height and shaped to support the child's back.

This piece of furniture is not designed for the possible rough handling a utilitarian chair would be subjected to. The legs are made from wooden elements that are 15 mm square in cross section. The horizontal stretchers are rectangular in cross section being 15 mm deep and 8 mm thick. The ends of these horizontal stretchers are cut with small tenons that fit into neatly chopped stopped mortises in the vertical legs that are fastened with small wooden pegs driven through the outer face of the leg and through the cheek of the tenon. The length of the "seat" easily accommodates one child but as a bench form "seat" it cannot accommodate two children sitting together.

Therefore, we should assume that a single child would sit in the centre of the platform. With the precise, almost model like jointing construction it would be unsuitable for the dynamic loads that it would be expected to safely resist if this piece of furniture were designed as a child's chair. Its length, 362 mm, would create unacceptable loading characteristics in the centre of the "seat" as the bending forces applied to the top horizontal rail flexes it under a dynamic load due to the pivotal points in the mortise and tenon joints being significantly further apart than would be normally expected in a chair.

Another interesting feature are the horizontal extensions of the platform and back panel bracket assembly. We see that these horizontal extensions extend to the front edge of the platform. This length of extension is not to be found on chairs, although it is seen on a similarly proportioned offering table, classified by Killen as type OTe that is depicted in the Theban tomb of Nebamun, TT65.[53] This offering table displays all those features seen in the Tutankhamun example, having a wide platform and short vertical back panel that are connected by a bracket. The bracket has a long horizontal extension that runs along the width of the platform and finishes close to the platform's front edge. This particular offering table is finished with a cavetto cornice moulding, which is mounted on a horizontal rail. Below this is strung a second horizontal stretcher supporting the frame. The construction of the offering table depicted in the tomb of Nebamun, TT65, and the example deposited in the tomb of Tutankhamun clearly show that they were specifically designed to support materials and goods that have static loading characteristics.

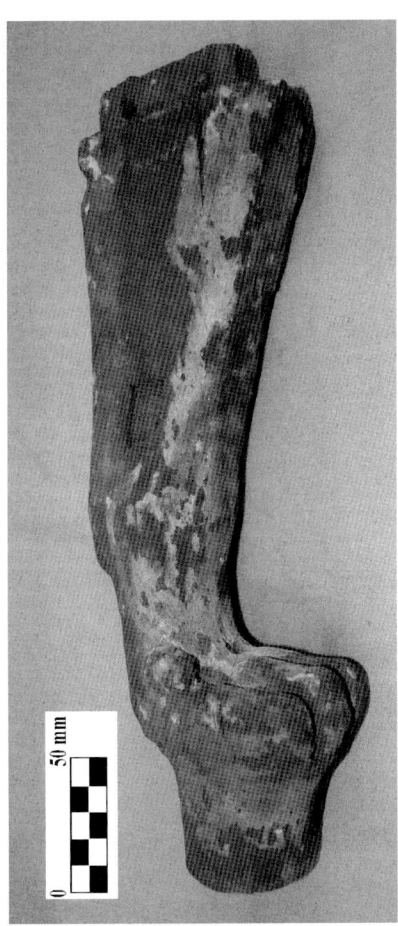

Plate 12. Chair leg. Garstang Museum, University of Liverpool, E. 7161. *Photographic credit: G. Killen.*

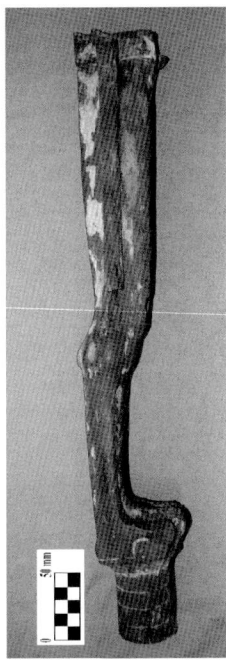

Plate 13. Chair leg (Form A), UC. 36478. Petrie Museum of Egyptian Archaeology, University College London. *Photographic credit: G. Killen.*

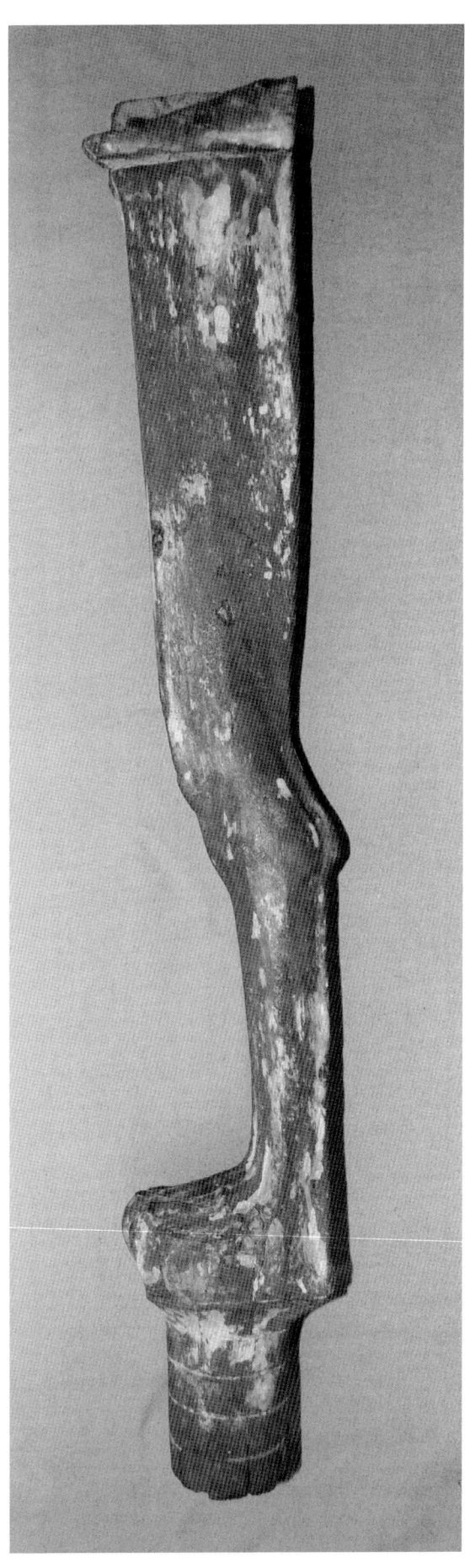

Plate 14. Chair leg (Form A), UC. 36478. Petrie Museum of Egyptian Archaeology, University College London. *Photographic credit: G. Killen.*

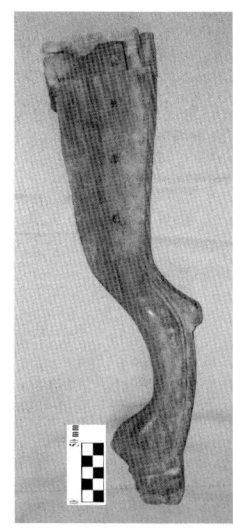

Plate 15. Chair leg (Form B). British Museum, London. EA. 49123. *Photographic credit: G. Killen.*

Plate 16. Statue of an official and his wife seated on a Cf type chair with a Form A leg. British Museum, London. EA 565. *Photographic credit: G. Killen.*

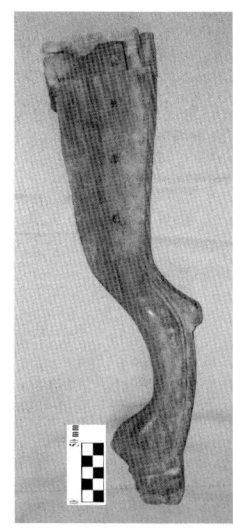

Plate 17. Statue of Yuny and his wife Renenutet seated on a Cp type chair with a Form B leg. MMA 15.12.1. © *Metropolitan Museum of Art, New York.*

This page: Plate 18. Chair. Louvre Museum, Paris. N 2950. *Photographic credit: G. Killen.*

Opposite: Plate 19. Chair. Louvre Museum, Paris. N 2950. *Photographic credit: G. Killen.*

Plate 20. Round legged stool. British Museum, London. EA 2473. *Photographic credit: G. Killen.*

Plate 21. Seat from a round legged stool. British Museum, London. EA 2517. *Photographic credit: G. Killen.*

Plate 22. Detail of seat (Plate 21). British Museum, London. EA 2517. *Photographic credit: G. Killen.*

Plate 23. Round legged stool. British Museum, London. EA 2474.
Photographic credit: G. Killen.

Plate 24. Detail of leg and stretcher joint. Round legged stool, British Museum, London. EA 2474. *Photographic credit: G. Killen.*

Plate 25. Detail of round
stool leg. UC 71984.
Petrie Museum of
Egyptian Archaeology,
University College London.
Photographic credit:
G. Killen.

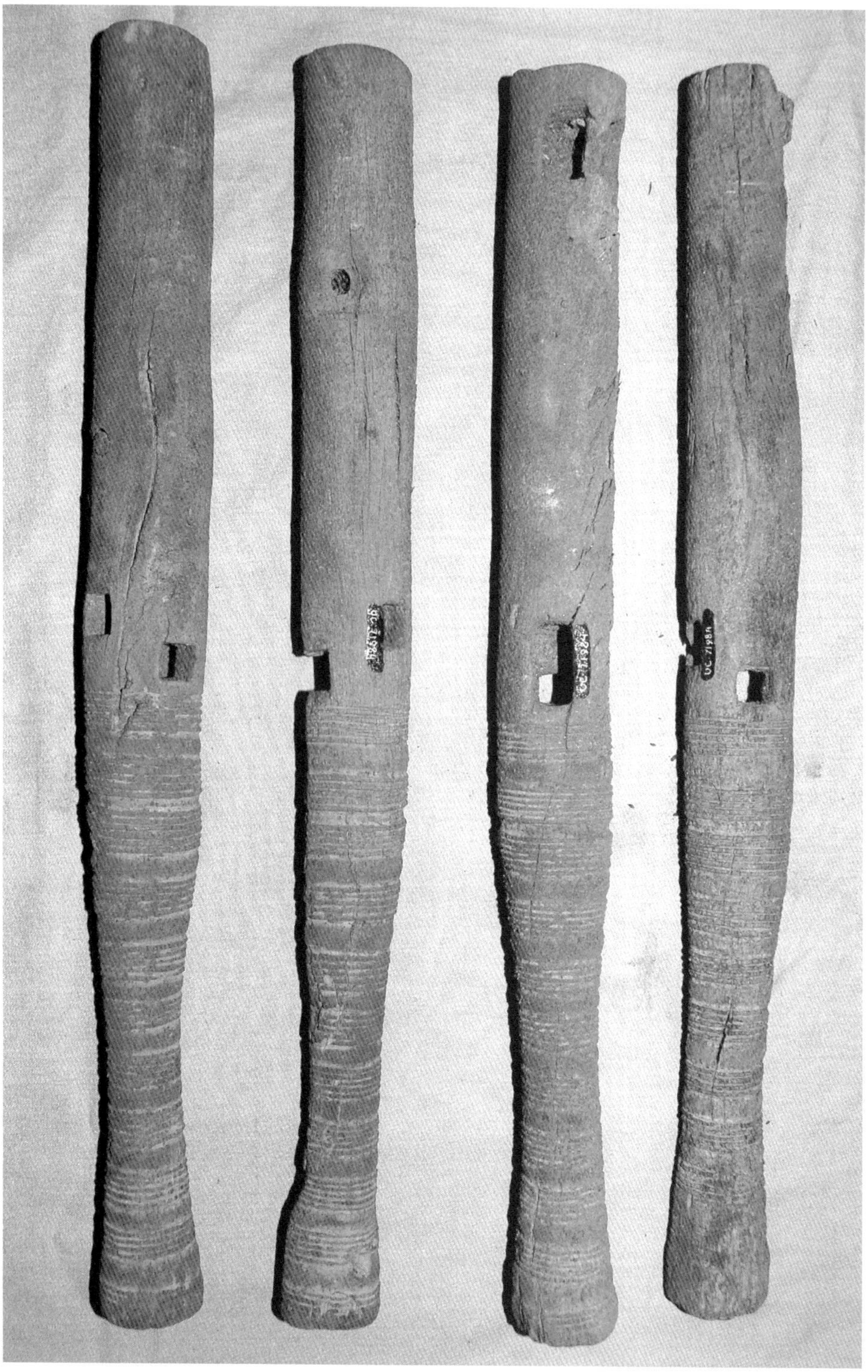

Plate 26. Round stool legs.
UC 71984. Petrie Museum
of Egyptian Archaeology,
University College London.
Photographic credit:
G. Killen.

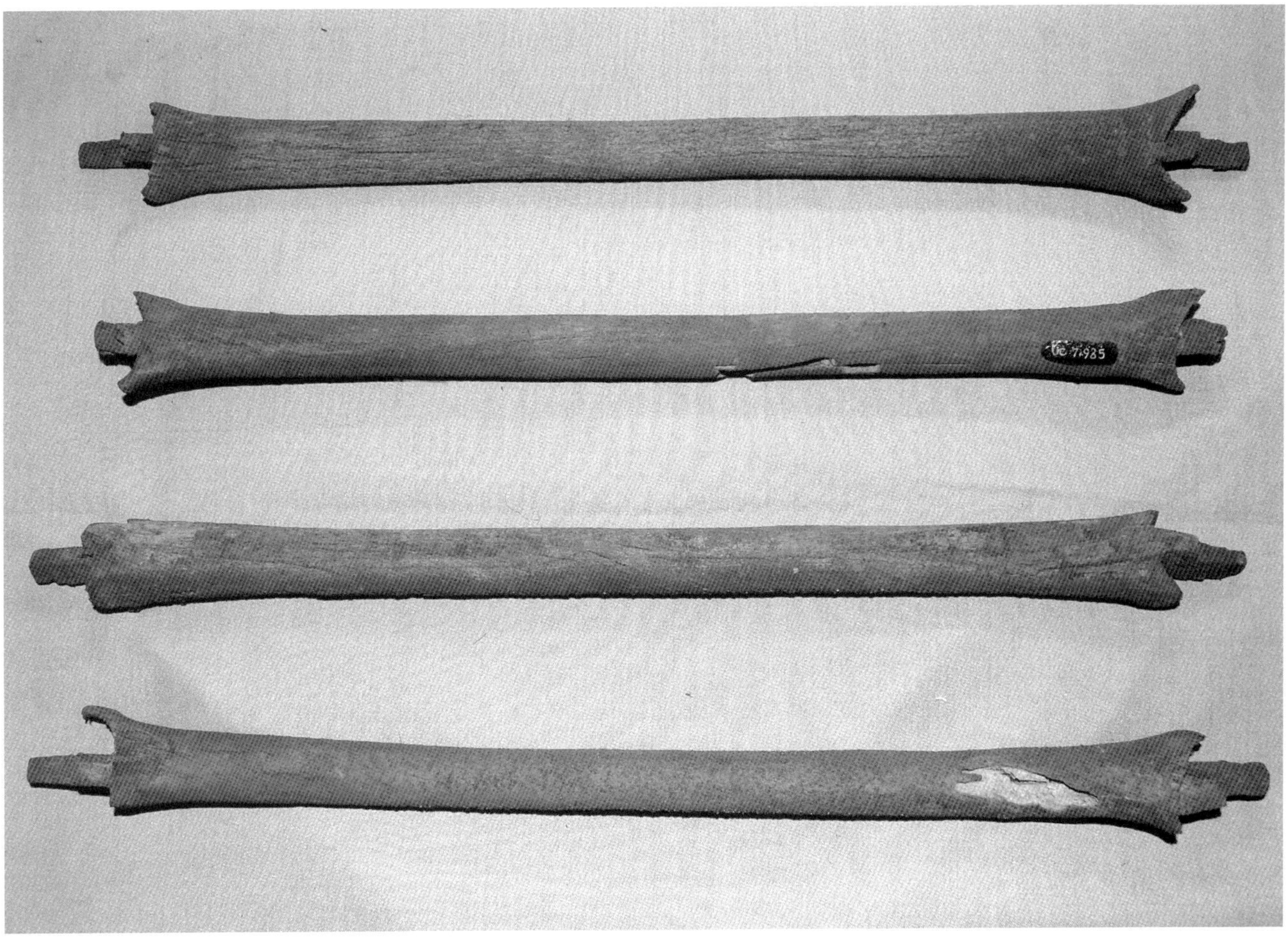

Plate 27. Stretchers from a round legged stool. UC 71985. Petrie Museum of Egyptian Archaeology, University College London. *Photographic credit: G. Killen.*

Plate 28. Detail of tenon on stretcher from a round legged stool. UCL. UC 71985. Petrie Museum of Egyptian Archaeology, University College London. *Photographic credit: G. Killen.*

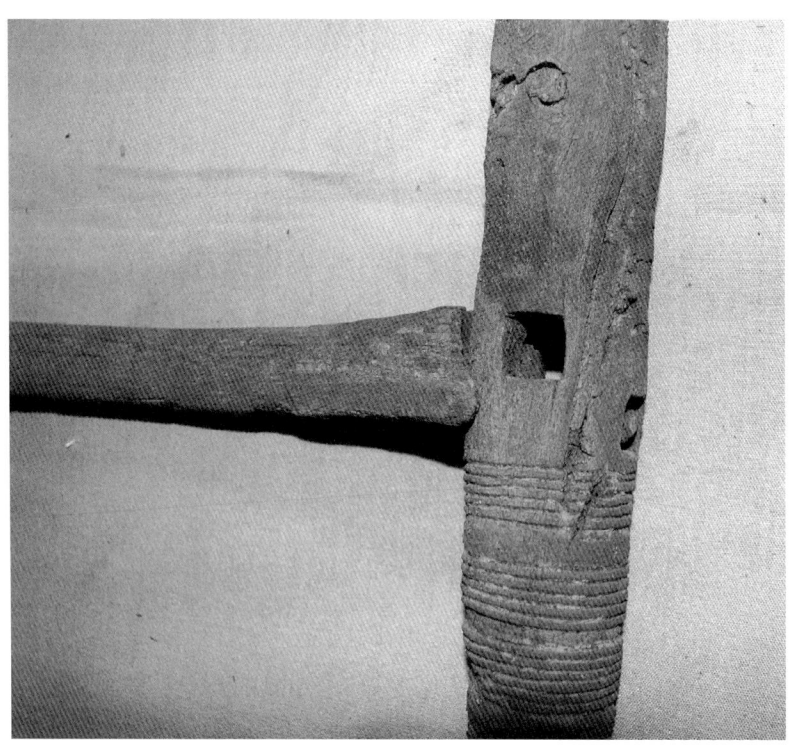

Plate 29. Detail of leg and stretcher joint. Leg. UC 71984; Stretcher UC 71985. Petrie Museum of Egyptian Archaeology, University College London. *Photographic credit: G. Killen.*

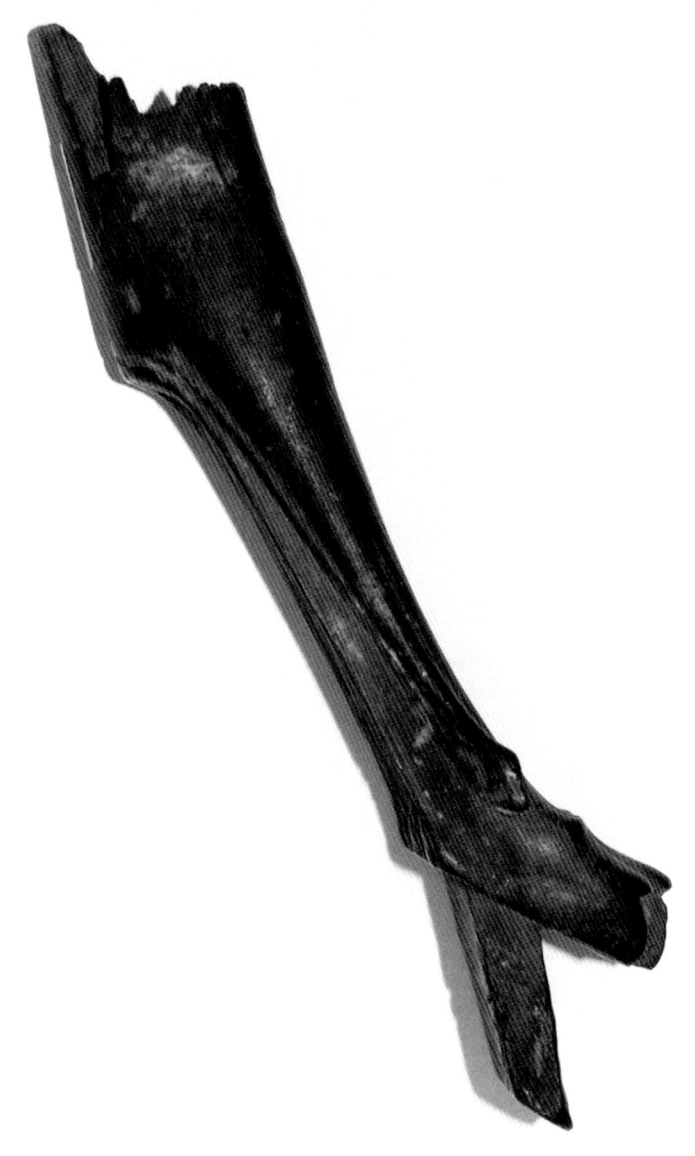

Plate 30. Folding stool leg fragment. British Museum, London. EA 2496. *Photographic credit: G. Killen.*

Plate 31. Folding stool, British Museum, London. EA 37406. *Photographic credit: G. Killen.*

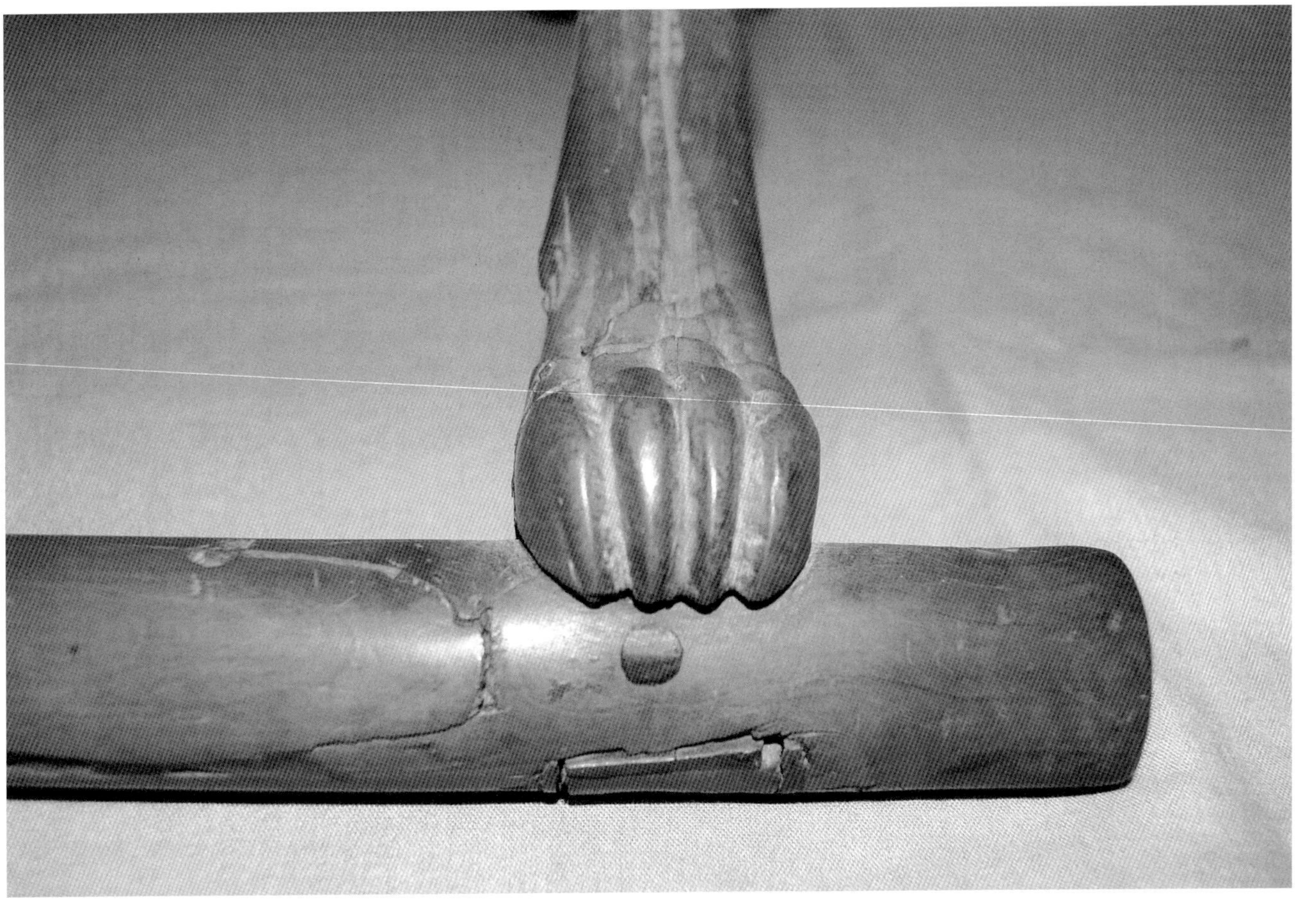

Plate 32. Folding stool, British Museum, London. EA 37406. *Photographic credit: G. Killen.*

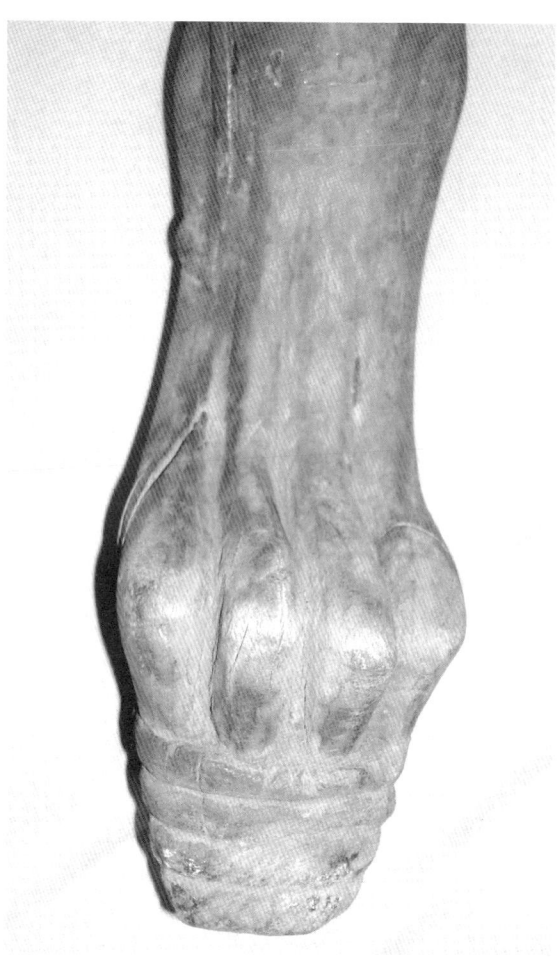

Plate 33. Chair leg, detail of foot. Garstang Museum, University of Liverpool, E. 7161. *Photographic credit: G. Killen.*

Plate 34. Chair leg, detail of foot. British Museum, London, EA 49123. *Photographic credit: G. Killen.*

Plate 35. Folding stool, British Museum, London. EA 37406. *Photographic credit: G. Killen.*

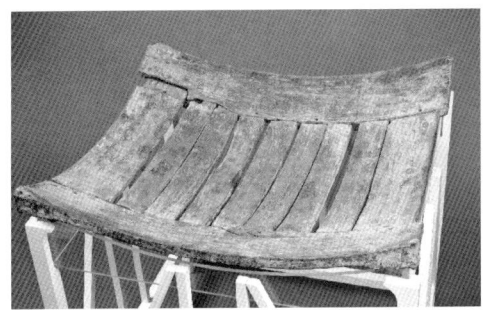

Plate 36. Lattice stool seat, Musées Royaux D'Art et D'Histoire, Brussels. Inv. No. 2411. © *Musées Royaux D'Art et D'Histoire, Brussels.*

Plate 37. Three-legged stool. British Museum, London. EA 2482. *Photographic credit: G. Killen.*

Plate 38. Stool, British Museum, London. EA 66652. *Photographic credit: G. Killen.*

Plate 39. Stool, British Museum, London. EA 66652. *Photographic credit: G. Killen.*

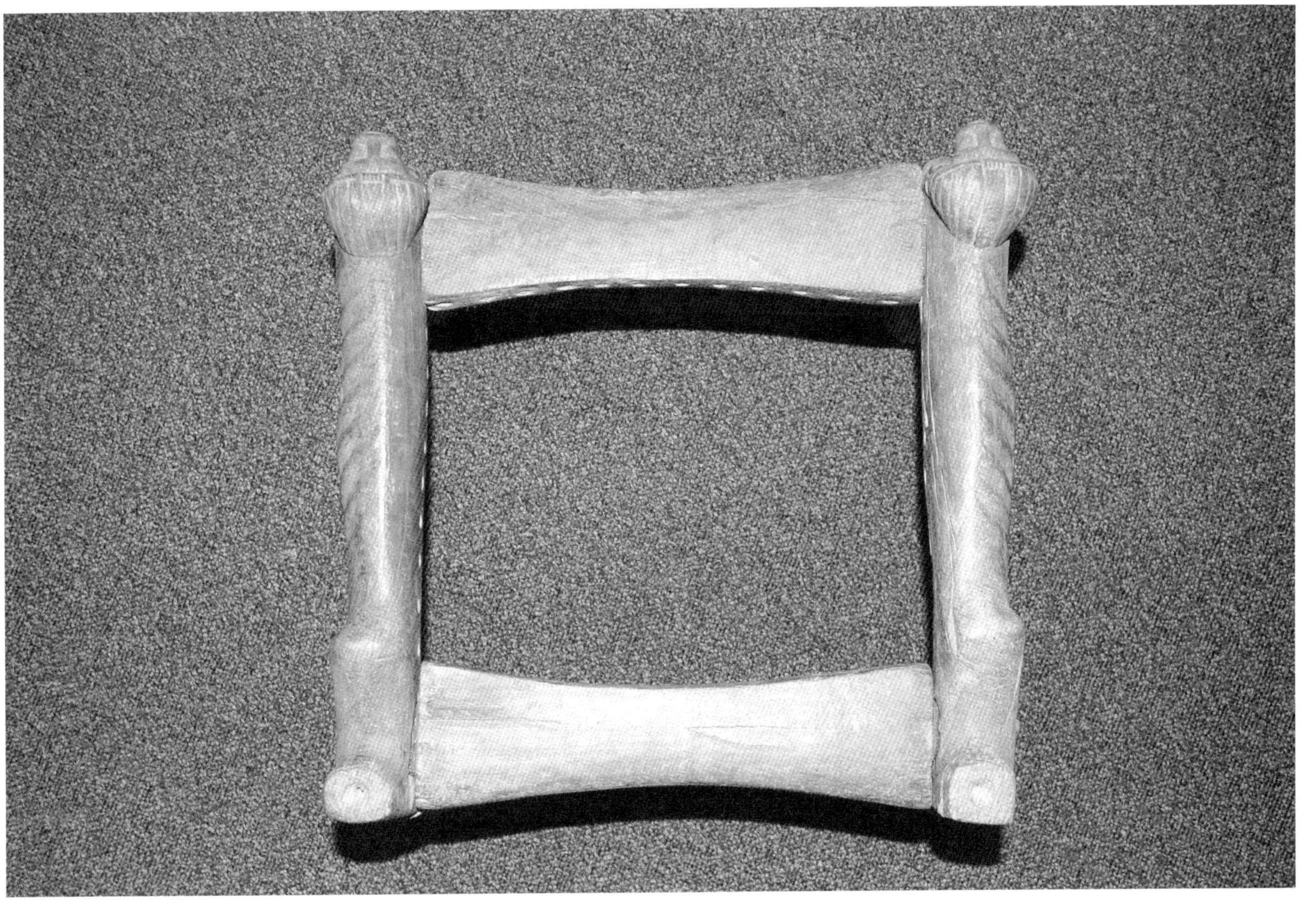

Plate 40. Stool, British Museum, London. EA 66652. *Photographic credit: G. Killen.*

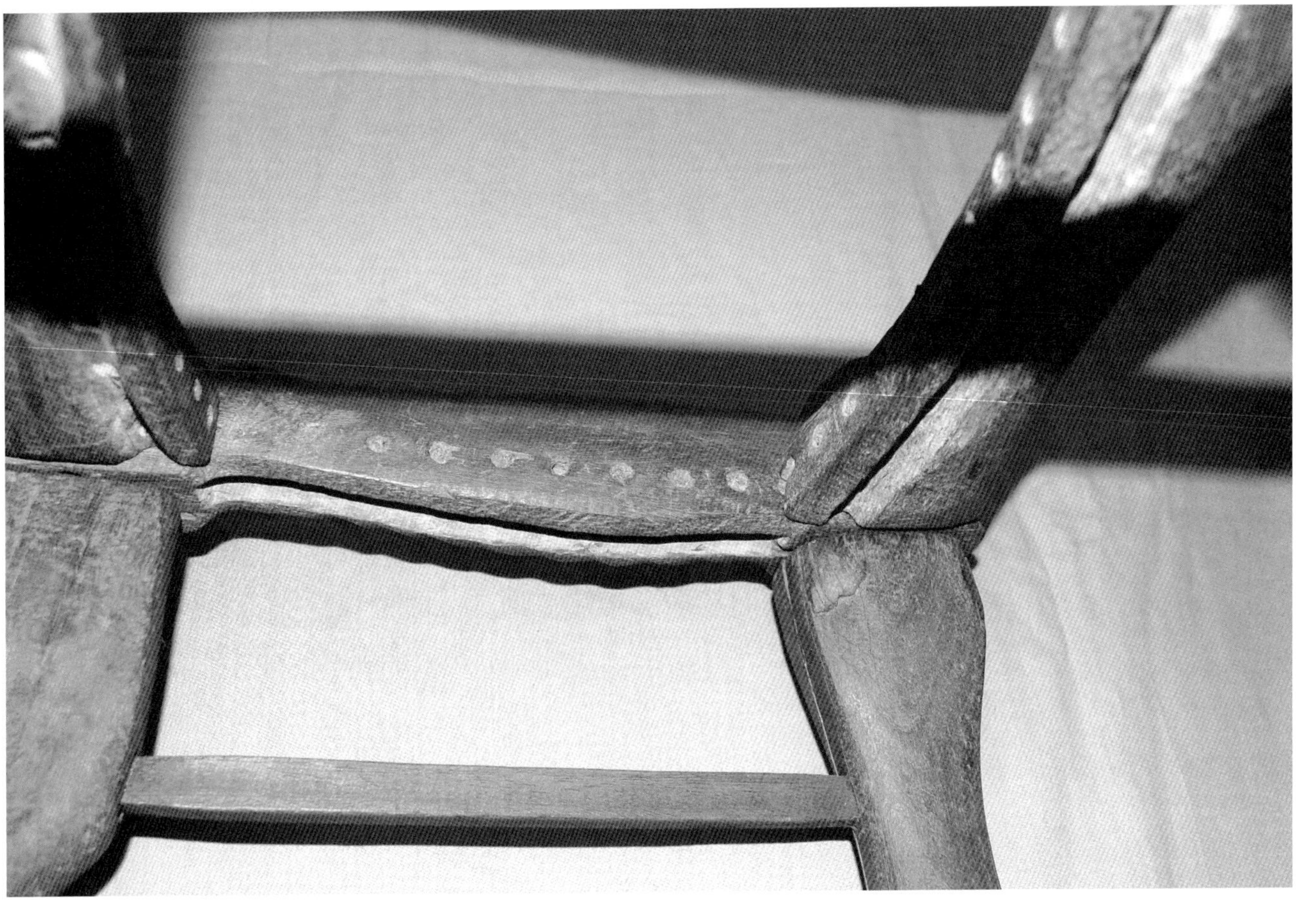

Plate 41. Stool, British Museum, London. EA 66652. *Photographic credit: G. Killen.*

Far left: Plate 42. Bed leg carved in the form of the God Bes. Rijksmuseum van Oudheden, Leiden. Inv. No. F. 1964/1.4. © *Rijksmuseum van Oudheden, Leiden. See also colour plates section.*

Left: Plate 43. Bed leg carved in the form of the God Bes. Rijksmuseum van Oudheden, Leiden. Inv. No. F. 1964/1.3. © *Rijksmuseum van Oudheden, Leiden. See also colour plates section*

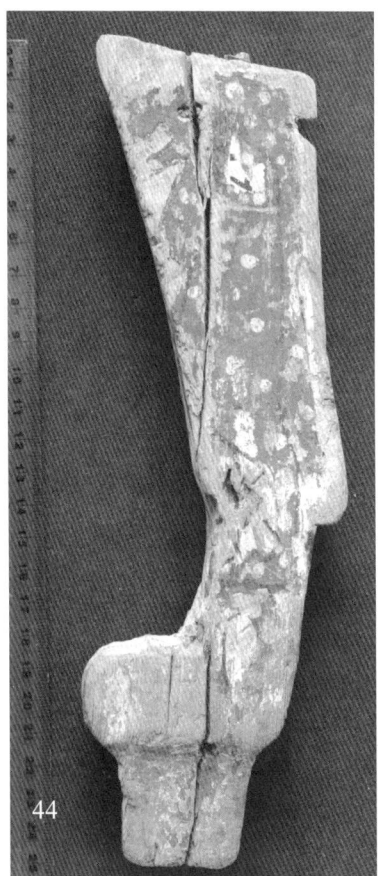
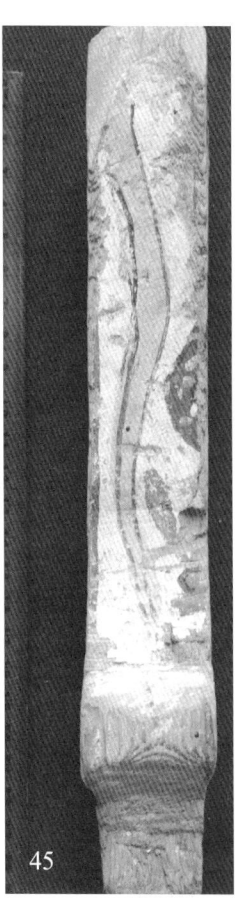
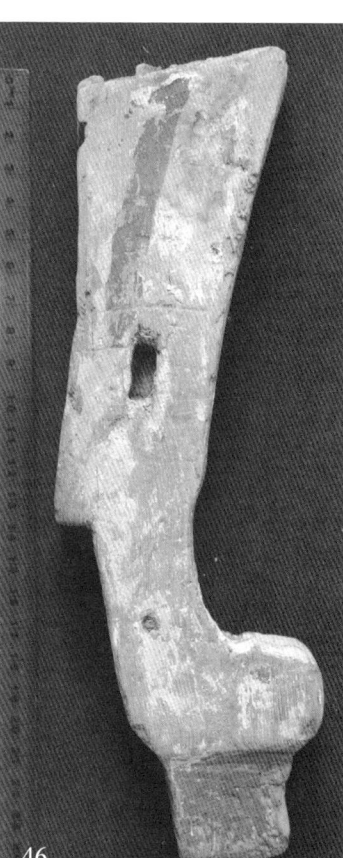

Plates 44–47. Lion leg with the painted depiction of Goddess Taweret. Egypt Centre, Swansea. Inv. No. W 2052b. © *Egypt Centre, Swansea.*

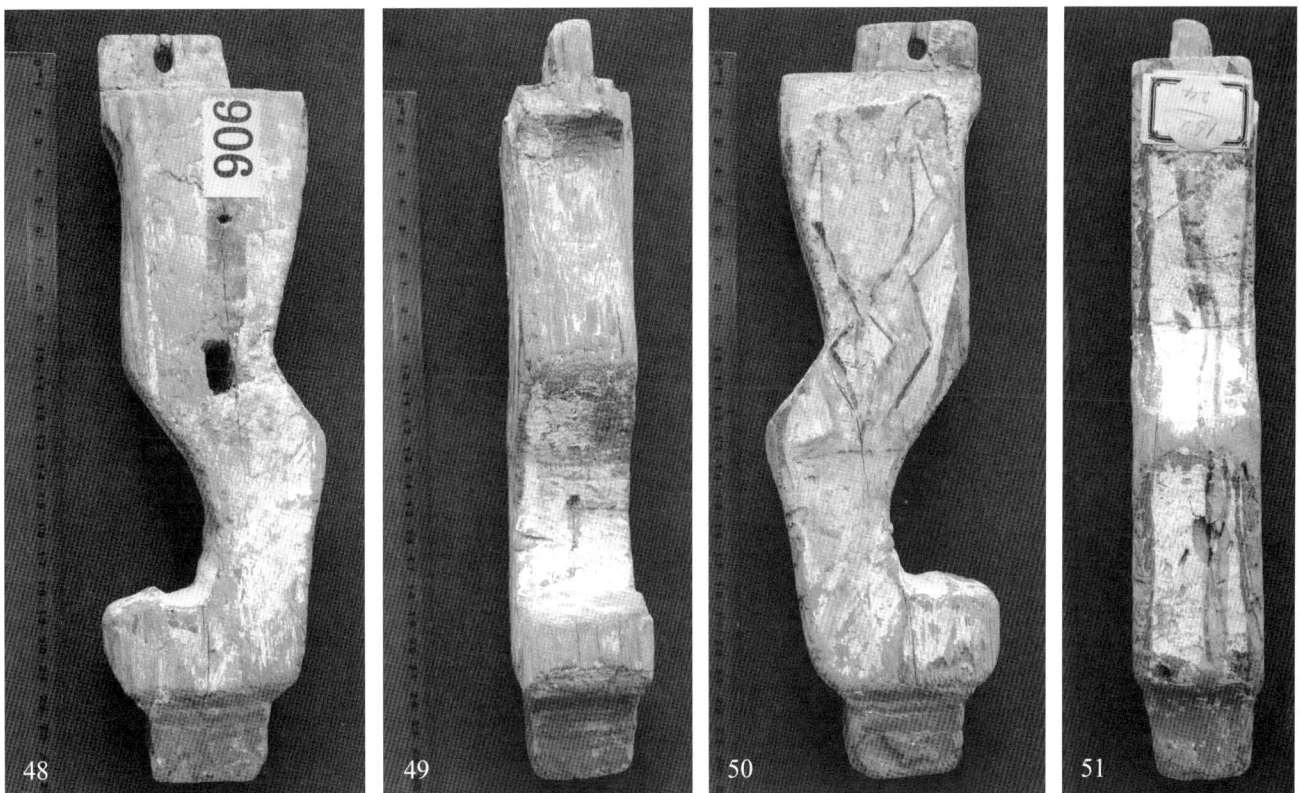

Plates 48–51. Lion leg with the painted depiction of God Bes. Egypt Centre, Swansea. Inv. No. W 2052a. © *Egypt Centre, Swansea. See also colour plates section.*

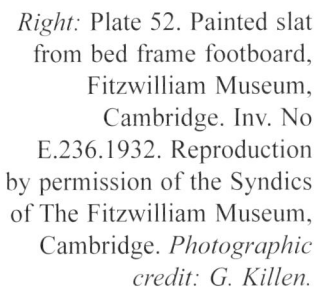

Right: Plate 52. Painted slat from bed frame footboard, Fitzwilliam Museum, Cambridge. Inv. No E.236.1932. Reproduction by permission of the Syndics of The Fitzwilliam Museum, Cambridge. *Photographic credit: G. Killen.*

Far right: Plate 53. Wooden element carved in the form of the God Bes, front, part of a bed frame footboard panel. Fitzwilliam Museum, Cambridge. Inv. No. E.GA.2681.1943. Reproduction by permission of the Syndics of The Fitzwilliam Museum, Cambridge. *Photographic credit: G. Killen.*

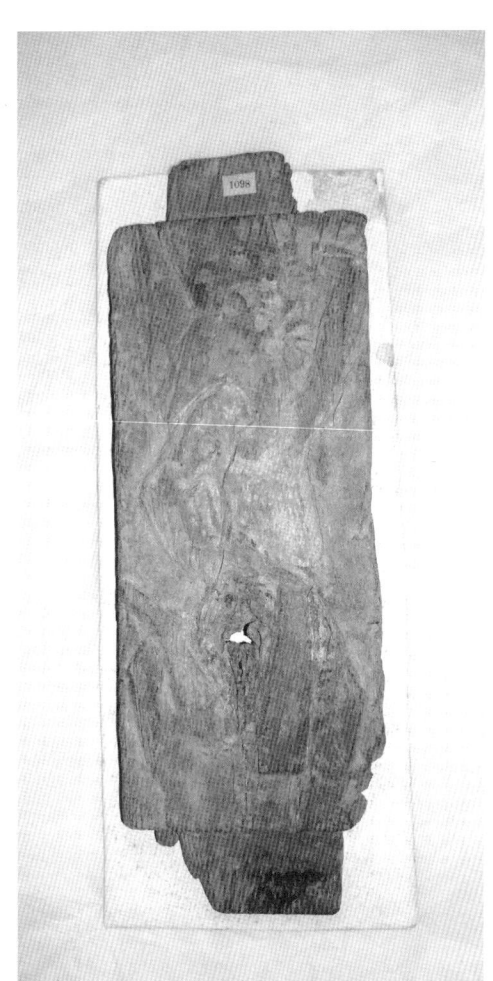

Plate 54. Facsimile of tomb wall painting depicting a round legged bedframe, Tomb of Ipuy, (TT217). Rogers Fund (30.4.116). © *Metropolitan Museum of Art, New York. See also colour plates section.*

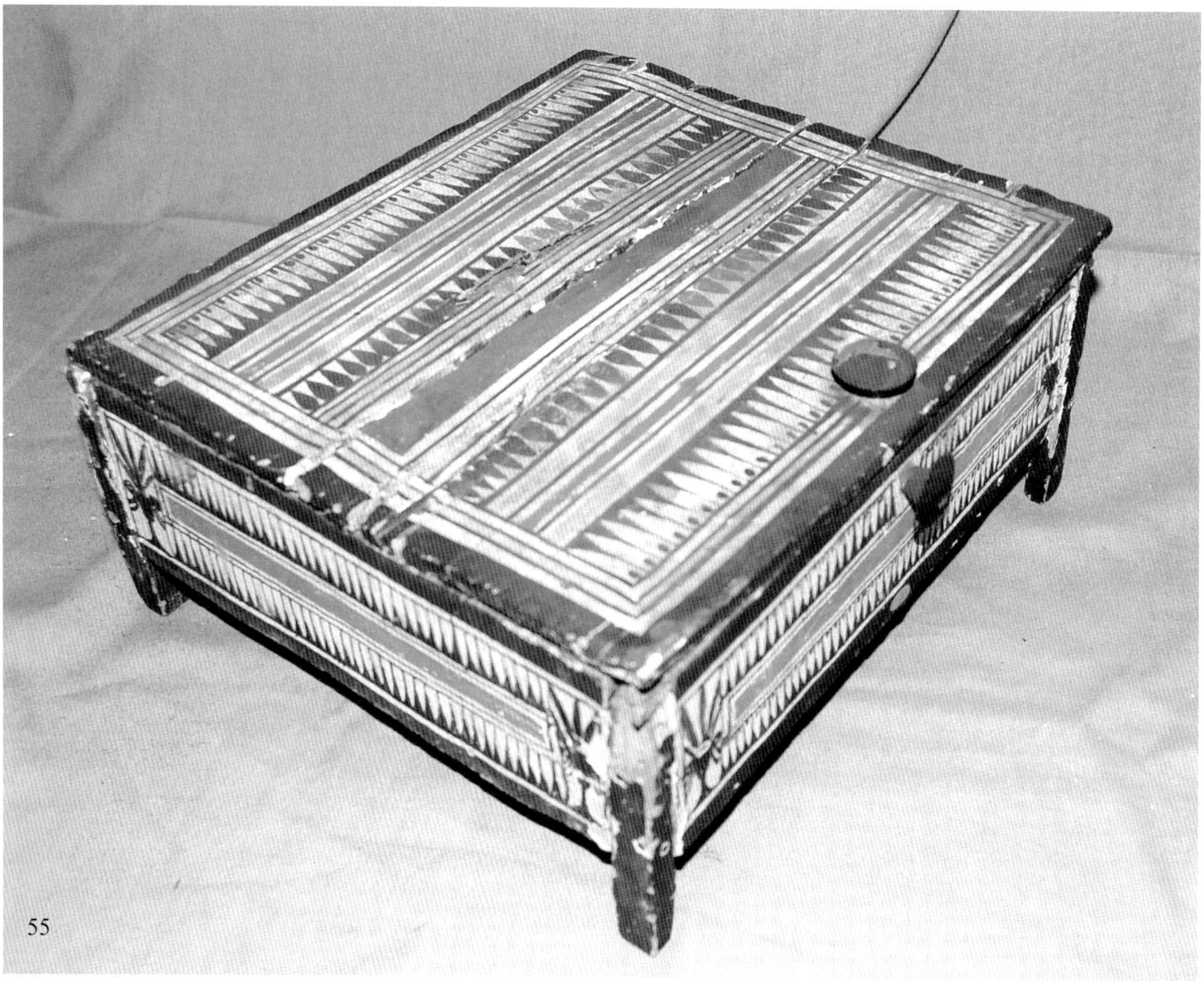

Above and opposite: Plates 55–62. Box with single lid, Ramesside Period. British Museum, London, EA 21818. *Photographic credit: G. Killen.*

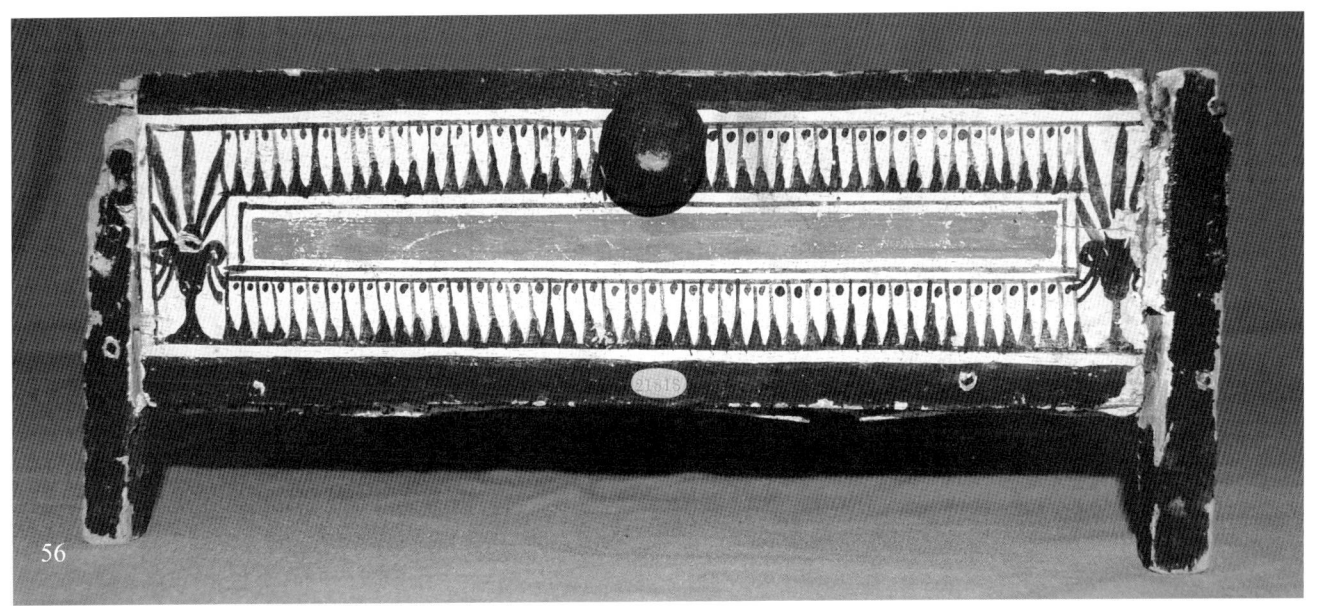

56

57

58

59

60

61

62

Plate 63. Box with shrine shaped lid, Ramesside Period. British Museum, London, EA 5907. *Photographic credit: G. Killen.*

Plate 64. Box with shrine shaped lid, Ramesside Period. British Museum, London, EA 5907. *Photographic credit: G. Killen.*

Plate 65. Box with shrine shaped lid, Ramesside Period. British Museum, London, EA 5907. *Photographic credit: G. Killen.*

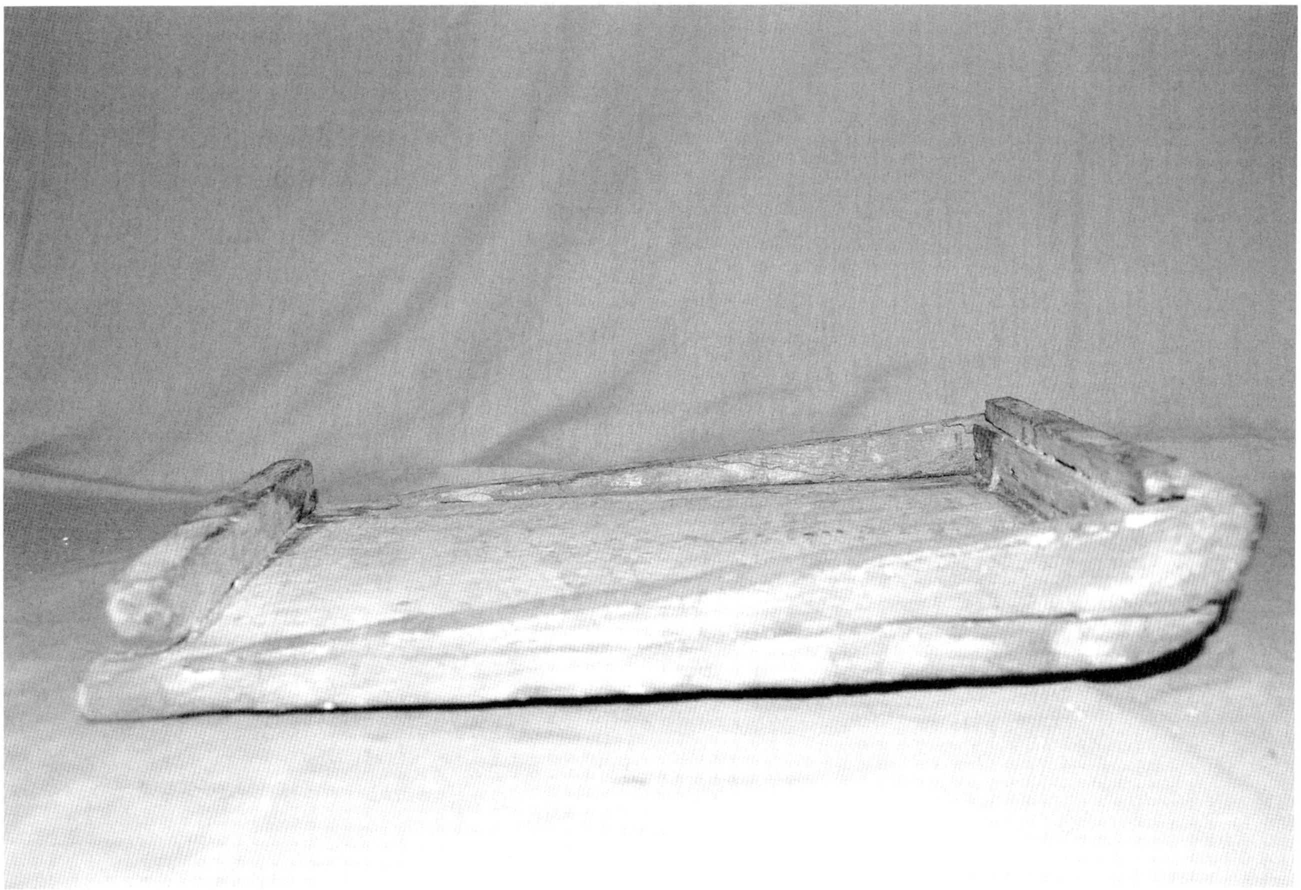

Plate 66. Box lid from shrine shaped box, Ramesside Period. British Museum, London, EA 5907. *Photographic credit: G. Killen.*

Plate 67. Box lid from shrine shaped box, Ramesside Period. British Museum, London, EA 5907. *Photographic credit: G. Killen.*

Plate 68. Vase stand. Louvre Museum, Paris. Inv. No. N 1391. *Photographic credit: G. Killen.*

Plate 69. Replica stand made by the author, based on a small table or stand from the Tomb of Tutankhamun, KV62. Egyptian Museum, Cairo. Carter No. 33, JE 62057 compared with a modern child's chair with a seat height of 210 mm. (BS EN 1729–1:2006, chair type 0, white feet, designed to be used by a child aged between eighteen months and two years).
© G. Killen.

Chapter 4

Royal and Temple Furniture

Illustrations of the round legged stools used by Rameses II

The wall sculptors who decorated the temples of Rameses II with the victory scenes of his reign often show the king seated on a round legged stool. The design of this stool was copied and rendered on temple walls throughout Egypt. The use of this stool reinforced the king's absolute power; however, it uses a form of construction not previously seen as the means to project the king's authority. Although earlier kings would have had or used round legged stools in their households, few would come to project their image by using such a piece of furniture.[1] An informal scene carved of Akhenaten and Nefertiti on a "house altar stela" discovered at Amarna shows the queen, comforting two of their daughters. She sits on a round legged stool which has a frieze of unification symbols below the seat. This stela shows the king seated on a simple lattice stool (classified by Killen as Sf type stool).[2] Perhaps the single round legged stool placed in the tomb of Tutankhamun, JE 62042, was designed to be used by Ankhesenamun.[3] The use of the round legged stool and later the use of a throne with round legs would come to characterise a royal preference for this type of seating in the Ramesside period and perhaps indicates that a new type of manufacturing technology, wood turning, was being practised in the royal workshops.

On the exterior wall of the first pylon at Luxor temple we have a carved image of a typical round legged stool that was used by Rameses II, (Plate 70). The legs are taller than those seen on other types of round legged stool; a deliberate design feature to elevate the seated king and allow him to place his feet upon a footstool. Between the seat rail and a leg bracing stretcher, there is a carved *Sema*, bound with the papyrus and upper Egyptian lily. At the seat rail joint the legs are parallel, however, lower down

the leg they have been shaped to a narrow waist which suggests that they were turned from wood.

Another round legged stool is to be found in a wall relief within the great hall, north wall – lower row, of the Great Temple at Abu Simbel (Plate 71).[4] A further wall relief on the first pylon in the Ramesseum shows Rameses II, (Plate 72), seated on a round legged stool, the legs have again been elongated to allow the king to rest his feet upon a box type footstool.[5] The top surface of the footstool is upholstered with a thick cushion while the sides of the footstool have been rendered with panels showing bound captives and a pair of bows, symbolising the king trampling on his enemies.

Royal Furniture of Rameses III

A rich collection of thrones that in their design surpass those found in the tomb of Tutankhamun, were rendered in paint and carved in relief in the tomb of Rameses III, KV11 and at his temple at Medinet Habu. Unfortunately, those furniture paintings in KV11 (five thrones, five footstools and two bedframes), which could be found in side chamber, Cg: (right wall, lower part; front wall, left part) have been destroyed. However, the quality of these wall paintings and the furniture they recorded can be seen through the paintings and illustrations of them recorded by artists who travelled to Egypt during the late 18th and early 19th centuries. The quality of those destroyed wall paintings can be judged by a small collection of furniture rendered as paintings that still can be seen in the tomb of Tausert (19th Dynasty) and Setnakht (20th Dynasty) (1198–1194 B.C.) (KV14). On the wall of burial chamber J1 (lower level, right wall) are three painted chairs. The legs of the centre chair, (Plate 73), are fashioned in a feline form; the chair has a cushioned seat and backrest and the space below the seat is filled with a *Sema* symbol bound with stems and flowers of the papyrus and upper Egyptian lily.

The furniture paintings once rendered on tomb walls of Rameses III were recorded before their destruction by the artist André Dutertre (1753–1842) who was a member of Napoleon's expedition survey team to Egypt in 1798. His artwork was subsequently engraved by Claude Joseph Pomel (1781–1839).[6]

Pomel's illustrations were to be popularly published by Albert Racinet (1825–1893), together with examples of funerary beds and plain biers. Today, it is possible to obtain these illustrations in poster form and they have inspired modern designers to create replicas of the furniture of the Ramesside period. These furniture illustrations can also to be found as hand coloured engravings in a work by Ippolito Rosellini published between 1832–1844.[7] He records two bedframes, the first (Plate 74 left), has lion shaped legs that together with the side rail are painted yellow to simulate a gilt finish. In the Rosellini engraving, pairs of gilt capped dowels are used to secure the joints of the bed legs to the side frame. Placed on this bedframe is a thick mattress that is covered with a blue fabric and on the mattress is a gilt headrest. Below the bedframe is a set of steps; similar to those seen in the tomb of Ipuy, TT 217 (Plate 54).

The other bedframe, (Plate 74, right), also has lion shaped legs but the frame has been painted brown to suggest a plain wooden frame. Some gold decorative plaques have been placed where the end grain of the foot and head rail tenons would have been located. The drums below each foot of this wooden bedframe are colour washed to give the impression it was also encased in gold foil.

A further set of illustrations from the tomb of Rameses III was published by the French traveller Frédéric Cailliaud (1789–1869).[8] Cailliaud arrived in Egypt in 1815 and accompanied Muhammed Ali's military expedition to the White Nile and into Nubia and Ethiopia. Those published illustrations, reinforce the accuracy of the work previously undertaken, and together with surviving carved furniture relief's of similarly designed furniture found at Medinet Habu, provide us with an intriguing glimpse into the types of throne and chairs once used by Rameses III and members of the royal court.

One major piece of furniture found illustrated in both KV11 and Medinet Habu is a throne based upon the concept of a folding frame that in reality would have been unable to fold as it was rigidly attached to a solid panelled wooden seat, similar in construction to an example discovered in the tomb of Tutankhamun[9]

Tutankhamun's throne has legs finished with carved ducks' heads that have been inlaid with ivory and African Blackwood, whereas the Rameses III examples have crossing legs that are feline in form.[10] The throne depicted in KV11 (Plate 75) is similar in construction to that carved in a wall relief on the third-floor, west wall of the king's private quarters within the eastern gateway at Medinet

Habu (Figure 28).[11] Both thrones are shown to have thick cushions that extend and cover the thrones backrest before rolling over the top back rail. The back support structure of both thrones are curved and supported by vertical pillars, this arrangement gives the typical triangulated form seen on New Kingdom chairs.

Set above the crossing legs of both thrones can be seen the front elevation of a cow's head. However, on the KV11 (Plate 75) example the cow's tail is shown in the foreground while on the Medinet Habu throne (Figure 28) the tail is hidden behind a circular disc, indicating that it is on the far side of the throne. The circular disc possibly formed part of the jointing mechanism of the throne's sub-frame. The common constructional arrangement seen on both thrones suggests that this design was known to those working in stone and paint at both centres, confirming that design principles had been established and were being rigorously followed by those artisans employed by Rameses III. The additional embellishment of the KV11 throne, with its bound captives below the seat would have been easier to achieve in paint and were not applied to the Medinet Habu example. It is clear that we are looking at a known piece of furniture.

Another throne, (Plate 76), illustrated in the KV11 furniture scenes, shows that the legs of this example have been painted blue, similar in colour to the chair preserved in the Louvre Museum, Paris, N 2950, (Plate 18), and suggests that chairs or thrones with this decorative form may be from a royal context. This type of finish was not used on any of the chairs or thrones placed in the earlier tomb of Tutankhamun. The arm support of this throne, (Plate 76), is modelled on the complete form of a lion; below the seat are two pairs of bound captives of Nubian and Asiatic origin, separated by a *Sema* symbol. Stems of the papyrus and upper Egyptian lily make the captives' bindings.

A further pair of thrones of similar construction are found, firstly, painted in the tomb of Rameses III (KV11), (Plate 77), and secondly in carved relief form, (Figure 29), in an earlier context within the temple at Beit el-Wali (entrance hall, south wall, west half), that dates to the reign of Rameses II.[12] The throne illustrated in KV11, (Plate 77), has a decorated panel below the seat bearing the cartouches of Rameses III that are protected by the outstretched wings of Horus. The Rameses II throne, (Figure 29), has the typical arrangement of unification symbols placed below the seat that is seen on a number of pieces of furniture deposited in the tomb of Tutankhamun.[13]

During the 18th Dynasty we see the introduction of round legged stools in a royal context, however, there is no evidence that this form of leg was incorporated into chair or throne design during that period and only one stool, with rounded legs, had been deposited in the tomb of Tutankhamun.[14] However, by the Ramesside Period the concept of constructing either thrones or chairs with rounded legs was well understood. Interestingly, round legged stools either seen in Ramesside private tombs or

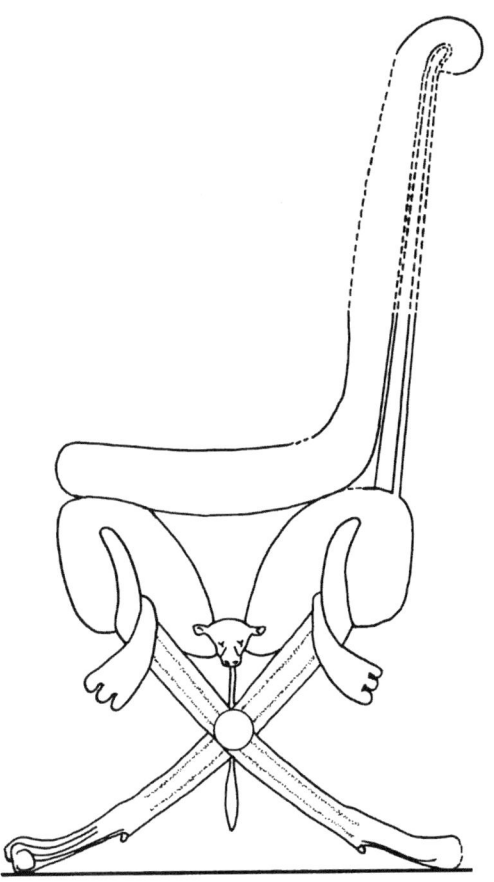

Figure 28. Line drawing of a folding type chair. Inner room of east fortified gate, Medinet Habu.

Figure 29. Chair. Temple at Beit el-Wali (entrance hall, south wall, west half), that dates to the reign of Rameses II.

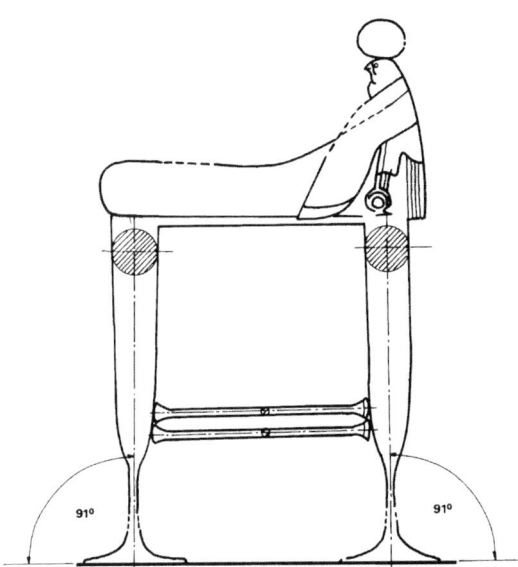

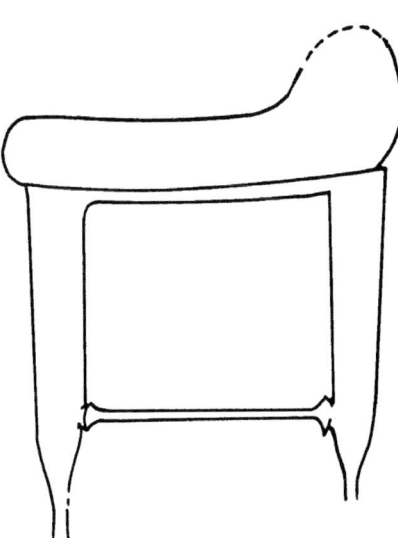

Figure 30. Line drawing of a round legged throne with falcon backrest. Inner room of east fortified gate, Medinet Habu.

Figure 31. Line drawing of a round legged stool. Inner room of east fortified gate, Medinet Habu.

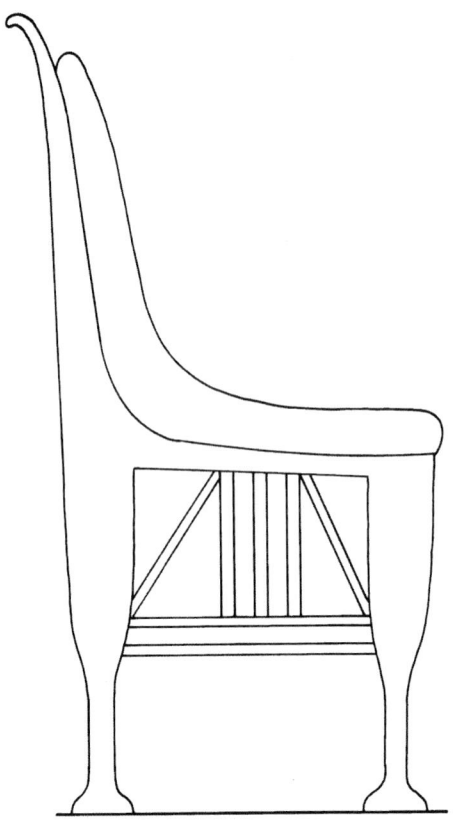

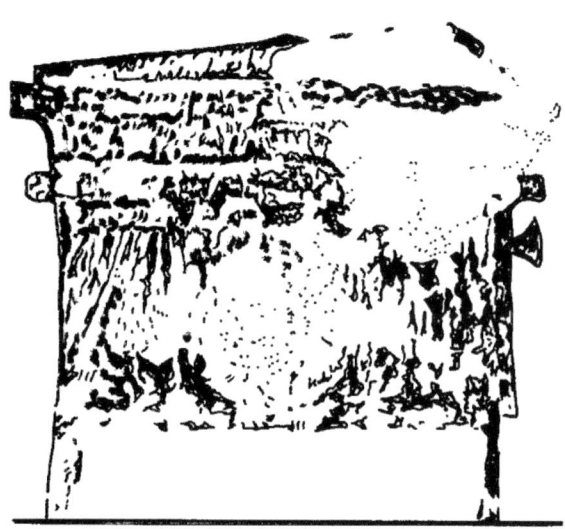

Left: Figure 32. Line drawing of a chair illustrated in a wall relief in the tomb of Penniut at 'Aniba.

Above: Figure 33. Line drawing of large shrine shaped box. Corridor B right wall. Tomb of Rameses VI. KV9.

incorporated as part of a seated pair statue were exclusively used by women (see Appendix D – Distribution of stools by gender as illustrated in the private Theban tombs). However, the use of such seating in a royal context was strictly reserved for the king.

Analysing those depictions of round legged thrones that were designed and manufactured in the workshops of Rameses III provides a glimpse of a pivotal moment in time when carpenters were capable of rounding wood accurately and were prepared to incorporate this technique into some of the most impressive pieces of furniture ever manufactured in ancient Egypt.

The king's throne illustrated in KV11, (Plate 78), has rounded legs that are incised with a feathered pattern and bands of lily petal decoration. Below the thick patterned cushion seat we can also see two rows of a herringbone pattern, indicating the method employed to string the seat. The artist has given the impression that the legs and frame were covered with burnished gold foil, as was the unification decoration below the seat. In the Dutertre engraving of the throne the unification symbol is not gilded and is not backed with a complementary material, suggesting as with Tutankhamun's golden throne that the intertwining stems of the papyrus and upper Egyptian lily together with the *Sema* sign were free standing and placed on the upper circular bracing stretcher.

A second throne that has accurately executed round legs is found in a finely carved wall relief at Medinet Habu, on the third floor, west wall of the north tower (Figure 30).[15] The author has superimposed the suggested sectional elements that were used in the construction of this throne.

The back support of this throne (Figure 30) is unusual as the god Horus with his outstretched wings is perched above the rear leg of the throne, providing a symbolic statement of the protection Horus gave to his representative on earth. Whether the figure of Horus was carved in wood or another material is unknown, although in the Petrie Museum Egyptian Archaeology, University College London, UC 27894, a similar hawk figure has been delicately carved from ivory and has splinters of wood on its flat back surface indicating that it had been glued to a wooden carcase and probably designed as a decorative furniture element.

Another round legged stool, (Figure 31), is also seen at Medinet Habu, west of the vestibule in the north tower.[16] The stretcher that braces the legs has its ends carved with papyrus shaped flowers. These typically form part of the scribed tenon that located in the mortise chopped in the round leg.

Chairs with round legs continued to be manufactured by carpenters and used by kings' throughout the Ramesside Period. Another example, (Figure 32), seen in a wall relief (east wall, north end) in the tomb of Penniut at 'Aniba, shows a seated Rameses VI.[17] This chair is shown to have a cushioned seat, which extends to form the backrest of the chair. The supporting latticework

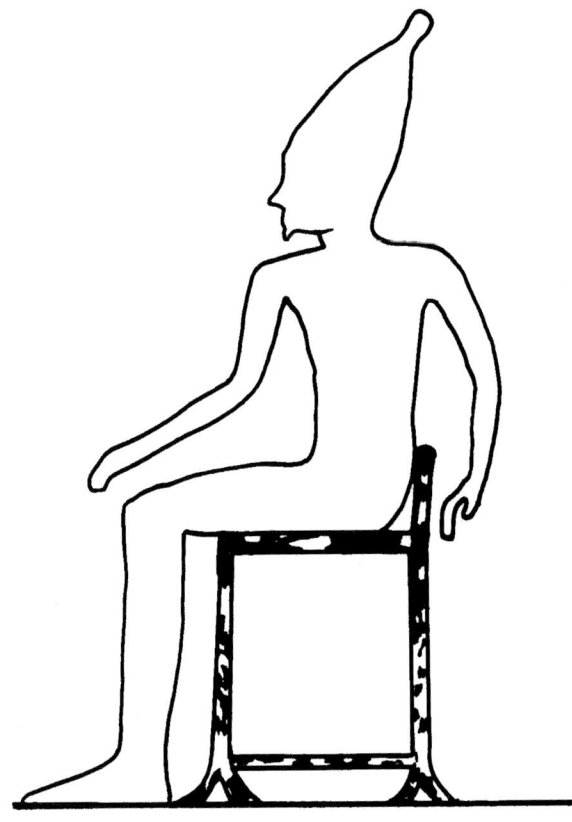

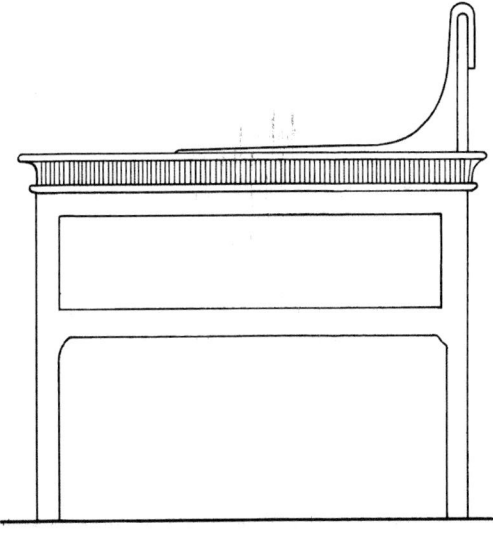

Left: Figure 34. Line drawing of chair, Corridor F right wall. Tomb of Rameses VI. KV9.

Above: Figure 35. Offering table. Chapel of Ra-Horakhty (north wall, western section). Abydos. Seti I.

arrangement below the seat is made from two horizontal stretchers and three vertical supports braced with a pair of angled braces.

The Furniture of Rameses VI

Furniture depictions in the tomb of Rameses VI (KV9) presents us with additional evidence of the type of furniture in use at this period. We see well known forms of furniture that were part of the common design canon as well as a range of furniture construction not seen in existing material forms.

Painted on the right wall of corridor B is a large shrine shaped box, (Figure 33), that has a mushroom-shaped knob on the front of the box though the area of paint where the lid knob would have been fixed is now lost.[18] This box has both a clearly defined cavetto cornice and a thick torus moulding.[19]

The tomb of Rameses VI also provides us with evidence of an unusual form of leg design that is used on stool, table and chair construction. The bottom part of the leg in contact with the ground is split to create a lambda "Λ" shape. The shape of the entire leg creates, whether intentionally or not, the "S 27" sign when both legs are paired together. The majority of the seats and tables are shown as a simple frame with two legs connected to a horizontal top rail, although one example found on the right wall of corridor F, is specifically depicted as a chair,

(Figure 34).[20] In this example the legs are additionally braced together with a horizontal stretcher and there is a small extension to the chair's back leg to create a low backrest.

LEG FROM A STAND (PLATE 79).

Petrie Museum of Egyptian Archaeology. University College London. UC 7920 Gurob
Length 555 mm, width at bottom of fork 350 mm.

Although the lambda "Λ" shape leg is uncharacteristic of Ramesside furniture the technical knowledge to manufacture a form of wooden element to this shape was known. This leads us to suspect that legs of the lambda "Λ" shape are more than an artist's impression.

Manufactured from a conveniently shaped forked branch this artefact, (Plate 79), was catalogued by Petrie as probably part of a stand, although Angela Thomas defines this element as "probably part of a plough" (Thomas 1981: 31).[21] The confusion derives from the lack of extant material and relies on pictorial evidence. Whether Petrie was aware of lambda "Λ" form legs in the Rameses VI tomb paintings is unknown. However, Petrie's initial classification is certainly credible when examining the element technically. Firstly, the acute angle formed by the forks in both the Rameses VI tomb paintings and UC 7920 are striking similar. Secondly, the peg that projects

Figure 36. Offering table. Chapel of Amun-Ra (north wall, western section). Abydos. Seti I.

Figure 37. Offering table. Chapel of Isis (north wall, western section). Abydos. Seti I.

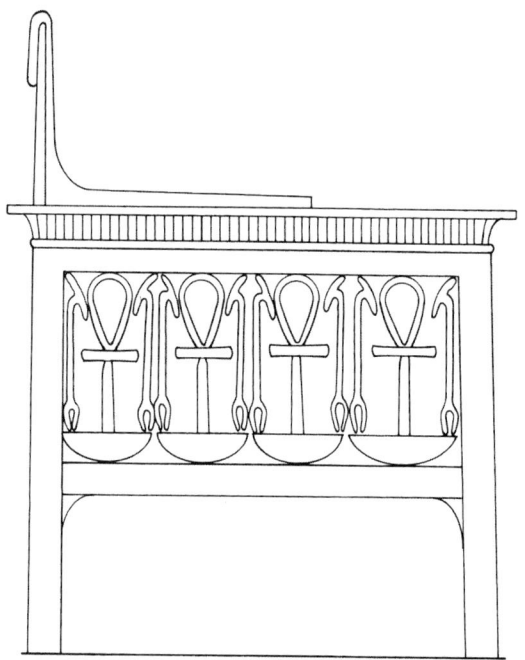
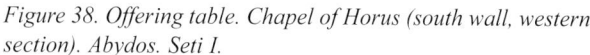

Figure 38. Offering table. Chapel of Horus (south wall, western section). Abydos. Seti I.

Figure 39. Offering table. (Sanctuary, south wall, west end). Beit el-Wali. Rameses II.

from the top of the fork is designed to locate in a hole of a vertical shaft; there is no indication that this joint was mechanically fixed indicating that only compressive loads were applied to the structure. In a plough assembly it would be reasonable to expect that not only compression loading would be applied to this assembly but also tensile and torsion forces would be exerted. Finally, the square mortise chopped through the apex of the "Λ" shape is indicative of a stretcher joint assembly that is seen in the Rameses VI tomb illustration of a chair, (Figure 34).

Temple Furniture

Wooden temple furniture can be separated into two generic forms. Firstly, stands and tables of a plain utilitarian design and secondly, elaborately decorated offering tables. The temple of Seti I at Abydos provides a good range of material to survey.

Offering tables at Abydos

The finely decorated offering tables seen in the temple of Seti I at Abydos, have a clear symbolic and ritualistic character.[22] Each table is laden with goods to be offered to the god; these are presented on a horizontal surface backed by a vertical backboard that visually presents the offering table as a symbolic throne.

In wall reliefs in the temple of Seti I at Abydos, examples of offering table are seen in the chapels of Ptah, Ra-Horakhty, Isis, Horus, Amun-Ra and in the second hypostyle hall. All are similar in construction, the plainest example being depicted in the Chapel of Ra-Horakhty (north wall, western section), (Figure 35), and is made from straight elements of wood that form the offering tables sub frame.[23] It has a single horizontal stretcher that braces the legs, and small right-angled brackets have been included to give the frame additional rigidity. The carved cavetto cornice with torus moulding has been attached to the top rail and the boards that make the offering platform. To the back of this platform has been fixed an upright back that is attached with a right-angled bracket to the platform. All offering tables exhibit similar characteristics having a wide platform on which to place the offerings, and a short back.

Another offering table found in the Chapel of Amun-Ra (north wall, western section), (Figure 36), has one side panel elaborately decorated; carved with two kneeling androgynous Hapi figures, each holding a tray with three vessels and papyrus flowers.[24] On their wrists hang a pair of *ankh* signs; they face towards the plumed cartouches of Seti I, and each are placed on an *nbw* sign. The use of Hapi, god of the annual Nile flooding is symbolic, as the inundation god provided the king with the food produce that could be presented during the offering ceremony.

An offering table depicted in the Chapel of Isis (north wall, western section), (Figure 37), has a panel fitted with the cartouches of Seti I flanked by pairs of uræi,

their heads support a sun disk while their tails enclose each cartouche.[25]

A final offering table depicted in the Chapel of Horus (south wall, western section), (Figure 38), has a panel filled with a frieze of *ankh* and *was* signs placed on a row of *nb* signs.[26]

Offering tables at Beit el-Wali

A painted wall relief at the temple of Beit el-Wali shows Rameses II standing behind an offering table before which is the god Amun-Ra, (sanctuary, south wall, west end). The side of this offering table, (Figure 39), has a panel which depicts the Nile god Hapi acting as the supporters of the plumed cartouches of Rameses II.[27]

The cavetto cornice and torus moulding have been removed from the back surface of this offering table; whether this was a deliberate constructional arrangement or it became necessary to artistically remove it because of the closeness of the vase that stands to the side of the offering table is difficult to resolve. The surfaces of the cornice and moulding with vertical lines of red paint have been applied to give the impression that both elements were carved with a ribbed pattern.[28]

OPENWORK PANEL FROM OFFERING TABLE (PLATE 80).

Petrie Museum of Egyptian Archaeology, UC 30579. Saqqara H5–503[1192]. From Sector 1, pit by south wall of courtyard.
Height 300 mm, width 100 mm, depth 17 mm.

The method of constructing the side panel of an offering table is seen in this openwork element, (Plate 80), which depicts the god Hapi in profile holding a tray on which stands a pair of *Hes*-vases that are separated with lotus flowers. Below the tray is placed a blank double plumed cartouche that stands on an *nbw*-sign. Unfortunately, the lack of an inscription makes it impossible to date this panel. However, its find spot would suggest it dates to the 7th–6th centuries B.C.[29]

This panel exhibits a striking parallel with the illustration of the panel that decorated the Beit el-Wali offering table, (Figure 39). The piercing and carving of the panel have been finely executed, as is the surface rendering. The anatomical details of the god Hapi are finely carved and he is shown wearing a tripartite wig with a papyrus head-dress, and attached to the god's chin is an Osirian beard. At the top and bottom of the panel are pairs of stub tenons that would have located in a pair of horizontal rails. There is evidence that gesso had been applied to the surfaces of the tenons, perhaps used as a fixing medium as there is no mechanical method of pinning this panel into position. The back of this panel is left plain and undecorated, emphasising that it was to be viewed from just one side and attached to the surface of a piece of temple furniture.

Plate 70. Rameses II seated on a round legged stool, relief from first pylon at Luxor temple. © *G. Killen*.

Plate 71. Rameses II seated on a round legged stool, relief from the north wall, great pillared hall, great temple of Rameses II, Abu Simbel. © *G. Killen.*

Plate 72. Rameses II seated on a round legged stool, relief from the first pylon at the Ramesseum. © *G. Killen.*

Plate 73. Painted chair illustrated as wall painting. Sarcophagus chamber of Tausert. Tomb of Tausert (19th Dynasty) and Setnakht (20th Dynasty) (1198–1194 B.C.) (KV14). © *G. Killen. See also colour plates section.*

Plate 74. Bed frames. Tomb of Rameses III, (KV11). Hand coloured engraving made by Ippolito Rosellini published between 1832–1844. Rosellini 1832–1844: pl. XCII. *See also colour plates section.*

Right: Plate 75. Folding type throne. Tomb of Rameses III, (KV11). Hand coloured engraving made by Frédéric Cailliaud (1789-1869). Cailliaud 1831 (bound volume, no plate numbers). *See also colour plates section.*

Far right: Plate 76. Throne. Tomb of Rameses III, (KV11). Hand coloured engraving made by Frédéric Cailliaud (1789–1869). Cailliaud 1831 (bound volume, no plate numbers). *See also colour plates section.*

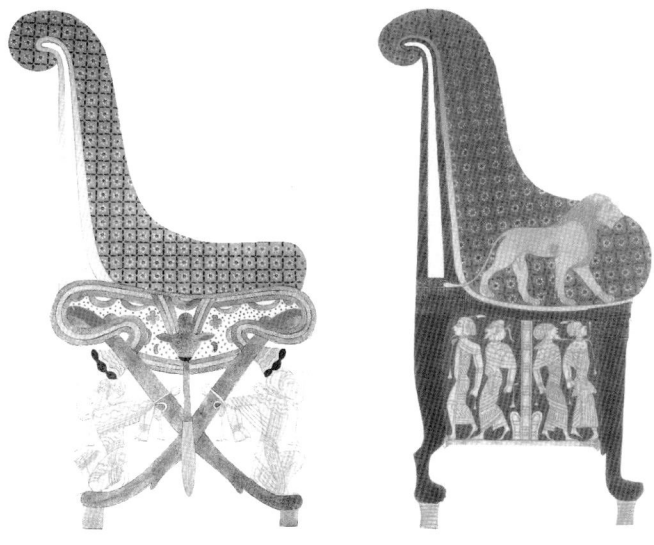

Right: Plate 77. Throne. Tomb of Rameses III, (KV11). Hand coloured engravings made by Frédéric Cailliaud (1789–1869). Cailliaud 1831 (bound volume, no plate numbers). *See also colour plates section.*

Far right: Plate 78. Round legged throne. Tomb of Rameses III, (KV11). Hand coloured engraving made by Frédéric Cailliaud (1789–1869). Cailliaud 1831 (bound volume, no plate numbers). *See also colour plates section.*

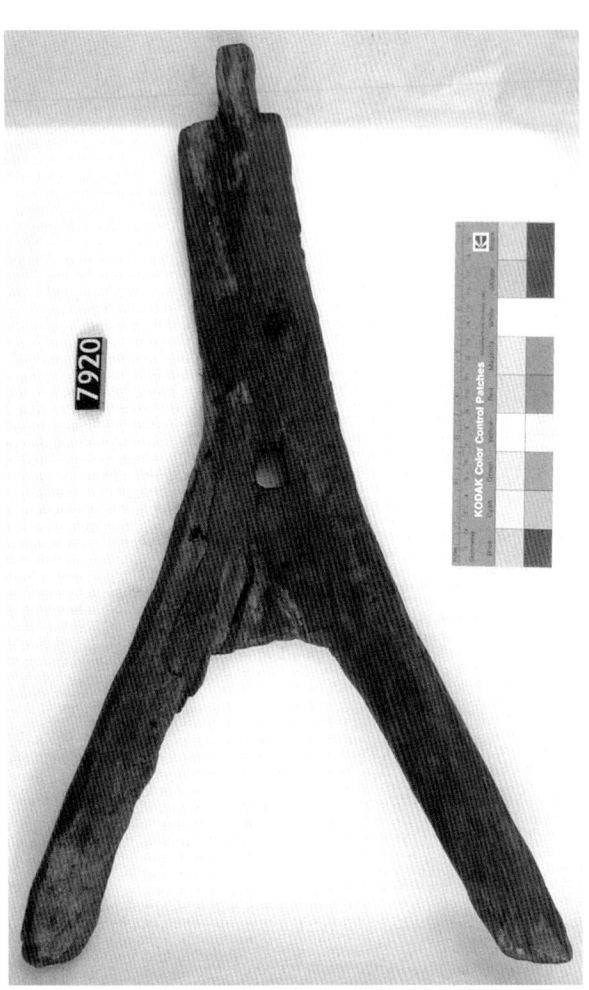

Plate 79. Leg from a stand. UC 7920. Gurob. © *Petrie Museum of Egyptian Archaeology, University College London.*

Plate 80. Openwork panel from offering table. UC 30579. © *Petrie Museum of Egyptian Archaeology, University College London.*

Notes

Chapter One: Deir el-Medina – A Community of Entrepreneurs?

1. O. Cairo 25670. Attributed to the 19th Dynasty. Wente 1967: 138 no.170 [translation]. "Provenance: found among the remains of the workmen's settlement at Abydos according to E.R. Ayrton, C.T. Currelly and A.E.P. Weigall, *Abydos III*, London 1902–04, 54. In view of the names and content, however, the text may be related to the community of workmen at Deir el-Medina. Dates attributed: dating to Dynasty XVIII by W. Spiegelberg (in E.R. Ayrton, C.T. Currelly and A.E.P. Weigall, *Abydos III*, London 1904, 38) is very unlikely" (http://www.leidenuniv.nl/nino/dmd/dmd.html). This ostraca indicates that skilled craftsmen may have been seconded to other communities for the purposes of training. (McDowell 1999: 66–67).
2. O. DeM 0418. Attributed to the 20th Dynasty. Wente 1967: 167, [no. 279] (translation).
3. An example of a royal cubit rod inscribed with a typical offering formula is dedicated to Any, a "Servant in the Place of Truth" a workman who once lived in the village of Deir el-Medina, and is preserved in the World Museum, Liverpool (M13825). Originally, being 525 mm in length, it is divided into seven palms (7 × 75 mm = 525 mm) and 28 digit/finger widths (28 × 18.75 mm = 525 mm), these divisions being marked as lines engraved across the rule. As with a modern rule one edge of this royal cubit rod is bevelled.
4. P. Turin 2002. Discusses the role workmen had in the placement of shrines in the tomb of Rameses IV. Černý 1973: 11–12.
5. The size of wooden scaffolding is seen in a fragment of painted tomb relief that dates to the 19th Dynasty, (Staaliche Museen zu Berlin, Preussischer Kulturbesitz, Ägyptisches Museen und Paprussammlung, Inv. No. 23731). The type of scaffolding shown in this tomb fragment would have been suitable for a wide range of secondary processed wooden products. Two carpenters are seen working on the scaffold, the elements that make the scaffold are made from planks of wood that range between four digits in width for the upright members and one palm two digits for the trestle planking. The scaffold is lashed together with rope, within the scaffold squats a carpenter whose appearance is quite unkempt; he has short spiky hair and heavy facial stubble. He is using an adze, which he holds in his right hand; it is unclear what type of technical operation he is engaged upon.
6. P. DeM 09. Attributed to the 20th Dynasty. Wente 1967: 168–169, [no. 285] (translation).
7. O. Glasgow D. 1925.68. Attributed to mid-20th Dynasty. McDowell 1993: 5–6, pls. IV–IVa, V–Va. (translation).
8. O. EA 5631. Attributed to the 19th Dynasty. Wente 1967: 146, [no. 196] (translation).
9. O. Michaelides 006. Attributed to the end of the 19th Dynasty. Allam 1973: 207–208, [no. 211] (translation).
10. P. DeM 18. Attributed to the 20th Dynasty. Wente 1967: 167–168, [no. 282] (translation).
11. O. DeM 0419. Attributed to the 20th Dynasty. McDowell 1999: 81, [no. 51] (translation).
12. O. Louvre E. 23554. Attributed to the 19th Dynasty. Andreu 1997: 154, fig. 71 (translation).
13. Approximately 300 mm in width and 411 mm in height.
14. A full analysis of the "Gurob Shrine Papyrus" Petrie Museum of Egyptian Archaeology, London. UC 27934 (i) and (ii). Smith and Stewart 1984: 54–64.
15. The three ostraca preserved in the Museo Archeologico, Florence; O. Florence 2628, O. Florence 2629 and O. Florence 2630 are examined in Killen and Weiss 2009: 137–158. The furniture classifications provided in that paper, e.g. (Ch), should now be read with those furniture forms illustrated in Appendix A of this work.
16. Schott photograph 8124.
17. Metropolitan Museum of Art Photograph, T. 1882 and T 1887.
18. O. Ashmolean Museum 119. Attributed to the 19th Dynasty. Allam 1973: 176, [no. 172] (translation).
19. O. Cairo CG 25800. Attributed to the 20th Dynasty. McDowell 1999: 230, [no. 181] (translation).
20. O. Turin N. 57040. Attributed to the 20th Dynasty. Helck 2002: 248 (translation).

21. O. P. DeM 03. Attributed to the 20th Dynasty. Wente 1967: 140, [no. 178] (translation).
22. O. DeM 0146. Attributed to the 20th Dynasty. McDowell 1999: 80, [no. 50] (translation).
23. O. Berlin P. 12343. Attributed to the 20th Dynasty. McDowell 1999: 81–82, [no. 52] (translation).
24. O. Brooklyn Museum 37.1880E. Attributed to the 20th Dynasty. McDowell 1999: 84–85, [no. 55] (translation).
25. O. DeM 0195 recto. Attributed to the 20th Dynasty. Allam 1973: 103, [no. 74] (translation).
26. Egyptian Museum, Cairo. JE 33833 (CG 24001). Daressy 1902: 1–3, pl. i.
27. This abstract sign should be compared with ZZG incised on a workbench (Bruyère 1939: pl. XXIV) and ZZI on a lamp, Tomb of Kha. (Schiaparelli 1927: 144, fig. 128). Killen and Weiss 2009: 156.
28. This abstract sign should be compared with ZZA found a piece of textile, Tomb of Kha. (Schiaparelli 1927: 93, fig. 63).

Chapter Two: An Analysis of Ramesside Furniture Used in Gurob and Memphis

1. Davies: 1927.
2. Kemp 1978: 130.
3. Kemp 1978: 122–133.
4. Tutankhamun's headrest, Egyptian Museum, Cairo. JE. 62023. Carter No. 403d.
5. Davies and Gardiner 1948: pl. XXIX.
6. Bruyère 1927: pl. VII.
7. Petrie 1927: 45, pl. XL [6].
8. See Emery 1949 and 1954.
9. See Reisner 1955.

Chapter Three: Ramesside Furniture Forms

1. Chair types Ckk, Cll, Cmm, Cnn, Coo, Cpp are depicted elsewhere:
   1. Ckk. Stela of Hori, Deir el-Medina. British Museum, London. EA 588.
   2. Cll. Stela, Petrie Museum of Egyptian Archaeology, London. UC 14354.
   3. Cmm. Stela, Memphis. Petrie Museum of Egyptian Archaeology, London. UC 14362.
   4. Cnn. Stela of Thutmes. Petrie Museum of Egyptian Archaeology, London. UC 14228.
   5. Coo. Depicted in the tomb of Khay, Ante chapel, south wall. Memphis. Martin 2001: pl. 14.
   6. Cpp. Block. Egyptian Museum, Berlin. Inv. No. 19782.
2. In the tomb of Rekhmira we see a woman seated on a low chair, her knees are raised above the height of the seat plane. Robins 1993: fig. 79. A young woman is shown kneeling on a low chair on the stela of Nenwaif, Abydos, 18th Dynasty, Baker 1966: 128, pl. 172. Metropolitan Museum of Art, New York, MMA 12.182.3. A chair with short legs measuring 190 mm in height is preserved in the British Museum EA 2480. Killen 1980: 57, fig. 30, pl. 88; Killen 2017A: 96–97, fig. 30, pl. 88).
3. Three Ramesside tomb scenes depict bench or double type seats:
   1. TT16 Panehesy, temp. of Rameses II. (Cy type, MMA Photographs T 1203 and T 1210).

2. TT184 Nefermenu, temp. of Rameses II. (Caa type, Schott Photograph 8625).
3. TT194 Thutemheb, 19th Dynasty. (Cy type, Seyfried 1995: Taf. XXV, XXVI, XXVIII).
4. Bench type seats can be found in scenes of usurped Theban tombs of the Ramesside Period.
   1. TT45 Djehuty, temp. of Amenophis II, usurped by Dhutemhab. (Caa type, MMA Photographs T 448, T 529, T 530; Cy type, T 532, T 533).
   2. TT112 Menkheperraseneb, temp. of Tuthmosis III, usurped by Ashefytemweset. (Caa type, MMA Photographs T 1663, T 1674; Cy type, T 1669, T 1674).
   3. TT127 Senemiah, temp. of Tuthmosis III, usurped during Ramesside times. (Caa type, MMA Photographs T 3577; Cy type, T 3569, T 3567, T 3576, T 3577, T 3578, T 3583, T 3596, T 3597, T 3602).
5. Depictions of royal furniture that once could be found in the tomb of Rameses III (KV11) were recorded by Andre Dutertre (1753–1842) and subsequently engraved by Claude Joseph Pomel (1781–1839) and published in *Description de l'Egypte* 1821: 178. pl. 89. The painting of royal chairs and thrones was established by the reign of Amenhotep III. In the tomb of Anen, TT120, at Sheikh el-Qurna, a scene shows the king seated on a throne its legs and arm panel are rendered in blue paint (Robins 1997: fig. 155).
6. The use of round legged stools used by men can be seen in a wall painting in the tomb of Amenhotep TT345. Cherpion 1999: pl. 38; Manniche 1988: 31. A round legged stool with its legs inscribed to Perpawty has been ascribed by the Rijksmuseum van Oudheden, Leiden as 18th Dynasty. Inv. No. AU 53. (Schneider 1997: no. 120).
7. A notable statue of a seated couple shows the woman seated on a round legged stool (classified by Killen as type Sk). Musée du Louvre, E. 3416.
8. Acquired in 1867 from the Cassis-Faraone collection.
9. Walter Segal drew both of Iyneferti's stools and these are published by Eaton-Krauss 1997: 183–184, figs. 2, 3, pl., II a–d. The drawings produced by Segal are useful dimensional sketches but are not constructional drawings. The dimensions of JE 27255B are recorded by Segal as height 320 mm, width 365 mm, depth 360 mm.
10. Purchased from Henry Salt. Sotheby's London auction, part of lot 661. Acquired 1835.
11. For an analysis of folding stools with duck head terminals, see. Killen 1980: 40–42, pls. 57-63; Killen 2017A: 62–63, pls. 57–63.
12. Sennedjem's folding stool. Egyptian Museum, Cairo, (JE 27288). Eaton-Krauss 1997: 180 - 183, 187, pl. 1.
13. I would like to thank Dr Sarah Durant, Research Fellow, Institute of Zoology, Zoological Society of London, for providing the information relating to the gross morphology of the cheetah.
14. Theban tomb of Paser, TT106. Metropolitan Museum of Art Photograph, T. 2931.
15. Bruyère 1937A: 101, figs. 43 and 44. Stool from the tomb of Setau, pit tomb 1352, Deir el-Medina.
16. Stool with lion shaped legs. Tomb of Kha, TT8, 18th Dynasty. Egyptian Museum, Turin. Inv. No. 8614. Killen 1980: 38–39, pl. 50; Killen 2017A: 60–61, pl. 50.
17. Prisse d'Avennes 1997: Industrial Art pl. II.87 and Industrial Art pl. II.89.

18. This type of bier has been classified by Killen as type BDa. Illustrations of this form of bier can be seen in the following Theban tombs. TT1 Sennedjem; TT106 Paser; TT214 Khawi; TT277 Amenemonet and TT292 Pesedu.

19. Curved tails have been attached to: The lion couch, JE 62011, Carter No. 35, Burton Photograph p. 0021. Also, the cow-headed couch, JE 62013, Carter No. 73, Burton Photograph p. 0015.

20. Steindorff 1937: Vol I. 123; Vol. 2. pl. 65.

21. Bruyère 1937B: 48, fig. 21 (top shelf right and left).

22. In mitigation the cemetery excavation (published in Spencer: 2002), was done in a short time at the very end of the 1938–1939 season and fragments of wood may well have been overlooked by the excavators. (per comm., email. Patricia Spencer, 9th November 2010).

23. I would like to thank Dr Neal Spencer for allowing access to the Amara West database. "The cemetery, especially tomb 201, yielded bags of wood, much of it eroded and crumbly, but with a number of diagnostic pieces likely to be from funerary beds. We have not finished studying or recording these yet, many will need proper illustrations" (per comm., email Neal Spencer, 17th November 2009). Therefore, since this material has not been published it is not possible to include this evidence in this work.

24. Spencer 2009: 58, pl. 24, wooden bed terminals (F9077, F9078) from the fill (9018) within the eastern chamber of Grave 201 (Cemetery C), and pl. 23, fragment of a coffin panel (F9118) from the fill (9019) within the western chamber of Grave 201 (Cemetery C).

25. Peterson 1973: 103, taf. 69. Limestone ostracon, 189 mm × 180 mm.

26. British Museum, EA 2371. Strouhal 1992: 18, fig. 15. The caption for figure 15 mistakenly references this object was being made from wood.

27. A further furniture leg carved in the form of the god Bes, but with his arms placed by his sides, was sold at auction in New York at Christies Rockefeller Plaza Sale Room on 3rd June 2009. (Sale 2174: Lot 27). Price Realised $8,750.

28. This form of footboard design can also be seen on a bedframe discovered in the tomb of Tutankhamun, JE 62016, Carter No. 47. The footboard of this bedframe is divided into three panels; each panel has the central figure of the God Bes flanked by two rampant lions. These figures compare in form and dress to the example preserved in the Fitzwilliam Museum E.GA.2681.1943.

29. Schiaparelli 1927: fig. 104, bedframe of Kha; fig. 105, bedframe of Merit. Both bedframes are now preserved in the Egyptian Museum, Turin. Kha's bedframe, Inv. No. 8327; Merit's bedframe Inv. No. 8629.

30. Archeologica Museum, Florence. Inv. No. 7945.

31. Louvre Museum, Paris. E 925. Greywacke, length 195 mm.

32. The bedframe recorded in O. EA 5861 verso (Figure 4.3), is awarded a quality mark of three-times *nfr*.

33. Two of Sennedjem's boxes that display each type of lid arrangement are preserved in the Metropolitan Museum of Art, New York. MMA 86.1.8. (single lid type), MMA 86.1.7 (double lid type). Killen 1994: 81, figs, 79, 80; Killen 2017B: 105–107, figs, 79, 80.

34. Another box with a confirmed Sennedjem provenance which is of an identical construction and decoration is now preserved in the Ägyptisches Museum, Staatliche Museen zu Berlin. ÄM 10195.

35. Bruyère 1933: 106–07, fig. 34.

36. The British Museum purchased this box from the Rev. Greville in 1887. The British Museum's database record for this object shows that it was found/acquired in Akhmim.

37. Porter and Moss 1960: 839.

38. A custom made games table (classified by Killen as a GTa type) is depicted in the tomb of Inherkhau, TT359, room 1, west wall. Bruyère 1933. pl. XI.

39. Table classified by Killen as type To is illustrated in the tomb of Amenemopet, TT265. Griffith Institute Photograph, DM. 265.4. Similar in design and construction to that preserved in the Metropolitan Museum of Art, New York. MMA 14.10.5. Killen 1980: 66, pl. 108; Killen 2017A: 119, pl. 108 and Brooklyn Museum, New York, 37.41E. Killen 1980: 66, pl. 109; Killen 2017A: 119, pl. 109.

40. Davies 1927: pls. XVI, XVII. Similar in design and construction to a three-legged table inscribed to Perpawty, British Museum, London. EA 2469. Killen 1980: 67, fig. 34, pls. 111–113; Killen 2017A: 119–120, fig. 34, pls. 111–113. This table is part of an 18th dynasty burial assemblage whose find spot is currently unknown. Other furniture from Perpawty's tomb consist of a round legged stool (previous discussed in Chapter 4.2), preserved in the Rijksmuseum van Oudheden, Leiden, Inv. No. AU 53. (Schneider 1997: no. 120); two gable lid boxes preserved in the Oriental Museum, Durham University, Inv. Nos. EG 4573 and EG 4572, (Killen 1994: 38–42, figs. 54–55, pls. 29–38; Killen 2017B: 49–52, figs. 54–55, pls. 29–39 and a gable lid box preserved in Archeologico Museo Civico, Bologna, Inv. No. EG 1970, (Killen 1994: 42–43, fig. 55, pl. 39; Killen 2017B: 52–53, fig. 55, pl. 39).

41. Vase stand classified by Killen as type STb is widely depicted in the Ramesside Theban tombs, see Appendix B. Similar in design and construction to that preserved in the British Museum, London. EA 2470, Killen 1980: 70, fig. 37, pls. 116–117; Killen 2017A: 127–129, fig. 37, pls. 116–117.

42. Mahmoud 2011: 295, Catalogue No.126. (Plate shows the nature of the lattice reinforcement below table top).

43. Davies 1927: pl. XXXIV.

44. Killen 1980: 67, fig 34, pls. 111–113; Killen 2017A: 119–120, fig 34, pls. 111–113. Three-legged table, British Museum, EA 2469.

45. Davies 1927: pl. XXX.

46. MMA Photographs, Griffith Institute, Oxford. T. 1913.

47. Ani's *Book of the Dead*. British Museum, EA 10470,6.

48. EA 1754. A number of other stele and objects from this tomb are preserved in the British Museum. (James 1970).

49. Carter Object Card for 033 describes this object as a "Wooden stand (?)". Griffith Institute, University of Oxford.

50. Eaton-Krauss 2008: 100–102, pl. XL (incorrectly referred to as pl. XI in the text).

51. This size of chair is classified as a Type 0 and is recognised in having white plugged feet (BS EN 1729-1:2006, Table A.1. The popliteal height is determined by the distance from underside of the seated thigh at the knee to the underside of the flat foot which is placed on the same plane as the feet of the chair.

52. Chair of Sitamum, has a seat height of 330 mm, discovered in the tomb of Yuya and Tuyu, KV46. Egyptian Museum, Cairo. JE 95342; CE 51113. Eaton-Krauss 1989: 81, fig. 2. Also, a child's chair discovered in the tomb of Tutankhamun, has a seat height of 320 mm, Egyptian Museum, Cairo. JE 62033;

Carter No. 39. Killen 1980: 61, pl. 99; Killen 2017A: 100, pl. 99. Using modern anthropometric data both these chairs would be suitable for use by children between 5 to 7 years of age. BS EN 1729-1:2006, fig. NA.1.

53. The tomb of Nebamun, temp of Hatshepsut. Usurped by Imiseba, temp. of Rameses IX. Offering table seen in MMA Photographs T. 1715. Griffith Institute, Oxford.

Chapter Four: Royal and Temple Furniture

1. A round legged stool was deposited in the tomb of Tutankhamun, Carter Nos. 142b and 149, JE 62042. (Eaton-Krauss 2008: 119–122, pls. LVI–LVIII). The technique involved in manufacturing these legs is discussed in Killen 2015: 91–111.

2. House altar stela', Neues Museum, Egyptian Museum and Papyrus Collection, Berlin. Inv. No. 14145.

3. Segal MSS 30 and 34, Griffith Institute, Ashmolean Museum, Oxford.

4. Rameses II is seen sitting on a typical round legged stool, covered with a thick cushion with *Sema* and intertwining papyrus and upper Egyptian lily decoration strung below the seat. The scene illustrates the Battle-record of Year 5 of his reign. This scene was also photographed during Breasted's 1905–1907 expedition to Egypt and the Sudan, The Oriental Institute of the University of Chicago, photograph P. 2439.

5. Description de l'Egypte 1821: pl. 31.

6. Description de l'Egypte 1821: pl. 89.

7. Rosellini 1832-1844: pls. XCI and XCII.

8. Cailliaud 1831.

9. Egyptian Museum, Cairo. JE 62030. Carter No. 351. Killen 1980: 61–62, pls. 100–101; Killen 2017A: 100–102, pls. 100–101.

10. Two similar examples of folding chair are seen on a lintel (E.13.2 discovered during the 1948–1949 EES season), in the temple at Amara West. (Spencer 1997: pl. 167 a–c).

11. Figure 28 is based on a line drawing. OIP 94, 1970: pl. 639.

12. Figure 29 is based on a line drawing. Ricke 1967: pl. 9.

13. Two notable pieces of furniture that belonged to Tutankhamun have or once had this unification symbol incorporated into their construction below the seat. A chair, but without the lion heads, JE 62032 (Killen 1980: 58 - 59, pl. 96; Killen 2017A: 98, pl. 96) and the gold throne JE 62028. (Killen 1980: 62, fig. 32, pl. 102; Killen 2017A: 102, fig. 32, pl. 102).

14. Round legged stool, JE 62042, Carter No. 149. Upper part of these legs were covered with gesso and then gold and bronze foil held in position with gold and bronze pins.

15. Figure 30 is based on a line drawing. OIP 94, 1970: pl. 639.

16. This wall relief has now been removed to the third floor room, south wall in the north tower. Figure 31 is based on a line drawing. OIP 94, 1970: pl. 646.

17. Figure 32 is based on a photograph taken during the 1905–1907 Breasted Expedition to Egypt and the Sudan. Chicago Oriental Institute, Tomb of Penniut, 'Aniba. P. 2543.

18. Figure 33 is based on a line drawing. Piankoff 1954: pl. 14.

19. A comparable box is seen in the tomb of Rameses IX, KV6. (Guilmant 1907: pl. LX). The preservation of this wall illustration is better than that seen in the tomb of Rameses VI. Piankoff 1954: pl. 14.

20. Figure 34 is based on a line drawing. Piankoff 1954: pl. 91.

21. Petrie 1927: 46.

22. The symbolic and ritualistic character of this type of offering table has been recognised by Quaegebeur. He is able to trace the use of this type of offering table to scenes from Medinet Habu, Amarna, Kom Ombo and Dendara. He links the titulature of Theban priests from the Third Intermediate Period to the Ptolemaic Period to this type of offering table where temple priests are responsible for the "great and pure offering table", (Quaegebeur 1994:155–173).

23. Figure 35 is based on a line drawing. Calverley 1935: pl. 15.

24. Figure 36 is based on a line drawing. Calverley 1935: pl. 5.

25. Figure 37 is based on a line drawing. Calverley 1933: pl. 19. A similar decorative frieze is seen on the sides of a box discovered in the tomb of Tutankhamun. Egyptian Museum, Cairo. JE 61476. Killen 1994: 72–74, pl. 59, fig. 75; Killen 2017B: 87, pl. 59, fig. 75.

26. Figure 38 is based on a line drawing. Calverley 1933: pl. 30. A similar decorative frieze is seen on the sides of a box discovered in the tomb of Tutankhamun. Egyptian Museum, Cairo. JE 61458. Killen 1994: 64–66, pl. 55, fig. 69; Killen 2017B: 79–80, pl. 55, fig. 69.

27. Figure 39 is based on a line drawing. Ricke 1967: pl. 44.

28. This offering table was also drawn by Hay. British Library, Hay MSS 29848 (156).

29. Green 1987: 18–19, figs. 26–28.

Appendix A

Ramesside Furniture Types

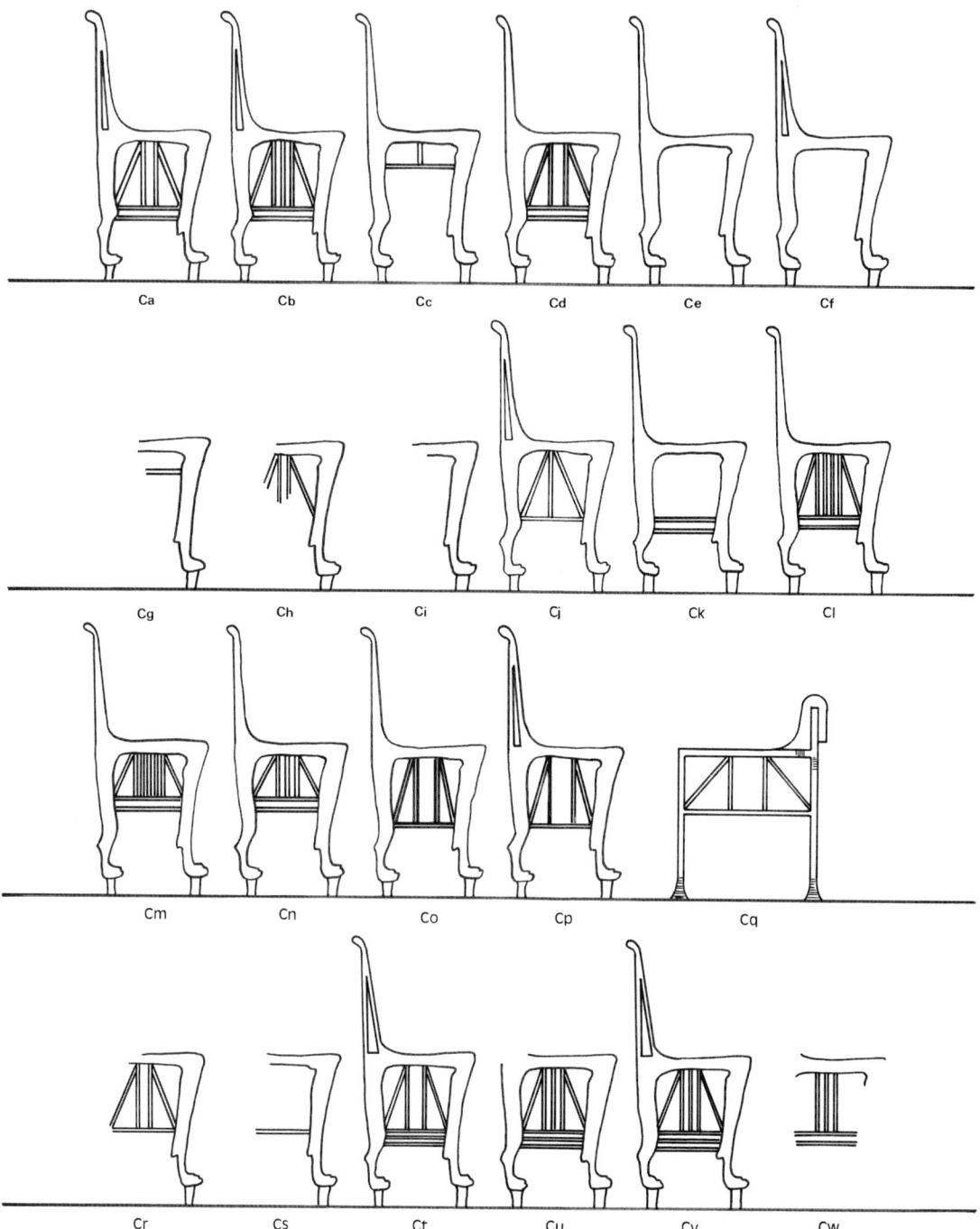

Ca　　Cb　　Cc　　Cd　　Ce　　Cf

Cg　　Ch　　Ci　　Cj　　Ck　　Cl

Cm　　Cn　　Co　　Cp　　Cq

Cr　　Cs　　Ct　　Cu　　Cv　　Cw

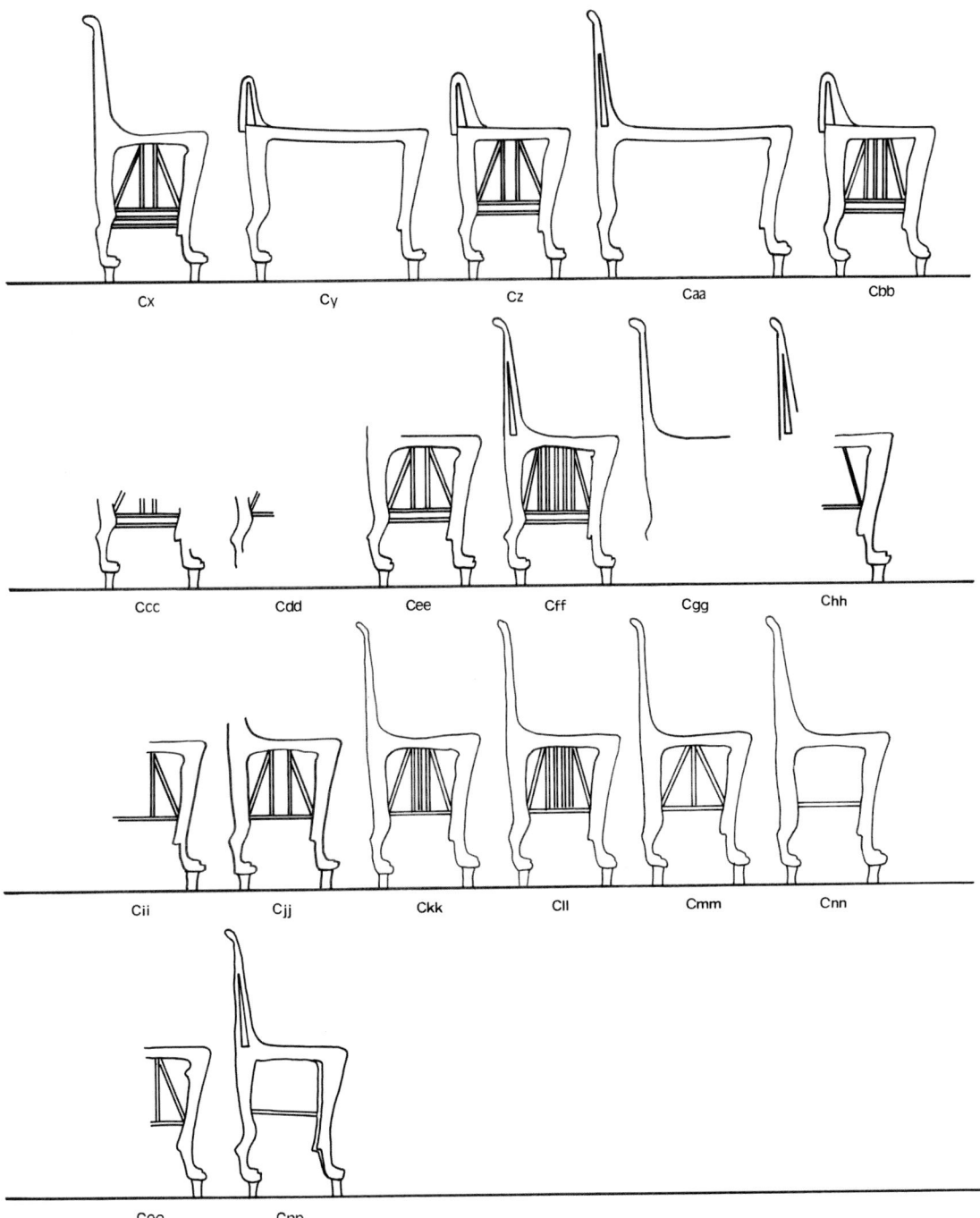

Cx   Cy   Cz   Caa   Cbb

Ccc   Cdd   Cee   Cff   Cgg   Chh

Cii   Cjj   Ckk   Cll   Cmm   Cnn

Coo   Cpp

Sa   Sb   Sc   Sd   Se   Sf

Sg   Sh   Si   Sj   Sk   Sl

Sm   Sn   So   Sp   Sq

Sr   Ss   St   Su   Sv

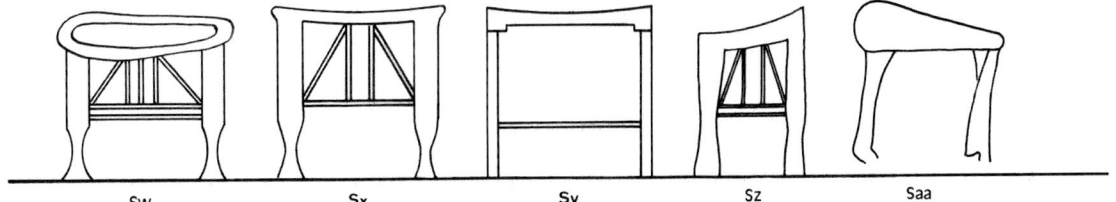

Sw   Sx   Sy   Sz   Saa

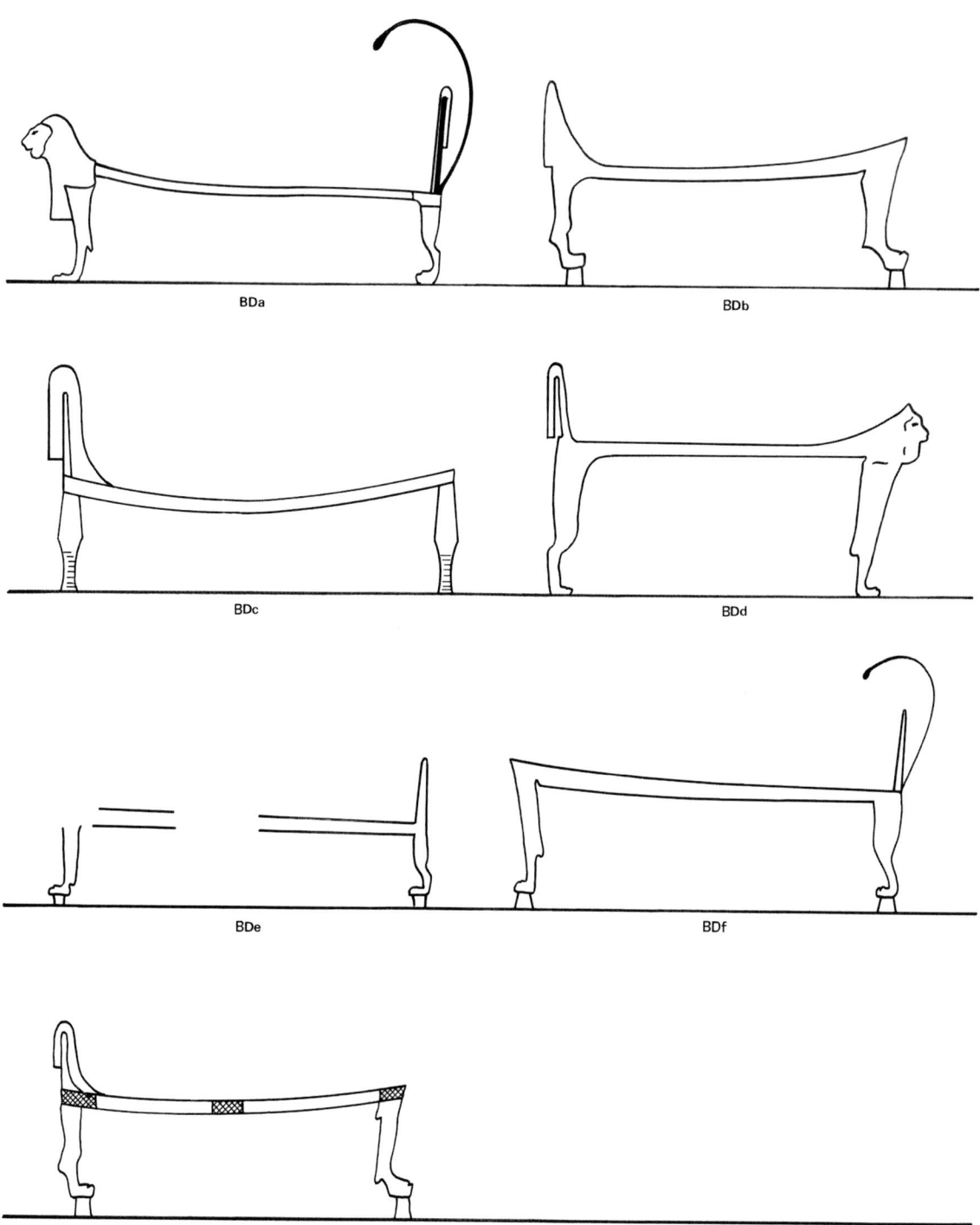

BDa

BDb

BDc

BDd

BDe

BDf

BDg

Bxa

Bxb

Bxc

Bxd

Bxe

Bxf

Bxg

Bxh

Bxi

Bxj

Bxk

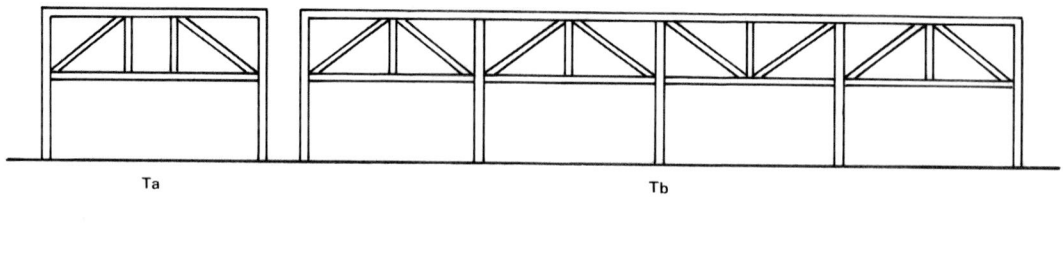

Ta   Tb

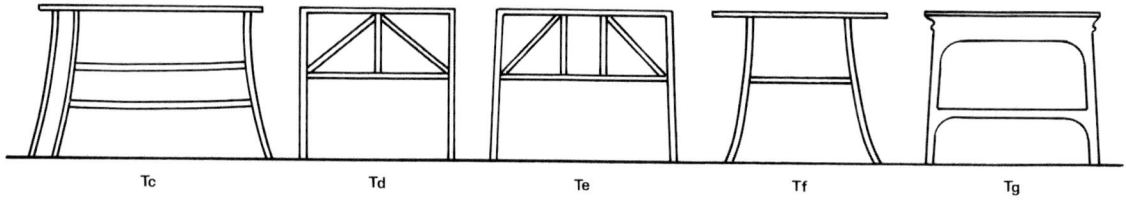

Tc   Td   Te   Tf   Tg

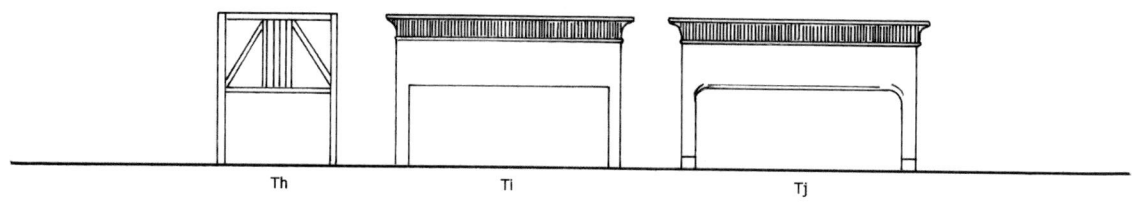

Th   Ti   Tj

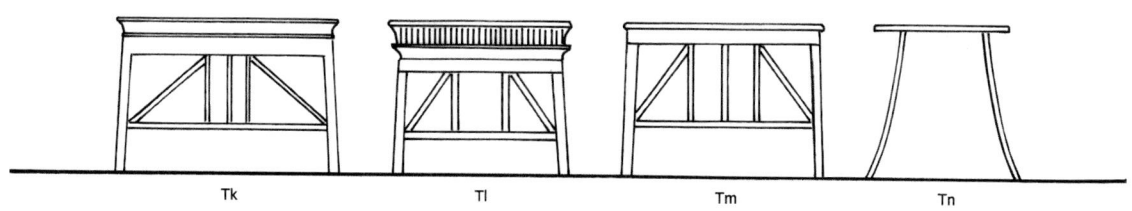

Tk   Tl   Tm   Tn

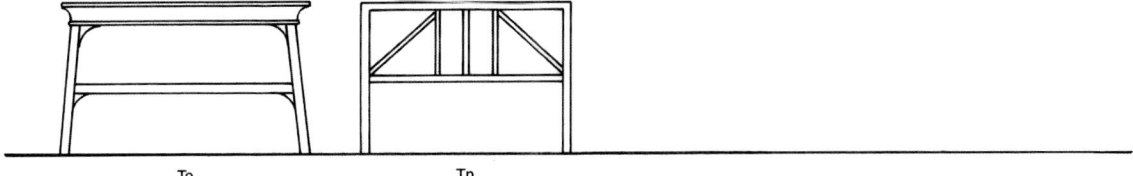

To   Tp

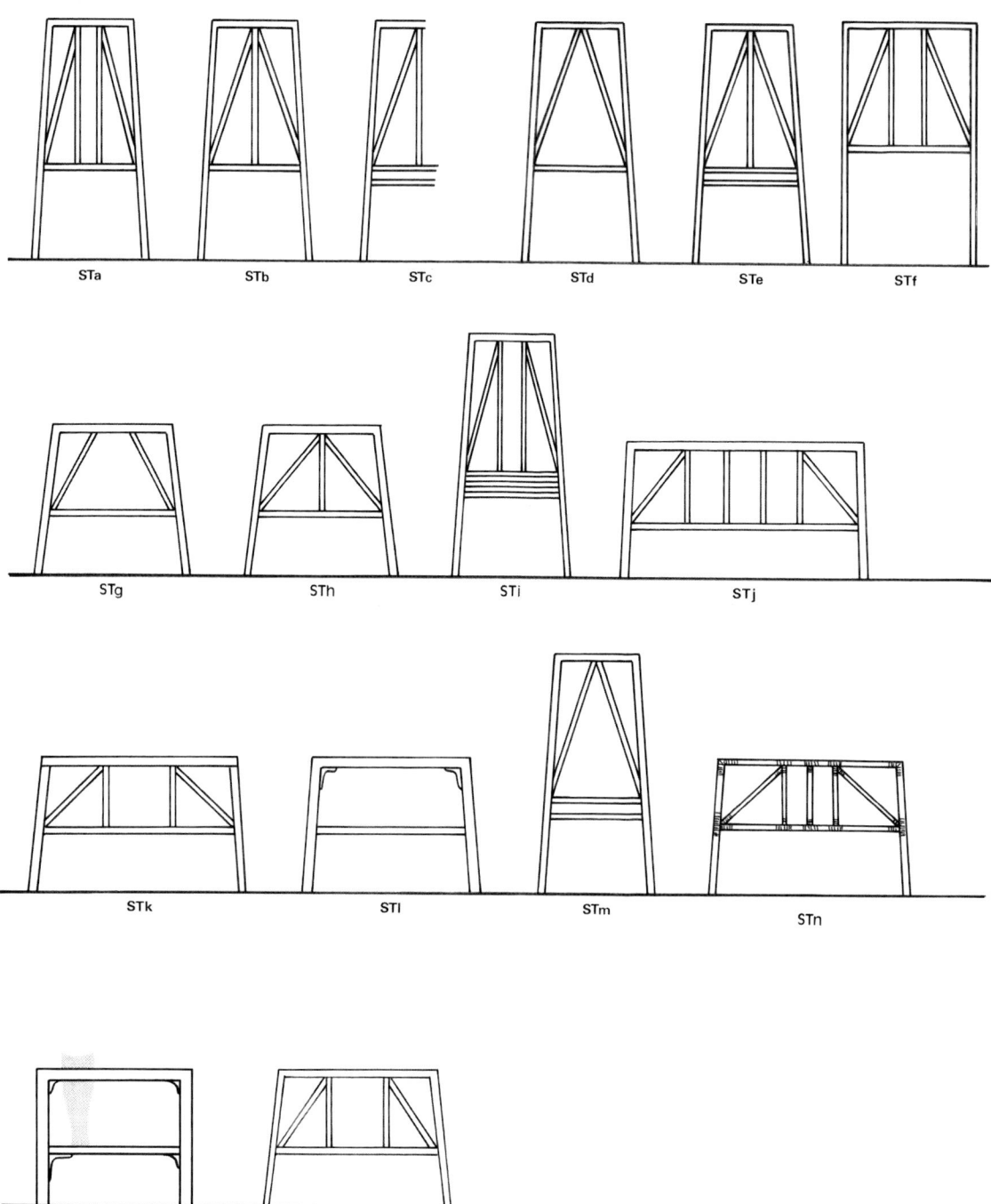

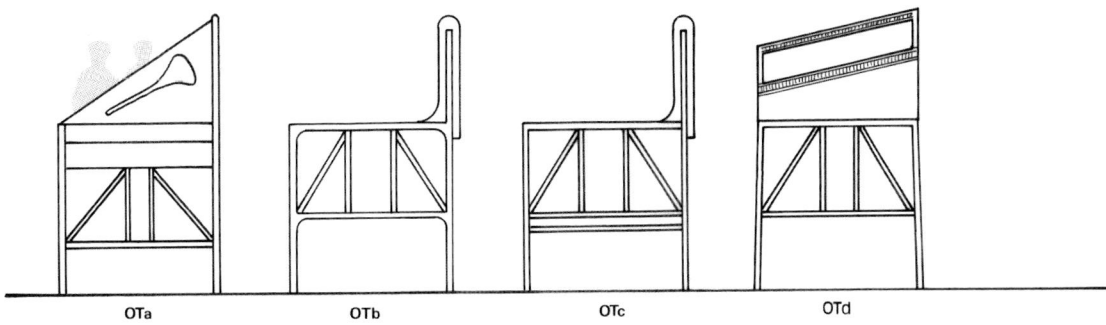

Appendix B

Furniture Types Illustrated in Ramesside Theban Tombs

Tomb	Owner	Reference	Chair and Thrones	Stool	Box	Bed	Tables, Stands, Offerings and Game Tables
1	Sennedjem *19th Dynasty* See Appendix C: Wooden Objects from the Tomb of Sennedjem	Bruyère 1959	(1) Cc, ♀, Column, Pl. XIV (1) Cg, ♂, Column, Pl. XIV (1) Cd, ♀, Entrance, Pl. XVII (2) (1) Ci, ♂, Entrance, Pl. XVII (2) (1) Cf, ♀, Wall M (lr), Pl. XXVI (2) Cf, ♂, Wall M (lr), Pl. XXVI (3) Cf, ♀, Wall U (lr), Pl. XXXII (3) Ci, ♂, Wall U (lr), Pl. XXXII (1) Ci, ♀, Wall U (lr), Pl. XXXII (1) Ci, ♂, Wall M, Pl. XXVI			(1) BDa, Wall Q, Pl. XXX (1) BDa, Wall U, Pl. XXXII	(1) STb, Entrance, Pl. XVII(2)
2	Khabekhnet *Rameses II*	Bruyère 1952				(1) BDf, North Wall, Scene 6, Pl. VII (1) BDf, South Wall, Scene 12, Pl. XII	
3	Pashedu *Ramesside*	Zivie 1979	(1) Ca, ♀, North Wall, Pl. 17 (1) Ca, ♂, North Wall, Pl. 17			(1) BDb South Wall, now lost – drawing Hay MSS, pl. 31	
4	Ken *Rameses II*	Griffith Institute Photographs	(1) Ca,♀, G.I.P. DM. 4.2 & 2010 (3) Ci,♀, G.I.P. DM. 4.2 & 2011 (4) Ci,♂, G.I.P. DM. 4.2 & 2011 (1) Ci,♂, (in boat), G.I.P. DM. 4.2 and 2011 (1) Ca,♀, (in boat), G.I.P. DM. 4.2 and 2011 (1) Ca,♀, DM. 4.3 & 2009 (1) Ch,♂, DM. 4.3 & 2009 (1) Ca,♀, DM. 4.3 & 2012 (1) Ci,♂, DM. 4.3 & 2012				
5	Neferabet *Ramesside*	Vandier 1935	(1) Ca, ♀, Room 1 South Wall, Pls, IV–V (1) Ci, ♂, Room 1 South Wall, Pls, IV–V				(1) STd, Room 1 South Wall, Pls, IV–V
6	Nefer.hotep *Rameses II*	Wild 1979					(1) STb –stand supporting games table. North Wall, Pl. 11 (2) STb, East Wall, Pl. 14

Tomb	Owner	Reference	Chair and Thrones	Stool	Box	Bed	Tables, Stands, Offerings and Game Tables
9	Amenmosi *Ramesside*	NR in Wilkinson MSS. V.119. dep. e. 59					
10	Penbuy and Kasa *Rameses II*	Griffith Institute Photographs	(1) Ccc, G.I.P. 1457 (1) Cdd, G.I.P. 1456				
13	Shuray *Ramesside*	NR					
14	Huy *Ramesside*	Griffith Institute Photographs		(1) Su, ♀, G.I.P. 1970			
16	Panehesy *Rameses II*	MMA Photographs	(1) Cγ, ♂♀, T. 1203; T. 1210		(1) Bxg, T. 1203, T. 1211		(2) Tl, T. 1205
19	Amenmose *Rameses I to Seti I*	MMA Photographs	(2) Ca, ♀, T. 1008 (2) Ch, ♂, T. 1008 (2) Ca, ♀, T. 1009 (1) Ci, ♂, T. 1009 (1) Ca, ♀, T. 1010 (1) Ch, ♂, T. 1010 (1) Cr. T. 1010		(6) Bxh, T. 1005 (1) Bxi, T1005 (2) Bxh, T. 1009		(3) STa, T. 1008 (1) STj, T. 1010
23	Thay *Merneptah*	MMA Photographs			(1) Bxj, T. 1911, T. 1912		
25	Amenemheb *Ramesside*	NR					
26	Khmememhab *Rameses II*	NR					
30	Khensmosi *Ramesside*	Schott Photographs					(1) STb. Supporting games box. Schott, 1923

Tomb	Owner	Reference	Chair and Thrones	Stool	Box	Bed	Tables, Stands, Offerings and Game Tables
31	Khons *Rameses II*	Davies and Gardiner 1948	(1) Co, ♀, Outer Hall – East Wall: South Side, Pl. XI (3) Cx, ♀, Outer Hall – East Wall: South Side, Pl. XI (1) Cx, ♂, Outer Hall – East Wall: South Side, Pl. XI (1) Ci, ♂, Outer Hall – East Wall: South Side, Pl. XI (1) Ci, ♀, Outer Hall, South Wall, Pl. XII (1) Co, ♀, Outer Hall, South Wall, Pl. XII (1) Co, Sex Unknown, Outer Hall, South Wall, Pl. XII (1) Cp, ♂, Outer Hall, North Wall, Pl. XV (1) Cp, ♀, Outer Hall, North Wall, Pl. XV (3) Cq, ♂, The Passage, South Wall, Pl. XVII		(1) Bxd, Outer Hall, East Wall: North Side. Pl. XVI		(1) Ti, Outer Hall –East Wall: South Side, Pl. XI (1) Tj, Outer Hall –East Wall: South Side, Pl. XI (1) STb, Outer Hall, South Wall, Pl. XII
32	Dhutmosi *Rameses II*	NR					
41	Amememipet Ipy *Rameses I to Seti I*	MMA Photographs. Assmann 1991. Right angle wooden furniture elbow. Nr 170. Taf. LXXI. Knob. 240–1 (171–172)	(2) Cf, ♀, T. 1878 (1) Cz, ♀, T. 1886		(1) Bxc. T. 1882; (1) Bxc. T. 1887; T. 1889; T. 1891; T. 1892; T. 1893		(1) Ti. T. 1897. (2) STb. Taf. 21.

Tomb	Owner	Reference	Chair and Thrones	Stool	Box	Bed	Tables, Stands, Offerings and Game Tables
44	Amenemhab *Ramesside*	El Saady 1996	(3) Ca, ♂, Left Half, North Wall (mr) Pl. 8b (1) Cb, ♂, Right Half, North Wall (lr) Pl. 20 (3) Ca, ♂, Right Half, North Wall (lr) Pl. 22 (1) Cb, ♀, Left Half, North Wall Pl. 35a (1) Co, ♂, Right Half, North Wall (lr) Pl. 22 (1) Cn, ♂, Right Half, North Wall (lr) Pl. 22	(1) Sb, ♀, Left Half, North Wall (mr) Pl. 8 (1) Sc, ♀, Right Half, North Wall (lr) Pl. 20 (1) Sc, ♀, Left Half, West Wall (ur) Pl. 39–40b			(4) OTa, Left Half, West Wall (lr) Pl. 47
45	Djehuty Temp. of Amenophis II Usurped by Dhutemhab *Rameses II*	MMA Photographs	(1) Caa, ♀♂, T 448, T 529, T 530 (1) Cb,♀, T 529 (1) Ci, ♂, T 529, T 530 (1) Cy, ♂, T 532 (1) Cy, ♀, T 533 (1) Cb, ♀, T 533 (1) Ci, ♂, T 533 (1) Ch, ♂, T 533 (1) Cbb, ♀, T 536 (1) Ci, ♂, T 536	(1) St, ♀, T 532			(1) STk, T 448, T 529 (4) STa, T 449 (2) STa, T 532
51	Userhet *Seti I*	Davies 1927	(3) Ca, ♀ North Wall, East Side, Pl. V (1) Cb, ♀ North Wall, East Side, Pl. V (1) Throne, North Wall, East Side, Pl. V (1) Cf, ♀, East Wall, Pl. IX (4) Ci, ♂, North Wall, East Side, Pl. V (1) Ci, ♂, East Wall, East Side, Pl. IX	(1) Sd, ♂, West Wall, Pl. XV	(2) Bxc, South Wall, West Side, Pl. XIII (1) Bxc, Stele from court, Pl. XIX (6)		(1) STa (Joints bound by Rush), North Wall, East Side, Pl. V (6) STb, South Wall, West Side, Pl. XIII. (6) Ta, South Wall, West Side, Pl. XIII (1) Tb, South Wall, West Side, Pl. XIII (3) Tc, North Wall, West Side, Pls. XVI–XVII (1) Ta, Stele from court, Pl. XIX (1) STa, North Wall, East Side. Pl. V

Tomb	Owner	Reference	Chair and Thrones	Stool	Box	Bed	Tables, Stands, Offerings and Game Tables
65	Nebamun Temp. of Hatshepsut. Usurped by Imiseba, temp., *Rameses IX.*	MMA Photographs					(1) STf, T. 1702 (2) Tm, T. 1702 (2) Ta, T. 1704 (2) STa, T. 1709 (1) OTe, T. 1715 (similar to Tutankhamun, Carter No. 33) (8) STn, T 1716 (1) STa, T. 1716
68	Perenkmun *20th Dynasty*	Schott Photographs					(1) Tl, Schott 7313
105	Khamipet *19th Dynasty*	MMA Photographs. Tomb in poor state of preservation. No furniture illustration preserved					
106	Paser Carpenters with wooden construction beyond. (6) MMA T 2905–2907 *Seti I–Rameses II*	MMA Photographs	(1) Ca, ♀, T. 2917 (1) Ch, ♂, T. 2917 (1) Ca, ♀, T. 2921 (1) Ca, ♂, T. 2935 (1) Ci, T. 2938 (1) Cs, T. 2939 (1) Ca, ♀, T. 2943	(1) Sr, ♀, T. 2931 (1) Sr, ♂, T. 2931 (1) Ss, T. 2958	(1) Bxc, T. 2893	(1) BDa, T. 2957	(2) STb, T. 2908 (1) STb, T. 2911
111	Amunwahsu *Rameses II*	Schott Photographs	(1) Cf,♀, Schott 8124 (2) Ci,♂, Schott 8124 (1) Ce,♀, Schott 8124				
112	Menkheperraseneb Temp. of Tuthmosis III. Usurped by Ashefytemweset. *Ramesside*	MMA Photographs	(1) Caa, ♂♀, T. 1663 (1) Ci, ♂, T. 1663 (3) Cy, ♂♀, T. 1669 (1) Caa, ♀♂, T. 1674 (1) Cy, ♀♂, T.1674				(1) Te, T. 1663 (1) Te, T. 1668
113	Kynebu *Rameses VIII*	Hay MSS	(1) Cff, ♂, 29822, 121–122. Also 29851B, 305	(1) Sw, ♀, 29822, 121–122. Also 29851B, 305			(1) Tp, 29822, 129-130 (1) STn, 29822, 121–122 Also 29851B, 306 (1) STb, 29851B, 307
114	Name unknown *20th Dynasty*	NR					

Tomb	Owner	Reference	Chair and Thrones	Stool	Box	Bed	Tables, Stands, Offerings and Game Tables
115	Name unknown *19th Dynasty*	NR					
127	Senemiah Temp. of Tuthmosis III. *Usurped during Ramesside times*	MMA Photographs	(1) Cy, ♀♂, T. 3569 (1) Cy, ♀♂, T. 3567 (1) Cy, ♀♂, T. 3576 (1) Cy, ♀♂, T. 3577 (1) Caa, ♀♂, T. 3577 (1) Cy, ♀♂, T. 3578 (1) Cf, ♂, T. 3578 (1) Cy, ♀♂, T. 3583 (1) Cy, ♀♂, T. 3596 (2) Cy, ♀♂, T. 3597 (1) Cy, ♀♂, T. 3602			(3) BDa, T. 3600 (1) BDa, T. 3601	(1) STl, T. 3574 (2) Te, T. 3579 (1) STl, T. 3579 (2) Te, T. 3584 (1) STl, T. 3593 (1) STl, T. 3596
135	Bekenamun *19th Dynasty*	NR					
136	Name unknown *19th Dynasty*	NR					
137	Mose *Rameses II*	NR					
138	Nezemger *Rameses II*	Schott Photographs	(1) Cb, ♀, Schott 8107 (1) Ce, ♀, Schott 8119	(1) Sq, ♂, Schott 7641 and 8106 (1) Sq, ♂, Schott 7642 and 8102			
141	Bekenkhons *Ramesside*	Baud 1935.	(1) Cw, ♂, fig. 74 (1) Ce, ♂, fig. 74	(2) Sn, ♀, fig. 74			
148	Amenemopet *Rameses II to V*	Schott Photographs	(3) Cf, ♀, Schott 6019 and detail 6020 (1) Cf, Schott 6580 (1) Cf, Schott 6581				
149	Amenmose *Ramesside*	NR					
152	Name unknown *Ursurped in Ramesside times*	NR					
153	Name unknown *Seti I*	NR					

Tomb	Owner	Reference	Chair and Thrones	Stool	Box	Bed	Tables, Stands, Offerings and Game Tables
157	Nebwenenet *Rameses II*	NR					
158	Tjanefer *Rameses III*	Seele 1959.	(1) Cr, ♂, Broad Hall, East Wall, North Doorway, Pl. 17 (1) Ch,♂, Broad Hall, East Wall, North Doorway, Pl. 17 (1) Cf, ♀, Broad Hall, West Wall, South of Doorway, lr. Pl. 20 (1) Ci, Broad Hall, West Wall, South of Doorway, lr. Pl. 20 (1) Ch, ♂, Broad Hall, West Wall, South of Doorway, lr. Pl. 21 (2) Cb, ♂, Broad Hall, West Wall, North of Doorway, lr. Pl. 22 (2) Cb, ♀, Broad Hall, West Wall, North of Doorway, lr. Pl. 22 (1) Cb, ♀, Passage, South Wall, First section from East, Pl. 30 (1) Cb, ♂, Passage, South Wall, First section from East, Pl. 30 (1) Cb, ♂, Passage, North Wall, First section from East, Pl. 35 (1) Cr, ♀, Passage, North Wall, First section from East, Pl. 35 (1) Ca, ♂, Passage, North Wall, Second section from East, Pl. 36 (1) Cs, Passage, North Wall, Third section from East, Pl. 37	(1) So, Broad Hall, South Wall, West of Statue, lr. Pl. 26			(2) STg, Court, South Wall, West Part, Pl. 5 (1) Tk, Broad Hall, East Wall, North Doorway, Pl. 17 (1) Te, Passage, North Wall, First Section from East, Pl. 35 (1) Ta, Passage, North Wall, Second Wall from East, Pl. 36
159	Raya *19th Dynasty*	Schott Photographs	(1), Cv,♀, Schott 5999				
163	Amennakht *19th Dynasty*	Spiegelberg Squeezes	(1) Ca,♂, Spie I (1) Ca,♂, Spie D1 (1) Ca,♂, Spie C1 (1) Cw,♂, Spie I (1) Ca,♂, Spie I (1) Ct,♂, Spie B3 (1) Cee,♂, Spie B3 (1) Cd,♀, Spie C1 (2) Ca,♀, Spie I (2) Ca,♀, Spie B3				

Tomb	Owner	Reference	Chair and Thrones	Stool	Box	Bed	Tables, Stands, Offerings and Game Tables
163 (cont.)			(1) Ci, Spie I (2) Cz♀♂ (tomb relief in British Museum, EA 55336)				
166	Ramose *20th Dynasty*	NR					
168	Any *19th Dynasty*	NR					
170	Nebmehyt *Rameses II*	NR					
173	Khay *19th Dynasty*	NR					
174	Ashakhet *9th Dynasty*	NR					
178	Neferrenpet also known as Kenro *Rameses II* Scenes showing workshop, warehouse and storerooms at Karnak temple	Hofmann 1995	(1) Cv, ♂, Room 1, North Wall, Pl. XVI (1) Cv, ♀, Room 1, East Wall, Pl. XVII (1) Cw, ♂, Room 1, East Wall, Pl. XVII (1) Cu, ♂, Room 1, East Wall, Pl. XVII (1) Cu, ♂, Room 1, East Wall, Pl. XVIII (1) Cv, ♀, Room 1, East Wall, Pl. XVIII (1) Cu, ♂, Room 1, East Wall, Pl. XIX (1) Cu, ♂, Room 1, North Wall, Pl. XXVI (1) Ca, ♂, Room 1, South Wall, Pl. XXIX (1) Ca, ♀, Room 1, South Wall, Pl. XXIX (1) Cv, ♂, Room 2, East Wall, Pl. XXXIII (1) Cb, ♀, Room 2, East Wall, Pl. XXXIII (1) Cb, ♂, Room 2, East Wall, Pl. XXXIV (1) Cb, ♀, Room 2, East Wall, Pl. XXXIV	(1) Sp, ♀, Room 1, East Wall, Pl. XIX (1) Sp, ♀, Room 1, North Wall, Pl. XXVI (4) Si, ♂, Workmen, Room 2, North Wall, Pl. XXXIX (1) Sf, ♂, Workman, Room 2, North Wall, Pl. XXXIX (1) Si, ♂, Room 2, West Wall, Pl. XL. (1) Sq, ♂, Room 2, West Wall, Pl. XL	(3) Bxf, Room 1, West Wall, Pl. XXVII (4) Bxe, Room 1, West Wall, Pl. XXVII (6) Bxc, Room 2, West Wall, Pl. 50. (2) Bxa, Room 2, West Wall, Pl. 50		(4) STh, Room 1, East Wall, Pl. XVII (1) STi, Room 1, East Wall, Pl. XIX (5), OTd, Room 1, West Wall, Pl. XXVII

Tomb	Owner	Reference	Chair and Thrones	Stool	Box	Bed	Tables, Stands, Offerings and Game Tables
180	Name unknown *19th Dynasty*	NR					
183	Nebsumenu *Rameses II*	NR					
184	Nefermenu *Rameses II*	Schott Photographs	(1)♀♂Caa, Schott 8625 (1) ♀, Cw, Schott 8626				
189	Nakhtdjehuty *Rameses II*	NR					
193	Ptahemhab *19th Dynasty*	Janssen 1955			(1) Bxc, Stela, Abb.3		(1) Tk, Stela, Abb.3
194	Thutemheb *19th Dynasty*	Seyfried 1995	(2) Cy, ♂, Taf. XXV (1) Cy, ♂♀, Taf. XXVI (1) Cy, ♂, Taf. XXVIII (1) Ci, ♀, Taf. XXVIII	(1) Su, ♀, Taf. XXVI (1) Su, ♀, Taf. XXVIII			
195	Bakenamun *19th Dynasty*	NR					
198	Riya *19th Dynasty*	NR					
202	Nekhtamun *19th Dynasty*	NR					
203	Wennefer *19th Dynasty*	NR					
206	Inpuemhab *Ramesside*	NR					
207	Horemheb *Ramesside*	NR					
208	Roma *Ramesside*	NR					
210	Raweben *19th Dynasty*	NR					
212	Ramosi *Rameses II*	NR					
213	Penamun *Ramesside*	NR					

Tomb	Owner	Reference	Chair and Thrones	Stool	Box	Bed	Tables, Stands, Offerings and Game Tables
214	Khawi *Ramesside*	Bruyère 1928 Bruyère 1952				(1) BDa, West Wall, Pl. III [left]	(1) STm, South Wall, Pl. XXVIII
215	Amenemopet *19th Dynasty* Seated stone statue Sl type Berlin, No. 6910 (pl. XXIX)	D'Abbadie and Jourdain 1939	(1) Cd, ♀, East Wall (Pl. XXIV)				
216	Neferhotep *Rameses II–Seti II* Statue fragment. Neferhotep seated on a chair (Cii) with his wife standing beside him: Bruyère (1925), Pl. XIII	MMA Photographs Bruyère 1925	(1) Cjj, Fig. 1.				(4) Tn, T. 1913.
217	Ipuy *Rameses II* Pls. XXXVI, XXXVII, XXXVIII, Woodworking Scenes	Davies 1927	(2) Ca, ♀♂, South Wall, Pls. XXV – XXVI(c) (2) Ca, East Wall, South Side, Pl. XXVIII (1) Ca, ♀, North Wall, Pl. XXXVI (2) Ca, North Wall, Pl. XXXVI (3) Ch, ♀, North Wall, Pl. XXXVI (6) Ci, ♀, North Wall, Pl. XXXVI (1) Ce, East Wall, South Side, Pl. XXVIII	(2) Se, East Wall, South Side, Pl. XXVIII (1) Sf, ♂, East Wall, South Side, Pl. XXVIII (1) Sg, ♂, East Wall, North Side, Pl. XXX (3) Sh, ♂, East Wall, North Side, Pl. XXX (2) Se, North Wall, Pl. XXXVI (2) Sf, North Wall, Pl. XXXVI (3) Sg, ♂ carpenter, North Wall, Pl. XXXVI (1) Si, ♂, Fragment North Wall, Pl. XL [3] (1) Sz,♂, North Wall, Pl. XXXVI	(4) Bxc, East Wall, South Side, Pl. XXVIII (5) Bxc, North Wall, Pls. XXXVI, XXXVIII	(1) BDb, East Wall, South Side, Pl. XXVIII (1) BDb, North Wall, Pl. XXXVI (1) BDc, North Wall, Pls. XXXVII, XXXVIII	(3) Ta, East Wall, South Side, Pl. XXVII (1) STb, East Wall, South Side, Pl. XXVII (1) Ta, East Wall, South Side, Pl. XXVIII (1) Td, East Wall, South Side, Pl. XXVIII (1) Ta, East Wall, North Side. Pl. XXX, XXXIV (1) Td, East Wall, North Side. Pl. XXX (2) Tf, East Wall, North Side. Pl. XXX (meat preparation) (1) Tg, North Wall, Pl. XXXVI (2) STa, North Wall, Pl. XXXVI

Tomb	Owner	Reference	Chair and Thrones	Stool	Box	Bed	Tables, Stands, Offerings and Game Tables
218	Amennakht *Ramesside*	Bruyère 1928 Schott Photographs Griffith Institute Photographs		(1) Su, ♀, Schott 8999 (1) Sv, ♂, Schott 8999	(3) Bxa, South Wall, Fig. 46	(1) BDd, South Wall, Fig. 56 Above Bed G.I.P. DM.218.b.5	(1) Ta, South Wall, Fig. 47 (1) STa, South Wall, Fig. 45 (1) STe, supporting games box, Schott 8999
219	Nebenmaet *Ramesside*	Maystre 1936	(3) Ca, ♀, Chapel North Wall, Pl. I (3) Ci, ♂, Chapel North Wall, Pl. I (1) Ca, ♀, Chapel East Wall, Pl. I (1) Ci, ♂, Chapel East Wall, Pl. I (4) Ca, ♀, Chamber East Wall, Pl. IV (7) Ci, ♂, Chamber East Wall, Pl. IV (2) Ch, ♀, Chamber East Wall, Pl. IV (4) Ci, ♀, Chamber East Wall, Pl. V (1) Ca, ♀, Chamber East Wall, Pl. V (1) Ci, ♂, Chamber East Wall, Pl. V	(1) Sk, ♀, Chamber South Wall, Pl. VI (1) Sf, ♂, Chamber South Wall, Pl. VI		(1) BDb, Chapel, South Wall, Pl. II (1) BDd, Chamber North Wall, Pl. V	(1) STe, Chamber South Wall, Pl. VI (1) OTe, Chamber West Wall, Pl. VII
221	Hormin *Ramesside*	NR					
232	Tjerwes *Ramesside*	NR					
233	Saroy *Ramesside*	NR					
235	Userhat *Ramesside*	NR					
236	Hornakht *Ramesside*	NR					
237	Wennefer *Ramesside*	NR					
244	Pakharu *Ramesside*	NR					

Tomb	Owner	Reference	Chair and Thrones	Stool	Box	Bed	Tables, Stands, Offerings and Game Tables
250	Ramosi *Rameses II*	Bruyère 1927	(1) Ch, ♂, North-East Wall, Pl. VII	(8) Sj, ♀, North-East Wall, Pl. VII (2) Sv, ♂, North-East Wall, Pl. VII (1) Sk, ♀, North-East Wall, Pl. VII			(1) STb, North-East Wall, Pl. VII
257	Neferhotep Temp. of Tuthmosis IV to Amenophis III, usurped by Mahu *Rameses II*	MMA Photographs	(1) Cf, T. 1111				
259	Hori *Ramesside*	Schott Photographs	(1) Ce, ♂, Schott 5977 (1) Cf, ♂, Schott 5978				
263	Piay *Rameses II*	MMA Photographs	(2) Ca, ♀, T. 3486 (2) Ci, ♂, T. 3486				(2) STb, T. 3486
264	Ipiy *19th Dynasty*	NR					
265	Amenemopet *19th Dynasty*	Griffith Institute Photographs	(1) Ce, ♀, DM. 265.4 (1) Ci, ♂, DM. 265.4			(1) BDd. DM. 265.2	(1) STb. DM. 265.4 (1) Te. DM. 265.4 (1) To. DM. 265.4
266	Amennakht *19th Dynasty*	NR					
267	Hay *20th Dynasty*	Valbelle 1975	(1) Cw, Pl. XIX (1) Ci, Pl. XXII				(1) Th, Pl. XIX
269	Name unknown *Ramesside*	NR					
270	Amenemwia *19th Dynasty* Tomb destroyed	NR					
272	Khamipet *Ramesside*	NR					
273	Sayemiotf	NR					
274	Amenwahsu *Ramesside*	NR					
275	Soebkemose *Ramesside*	NR					

Tomb	Owner	Reference	Chair and Thrones	Stool	Box	Bed	Tables, Stands, Offerings and Game Tables
277	Amenemonet *Ramesside*	Vandier 1954	(4) Ch, ♂, Wall C (lr), Pl. VIII	(2) Sb, ♀, Wall C (lr), Pl. VIII	(1) Bxa, Wall D, Pl. X (4) Bxb, Wall D, Pl. X. Carried on poles, sides of boxes decorated	(1) BDa, Wall E, Pl. XIV. Head of lion crowned with lily flower	
278	Amenemhab *Ramesside*	Vandier 1954.	(1) Cb, ♀, Wall C, Pl. XXXII (1) Cg, ♂, Wall C, Pl. XXXII (1) Cb, ♀, Wall E, Pl. XXXV (1) Ci, ♀, Wall E, Pl. XXXV				
283	Roma *Rameses II to Seti II*	NR					
284	Pahemneter *Ramesside*	NR					
285	Iny *Ramesside*	NR					
286	Niay	NR					
290	Irinufer *Ramesside*	Bruyère and Kuentz 1926	(1) Cj, ♂, Stela, Pl. XVIII (3) Chh, ♂, Stela, Pl. XVIII (2) Chh, ♀, Stela, Pl. XVIII	(1) Sn, ♀, Stela, Pl. XVIII			
291	Nu and Nakhtmin *Late 18th Dynasty– Ramesside*	Bruyère and Kuentz 1926	(2) Cf, ♀, Chapel West Wall, Pl. III (2) Ci, ♂, Chapel West Wall, Pl. III (2) Cf, ♀, Stela (Turin, Inv. No. 99), Pl. XI (2) Ci, ♂, Stela (Turin, Inv. No. 99), Pl. XI				
292	Pesedu *Seti I–Rameses II*	Griffith Institute Photographs				(1) BDa. G.I.P. DM. 292.5	
293	Ramesesnakht *Rameses IV*	NR					

Tomb	Owner	Reference	Chair and Thrones	Stool	Box	Bed	Tables, Stands, Offerings and Game Tables
294	Amenhotep *Ramesside*	Strudwick 1996. Some furniture fragments found in tomb.	(1) Cf, ♀, Pl. IX. (1) Ci ♂, Pl. IX. (1) Cf, ♀, Pl. X. (1) Cf, ♂, Pl. X. Pl. IX shows Sendjehuty and his wife. Pl. X shows Zahi and his wife.				(1) STo, Pl. IX (1) STo, Pl. X. Similar bracket to that used on STo, Volume I, Ct 133, p. 107, Pl. 48
296	Nefersekheru *Ramesside*	MMA Photographs	(1) Ca, ♂, T. 2146 (1) Ch, ♂, T. 2146 (1) Ch, ♂, T. 2147 (3) Ch, T. 2149 (1) Ch, ♂, T. 2150 (1) Cf, ♀, T. 2150	(2) So, ♀, T. 2146 (1) So, ♀, T. 2147 (1) So, ♀, T. 2149			
298	Baki *Ramesside*	Bruyère 1928				(1) BDe, North Wall, Fig. 61	
299	Inherkhau *Rameses III–IV*	NR					
300	Anhetep *Ramesside*	NR					
301	Hori *Ramesside*	NR					
309	Name unknown *19th–21st Dynasty*	NR					
321	Khamipet *Ramesside*	NR					
322	Penmenab *Ramesside*	NR					
323	Pashedu *Seti I*	NR					

Tomb	Owner	Reference	Chair and Thrones	Stool	Box	Bed	Tables, Stands, Offerings and Game Tables
324	Hatiay *Ramesside*	Davies and Gardiner 1948 Find: Triple Statue Group, deceased, wife and mother (heads lost); right hand female seated on Sn type stool Cairo Museum. CE 71965		(1) Sn ♀, Outer Hall, North Wall. Pl. XXXI (2) Sd, ♂, Outer Hall, East Wall, Pl. XXXII (1) Sf, ♂, Outer Hall, North Wall, West Side Top. Pl. XXXIII			
326	Pashedu *Ramesside*	Bruyère 1924	(1) Cd, ♂, Pl. XII [top] and P. XIIIa				
327	Turobay *Ramesside*	NR					
328	Hay *20th Dynasty*	NR					
329	Mose *Ramesside*	NR					
330	Ker *19th Dynasty*	NR					
331	Penniut Suneo *Ramesside*	Davies and Gardiner 1948	(1) Cb, ♂, Outer Doorway, East Reveal, Lower Part. Pl. XXXVI	(1) Sl, ♀, Outer Doorway, East Reveal, Lower Part. Pl. XXXVI			
332	Penemutet *Ramesside*	NR					
335	Nekhtamun *19th Dynasty*	Schott Photographs Bruyère 1926	(1) Ca, ♀, Fig. 82 (1) Ci, ♂, Fig. 82 (2) Ca, ♀, Figs. 83 and 84 (1) Ca, ♀, Fig. 84			(1) BDb. Schott 5601 and 5603	(1) OTb, Fig. 91

Tomb	Owner	Reference	Chair and Thrones	Stool	Box	Bed	Tables, Stands, Offerings and Game Tables
335 (cont.)			(2) Ca, ♀, Fig. 85 (1) Ca, ♂, Fig 89 (1) Ca, ♂, Fig 90 (1) Ci, ♂, Fig 90 (2) Ca, ♀, Fig 91 (1) Ca, ♀, Fig 92				
336	Neferrenpet *19th Dynasty*	Bruyère 1926	(3) Ca, ♀, Fig. 59 (1) Cee, ♀, Fig.59 (2) Ca, ♀, Fig. 60 (1) Cd, ♀, Fig. 66 (1) Ci, ♂, Fig. 66			(1) BDg, Figs. 55 and 72	(1) Te, Fig. 59
337	Qen *Ramesside*	NR					
339	Huy and Peshedu *Rameses II*	Bruyère 1928 Bruyère 1926	(1) Co, ♀, South Wall, Fig. 82 (1) Ci, ♂, South Wall, Fig. 82 (3) Co, ♀, East Wall, Fig. 82 (2) Ci, ♂, East Wall, Fig. 82 (1) Ch, ♂, East Wall, Fig. 82	**Furniture discovered in tomb** (1) Se. Belonging to Peshedu, Pl. V [3] (1) Sx. Pl. V. [2] (1) Sy. Pl. V. [1].	**Furniture discovered in tomb** (1) Bxk, Pl. V [4]		
341	Nakhtamun *Rameses II*	Davies and Gardiner 1948	(1) Ca, ♂, Inner Room, East and South Walls. Pl. XXVIII (1) Ca, ♀, Inner Room, East and South Walls. Pl. XXVIII	(1) Sl, ♀, Inner Room, East and South Walls. Pl. XXVIII (1) Sm, ♀, Inner Room, North Wall, Pl. XXIX	(1) Bxe, (panels decorated). Outer Hall, East Wall: South Side. Pl. XXV (1) Bxc, Outer Hall, South Wall and Adjoining West Wall. Pl. XXVI (2) Bxf, Outer Hall, East Wall: South Side. Pl. XXV		(1) STf, Outer Hall, East Wall and Adjoining North Wall. Pl. XXIV (1) Te, Outer Hall, South Wall and Adjoining West Wall. Pl. XXVI (4) Te, Inner Room, East and South Walls. Pl. XXVIII (3) STa, Inner Room, East and South Walls. Pl. XXVIII (1) STb, Inner Room, East and South Walls. Pl. XXVIII

Tomb	Owner	Reference	Chair and Thrones	Stool	Box	Bed	Tables, Stands, Offerings and Game Tables
346	Amenhotep *Rameses IV*	Davies and Gardiner 1948	(1) Ce, ♂, Outer Doorway, North Jamb. Pl. XL				
347	Hori *Ramesside*	NR					
348	Name Unknown *22nd Dynasty*	NR					
351	Abau *Ramesside* Tomb inaccessible	NR					
352	An Overseer of the granary of Amun *Ramesside* Tomb inaccessible	NR					
355	Amunpahapy *20th Dynasty*	NR					
356	Amenemwia *19th Dynasty*	Bruyère 1929. Griffith Institute Photographs	(1) Ca, ♀, East Wall, Fig. 46 (1) Ci, ♂, East Wall, Fig. 46 The Ca is also shown in G.I.P. DM.356.10 The Ci is also shown in G.I.P. DM. 356.10			(1) BDb, West Wall, Fig. 49 Also G.I.P. DM. 356.6	(1) OTb, East Wall, Fig. 46 Also G.I.P. DM 356.10
357	Dhutihirmaktuf *19th Dynasty* Fragment of mushroom-shaped knob, Bruyère, 1930, p.77, Fig 35 [3] Stool/Stand fragment, painted white with text in red, Bruyère, 1930, p.77. [IVI]	Bruyère 1930	(2) Co, ♂♀, East Wall, Fig. 31				

Tomb	Owner	Reference	Chair and Thrones	Stool	Box	Bed	Tables, Stands, Offerings and Game Tables
359	Inherkhau *Rameses III–Rameses IV*	Bruyère 1933	(1) Cl, ♂, Room 1, West Wall, Pl. X (2) Cm, ♀, Room 1, West Wall, Pl. X (1) Ci, ♂, Room 1, West Wall, Pl. X (1) Cn, Room 1, West Wall, Pl. XI (1) Cn, ♀, Room 1, West Wall, Pl. XI (1) Cm, Room 2, North Wall, Pl. XV (2) Cb,♀, Room 2, North Wall, Pl. XVI–XVII (1) Ch, ♂, Room 2, North Wall, Pl. XVI (2) Cl, ♀, Room 2, South Wall, Pl. XXII–XXIII (1) Ch, ♂, Room 2, South Wall, Pl. XXII–XXIII (1) Cn, ♀, Room 2, South Wall, Pl. XXII				(1) GTa, Room 1, West Wall, Pl. XI (1) STa, Room 2, North Wall, Pl. XVI–XVII (1) STc, Room 2, North Wall, Pl. XVI (1) Th, Room 2, South Wall, Pl. XXII
360	Qeh (Kaha) *Rameses II* Tomb contained two boxes with pairs of lids; fragment of seat; two bed legs; two lion shaped bed legs, painted red. Bruyère, B. 1933, pp. 106–107, Fig. 34 Boat building scene, Pl. XXVI *Rameses II*	Bruyère 1933	(1) Ck, ♀, East Wall, Pl. XXVI (2) Cd, ♀, South Wall, Pl. XXVII (1) Ca, ♀, East Wall, Pl. XXVIII (1) Ci, ♂, East Wall, Pl. XXVIII			(1) BDf, North Wall, Pl. XXIX	
361	Huy *Seti I* Great Carpenter in the Place of Truth	Bruyère 1933	(1) Ce, ♂, Column at entrance to chapel, Fig. 22				

Tomb	Owner	Reference	Chair and Thrones	Stool	Box	Bed	Tables, Stands, Offerings and Game Tables
369	Kaemweset *19th Dynasty*	NR					
370	Name Unknown *Ramesside*	NR					
371	Name Unknown *Ramesside*	NR					
373	Amenmessu No furniture illustrated in this badly-preserved tomb *Ramesside*	Seyfried 1990 Knob, 258 (2028)					
374	Amenemopet *Ramesside*	NR					
377	Name Unknown *Ramesside*	NR					
379	Name Unknown *Ramesside*	NR					
381	Amenemonet *Ramesside*	NR					
382	Usermentu *Ramesside*	NR					
384	Nebmehyt *19th Dynasty*	NR					
385	Hunufer *Ramesside*	NR					
387	Meryptah *Ramesside*	NR					
394	Name Unknown *Ramesside*	NR					
395	Name Unknown *Ramesside*	NR					
399	Name Unknown *Ramesside*	NR					
408	Bekenamun *Ramesside*	NR					

Tomb	Owner	Reference	Chair and Thrones	Stool	Box	Bed	Tables, Stands, Offerings and Game Tables
409	Samut Kyky *Rameses II*	Negm 1997.	(1) Ca, ♂, Wall H (lr), Pl. IX (3) Ca, ♂, Wall M (lr), Pl. XV (6) Ca, Wall F (ur), Pl. XXI (1) Ca, ♂, Column to second chamber, Pl. XXIX (1) Cb, ♂, Column to second chamber, Pl. XXIX	(1) Sa, ♀ , Wall H (lr), Pl. IX (3) Sb, ♀, Wall M (lr), Pl. XV (1) Sb, ♀, Wall F (ur), Pl. XXI			(3) Ta, Wall F (lr), Pl. XXIII (1) Te, Wall F (lr), Pl. XXIII (3) Te, Wall G (lr), Pl. XXV (1) STa, Wall M (lr), Pl. XV (1) STb, Wall M (ur), Pl XI (1) STe, Pl. LV
A6	Dhutnufer *20th Dynasty*	NR					
A12	Nebwenenef	NR in Wilkinson MSS V. 208 dep. e. 59					
A14	Unknown *Rameses II*	NR					
A15	Amenemib	NR in Wilkinson MSS V. 211, 212. dep. e. 59					
A16	Dhutihotp *Ramesside*	NR					
A18	Amenemipet *Ramesside*	Hay MSS	(1) Cgg, ♂, 29816, 136				
A26	Name Unknown *Ramesside*	NR					
C7	Harmosi *Rameses II*	NR					
C8	Nakht *19th Dynasty*	NR					

Appendix C

Furniture Types Illustrated in Ramesside Memphite Tombs

Tomb	Owner	Reference	Chair and Thrones	Stool	Box	Bed	Tables, Stands, Offerings and Game Tables
	Iurudef Wooden mirror handle, shaped as a papyrus fragment (height 121 mm, dia. 31 mm) Cat. No. 40 Discovered in chamber B, Pl. 40	Raven 1991					
	Khay	Martin 2001	(1) Cd♀, Ante Chapel, North Wall, Pl. 7 (1) Cii ♂, Ante Chapel, North Wall, pl. 7 (1) Co ♀, North Chapel, West Wall, pl. 9 (1) Ci ♂, North Chapel, West Wall, pl. 9 (1) Ce ♀, South Chapel, South Wall, pl. 13 (1) Ci ♂, South Chapel, South Wall, pl. 13 (1) Cd ♀, Ante Chapel, South Wall, pl. 14 (1) Coo ♂, Ante Chapel, South Wall, pl. 14	(1) Saa ♂, South Chapel, North Wall, pl. 11			
	Pabes NR	Martin 2001					
	Tia and Tia	Martin 1997	(1) Ce ♀, Apis chapel, South wall, pl. 47				(1) STa Chapel Entrance, in west wall of Second courtyard – west wall south wing. Pl. 37

Tomb	Owner	Reference	Chair and Thrones	Stool	Box	Bed	Tables, Stands, Offerings and Game Tables
	Paser Wooden Mallet, Cat. 26. pl. 32 Wood fragment turned on a lathe Uncontexted surface fine over the tomb of Paser (81-S80) Coptic Period 500–850 AD	Martin 1985	(1) Cn ♀, Ante chapel, pl. 11 (1) Ci ♂, Ante chapel, pl. 11				

Appendix D

Distribution of Stool Type by Gender as Illustrated in Private
Ramesside Theban Tombs

Tomb	Sa	Sb	Sc	Sd	Se	Sf	Sg	Sh	Si	Sj	Sk	Sl	Sm	Sn	So	Sp	Sq	Sr	Ss	St	Su	Sv	Sw	Sx	Sy	Sz
14																					1♀					
44		1♀	2♀																							
45																				1♀						
51				1♂																						
106																		1♂+1♀	1							
113																							1♀			
138																	2♂									
141														2♀												
158															1											
178						1♂			5♂							2♀	1♂									
194					4	2♀+1♂	4♂	3♂													2♀					
217									1♂																	1♂
218											1♀										1♀	1♂				
219						1♂																				
250											1♀											2♂				
277		2♀								8♀																
290						1♂								1♀												
296															4♀ 1♂											
324				2♂																						
331												1♀														
339													1♀											1*	1*	
341												1♀														
409	1♀	4♀																								
Total ♀	*1*	*7*	*2*			*2*				*8*	*2*	*2*	*1*	*3*	*5*	*2*		*1*	*1*	*1*	*4*		*1*			
Total ♂				*3*	*4*	*4*	*4*	*3*	*6*						*1*		*3*	*1*				*3*				*1*
Total	**1**	**7**	**2**	**3**	**4**	**6**	**4**	**3**	**6**	**8**	**2**	**2**	**1**	**3**	**6**	**2**	**3**	**2**	**1**	**1**	**4**	**3**	**1**	**1***	**1***	**1**

* Furniture found in tomb not tomb illustration.

Appendix E

Distribution List of Replica Wooden Products Manufactured by the Author and Preserved in Museums and Private Collections

Product Type	Product Influence	Location	Plate No.
Folding stool with duck head terminals	British Museum, London: EA 29284; also fragment of duck head, World Museum, Liverpool: M11841	World Museum, Liverpool	
Folding stool with duck head terminals	British Museum, London: EA 29284; also fragment of duck head, Egypt Centre, Swansea: W2060	Egypt Centre, Swansea	81
Headrest	Egypt Centre, Swansea: AB80	Egypt Centre, Swansea	82
Chair	Egypt Centre, Swansea: W2059	Egypt Centre, Swansea	83
Chair	Ipswich Museum: 1932.27.1	Ipswich Museum, Ipswich	
Chair	Garstang Museum, University of Liverpool: E 7240, E 7241, E 7242	Garstang Museum, University of Liverpool	
Qersu coffin post and stub side panels	Irethereru; Fitzwilliam Museum: E.14.1926	Fitzwilliam Museum, Cambridge	85
Coffin section	Nespawershefyt; Fitzwilliam Museum: E.1.1822	Fitzwilliam Museum, Cambridge	84
Coffin section	Pakepu; Fitzwilliam Museum: E.2.1869	Fitzwilliam Museum, Cambridge	
Coffin corner panel mitre joint	Nakht; Fitzwilliam Museum: E.68.1903	Fitzwilliam Museum, Cambridge	
Kohl pot	Fitzwilliam Museum: E.GA.4575.1943	Fitzwilliam Museum, Cambridge	86
Carved hand for coffin lid	Fitzwilliam Museum: E.GA.2861.1943	Fitzwilliam Museum, Cambridge	87
Headrest	University Museum, Manchester: Inv. No. 3722	Fitzwilliam Museum, Cambridge	
Folding headrest	Petrie Museum of Egyptian Archaeology, UCL: UC 16756	Author's collection	3
Folding headrest	Petrie Museum of Egyptian Archaeology, UCL: UC 16756	University Museum, Manchester	88
Carved duck head	World Museum, Liverpool: M11841	University Museum, Manchester	
Stool leg	Garstang Museum, University of Liverpool: E 7242	University Museum, Manchester	
Box	Based on fragments excavated from the spoil pits at Abydos	Author's collection	
Offering table	Egyptian Museum, Cairo: JE 62057	Author's collection	69
Wood brick mould	University Museum, Manchester: Inv. No. 51	Private collection	
Replica Egyptian woodworking tool	Originals in British Museum	Author's collection	89

Plate 81. Replica folding stool with duck head terminals. Product influence: British Museum, London: EA 29284. Also fragment of duck head, Egypt Centre, Swansea. W2060. Location (2017): Egypt Centre, Swansea.© *G. Killen*

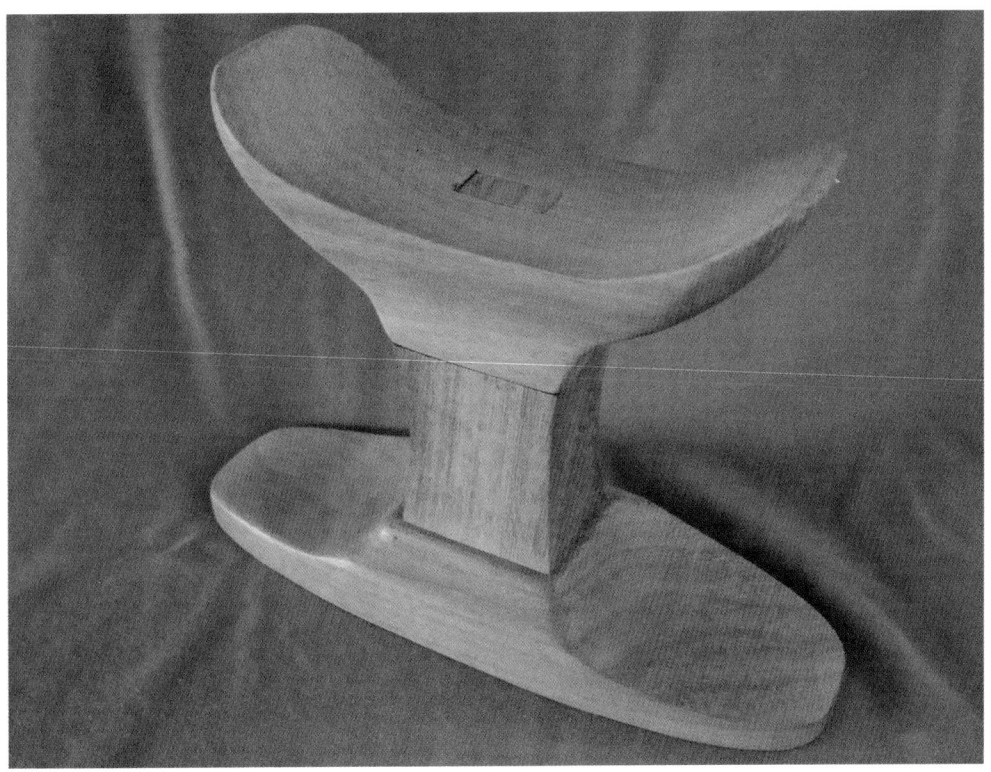

Plate 82. Replica headrest. Product influence: Egypt Centre, Swansea: AB80. Location (2017) Egypt Centre, Swansea. © *G. Killen*

Plate 83. Replica chair. Product influence: Egypt Centre, Swansea: W2059. Location (2017): Egypt Centre, Swansea. © *G. Killen*

Plate 84. Replica coffin section (Decoration: Elsbeth Geldhof, Historic paint conservator). Product influence: Nespawershefyt. Fitzwilliam Museum: E.1.1822. Location (2017): Fitzwilliam Museum, Cambridge. © *Lorraine March-Killen*

Plate 85. Replica Qersu coffin post and stub side panels (left). Product influence: Irethereru. Fitzwilliam Museum: E.14.1926. Location (2017): Fitzwilliam Museum, Cambridge. *© Lorraine March-Killen*

Left: Plate 86. Replica Kohl pot. Product influence: Fitzwilliam Museum: E.GA.4575.1943. Location (2017): Fitzwilliam Museum, Cambridge. © *G. Killen*

Below: Plate 87. Replica carved hand for coffin lid. Product influence: Fitzwilliam Museum: E.GA.2861.1943. Location (2017): Fitzwilliam Museum, Cambridge. © *G. Killen*

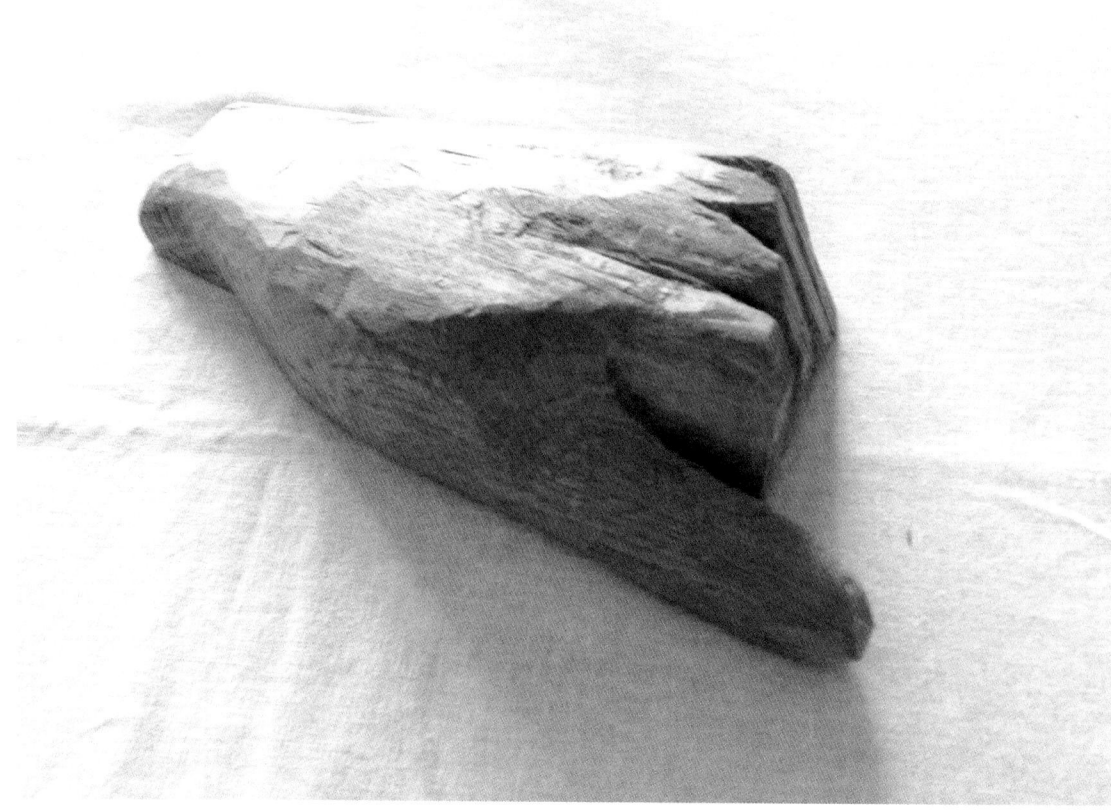

Plate 88. Replica folding headrest. Product influence: Petrie Museum of Egyptian Archaeology. UCL. UC 16756. Location (2017): University Museum, Manchester. © *Courtesy of Manchester Museum, University of Manchester.*

Plate 89. Replica Egyptian woodworking tools. Product influence: Originals in British Museum. Location (2017): Author's collection. © *Lorraine March-Killen*

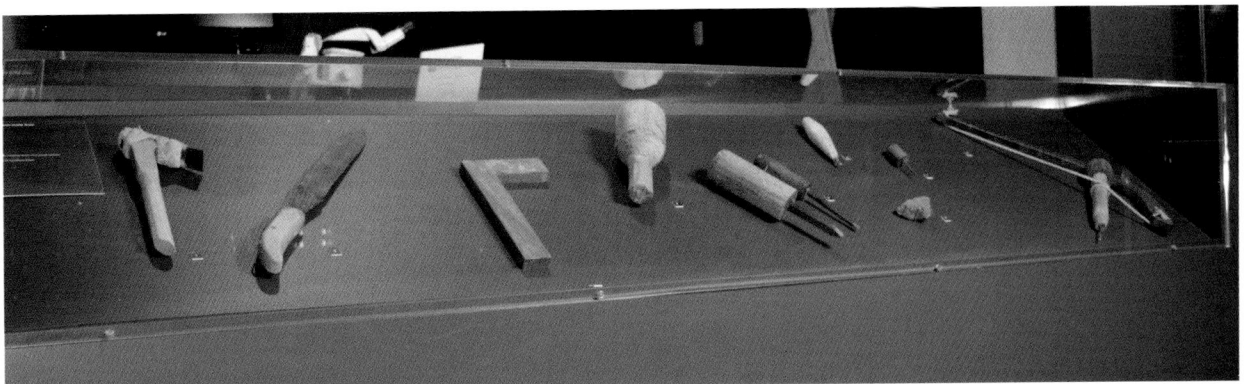

Plate 2. Folding headrest. Gurob. Petrie Museum of Egyptian Archaeology, UCL. UC 16756. *See also page 37.*

Plate 42 (far left). Bed leg carved in the form of the God Bes. Rijksmuseum van Oudheden, Leiden. Inv. No. F. 1964/1.4. *See also page 78.*

Plate 43. Bed leg (left) carved in the form of the God Bes. Rijksmuseum van Oudheden, Leiden. Inv. No. F. 1964/1.3. *See also page 78.*

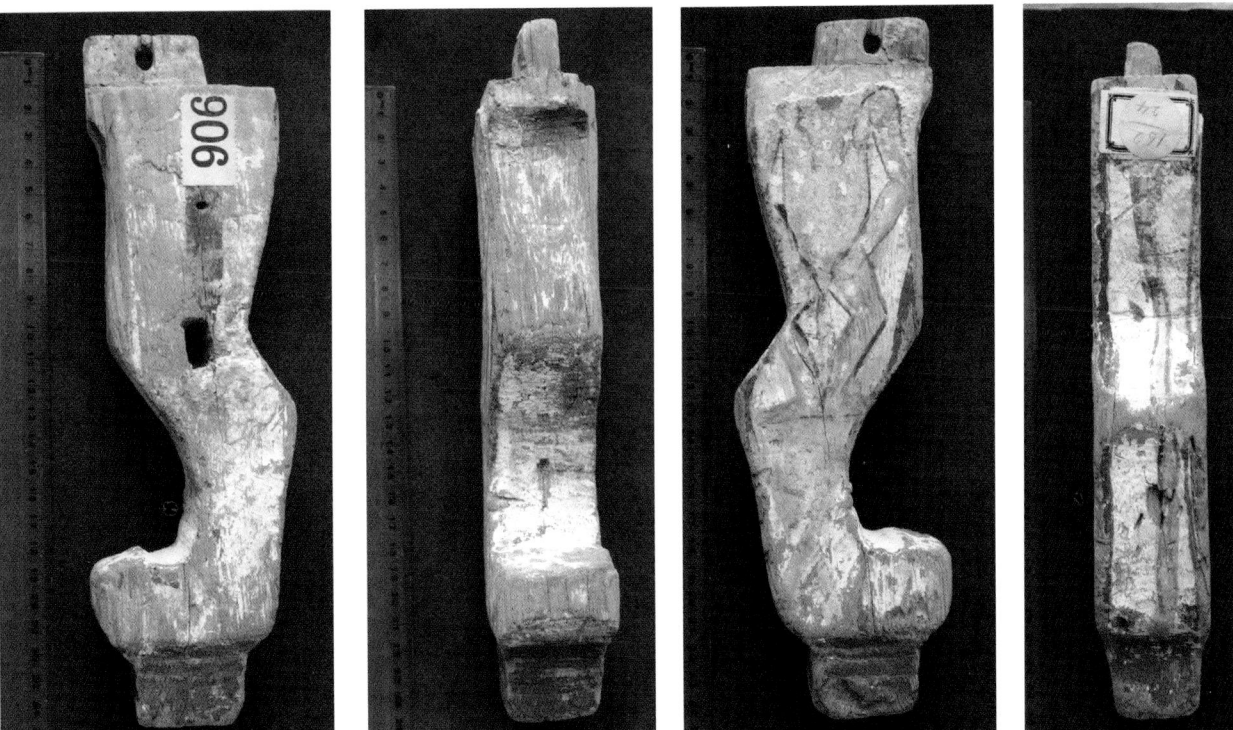

Plates 48–51. Lion leg with the painted depiction of God Bes. Egypt Centre, Swansea. Inv. No. W 2052a. *See also page 79.*

Plate 73. Painted chair illustrated as wall painting. Sarcophagus chamber of Tausert. Tomb of Tausert (19th Dynasty) and Setnakht (20th Dynasty) (1198–1194 B.C.) (KV14). *See also page 96.*

Left: Plate 54. Facsimile of tomb wall painting depicting a round legged bedframe, Tomb of Ipuy, (TT217). *See also page 80.*

Below: Plate 74. Bed frames. Tomb of Rameses III, (KV11). Hand coloured engraving made by Ippolito Rosellini published between 1832–1844. Rosellini 1832–1844: pl. XCII. *See also page 97.*

Plates 75–78. Various thrones. Tomb of Rameses III, (KV11). Hand coloured engraving made by Frédéric Cailliaud (1789–1869). Cailliaud 1831: (Bound volume no plate numbers). *See also page 97.*

Catalogue of Museum Collections

FRANCE: MUSÉE D'ARCHÉOLOGIE MÉDITERRANÉENNE, MARSEILLE

Inventory number	Description	Material	Date	Size in mm	Plate	Figure
93/2/1	Box	Painted wood	19th or 20th Dynasty	h. 420 l. 500 w. 350		
287	Chair, Deir el-Medina, Clot-Bey collection.	Painted wood	N.K.	h. 470 w. 330 d. 300		
288	Folding stool, Thebes, Clot-Bey collection	Wood	N.K.	h. 330 w. 450		

GERMANY: STAATLICHE MUSEEN ZU BERLIN, ÄGYPTISCHES MUSEUM BERLIN

Inventory number	Description	Material	Date	Size in mm	Plate	Figure
ÄM 625/630	Box, painted.					
ÄM 20472	Box					
ÄM 761	Small box with round lid					
ÄM 733	Box					
ÄM 723	Box					
ÄM 18610	Stool leg, bovine form	Ivory	1st Dynasty			

INDIA: GOVERNMENT CENTRAL MUSEUM, ALBERT HALL, JAIPUR

Inventory number	Description	Material	Date	Size in mm	Plate	Figure
10719	Box, inscribed to Iyneferti	Wood, painted	19th Dynasty	l. 259 w. 260 h. 120		V.III. 23

ITALY: EGYPTIAN MUSEUM, FLORENCE

Inventory number	Description	Material	Date	Size in mm	Plate	Figure
2681	Stool, square legs	Wood	N.K.			
2684	Stool, low with square legs	Wood	N.K.			
6898	Stool, lion legs, seat rails modern	Wood	N.K.			
6900	Stool, round legs	Wood	N.K.			
6901	Low stool. with shaped legs	Wood	N.K.			

Inventory number	Description	Material	Date	Size in mm	Plate	Figure
7945	Two panelled footboards from bedframes	Wood	N.K.			
6906	Chair or stool leg in lion form	Wood	N.K.			
6895	Bedframe	Wood	N.K.	l. 1,260 w. 670 h. 320		
2680	Chair	Wood, from Luxor	N.K.	h. 660 w. 495 d. 396		
6899	Chair or stool leg in lion form.	Wood	N.K.			
9484	Stool leg, bovine form	Wood	E.D.P.			
6904	Stool leg	Wood	N.K.			
9500	Stool leg	Wood	N.K.			
6905	Lion paw fragment from a stool leg	Wood	N.K.			
7933	Box	Reed and rush	N.K.			
645	Front leg of stool in form of lion's fore body	Wood	L.P.			
2682	Stool, low with straight legs	Wood				
6902	Chair, side seat stretcher with inlaid bracket	Wood and ivory				
6831	Stool leg, straight with crossing mortises for seat rails	Wood				
6896	Stools legs (pair), straight with crossing mortises for seat rails					

JAPAN: MIDDLE EASTERN CULTURE CENTER OF JAPAN, TOKYO

Inventory number	Description	Material	Date	Size in mm	Plate	Figure
M 00449	Stool, legs of lion form	Wood	19th Dynasty			

SPAIN: EGYPTIAN MUSEUM, BARCELONA

Inventory number	Description	Material	Date	Size in mm	Plate	Figure
E. 434	Bedframe, bovine form legs	Wood	O.K.	l. 2,030 w. 900 h. 330		

UNITED KINGDOM: BRITISH MUSEUM, LONDON

Inventory number	Description	Material	Date	Size in mm	Plate	Figure
EA 63533	Stool, Amarna	Limestone	N.K.	l. 115 w. 1,227		
EA 55067	Stool, three legged	Limestone	N.K.	l. 330 w. 250 h. 100		
EA 59728	Bedframe	Wood	N.K.	h. 305 w. 933 l. 2,030		
EA 72216	Furniture leg, lathe turned	Wood	L.P.	h. 387 dia. 60 w. 108		
EA 58470	Stool	Limestone	N.K.	h. 205 l. 320 w 245		
EA 61611	Bedframe fragment, cow head terminal	Wood and resin	N.K.	h. 260 l. 570 w. 240		
EA 61607	Bedframe fragment, hippopotamus head terminal	Wood and bitumen	N.K.	h. 250 l. 520 w. 150		
EA 21818	Box, with single flat lid	Wood	N.K.	l. 270 w. 275 h. 140	V.III. 55–62	V.III. 24
EA 34228	Furniture fragment	Wood	N.K.	l. 302 w. 23		
EA 65849	Furniture fragment	Wood, painted	N.K.	h. 49 d. 15 w. 5		
EA 24656	Bed leg, Sphinx form	Wood	25th Dynasty	h. 423 w. 70		
EA 38550	Chair backrest	Wood, painted	N.K.	h. 241 w. 265		
EA 20928	Stool leg	Wood	N.K.	h. 128 w. 48		
EA 20927	Stool leg	Wood	N.K.	h. 129 w. 53		
EA 20926	Stool leg	Wood	N.K.	h. 129 w. 53		
EA 20783	Stool fragment	Wood	L.P.	h. 330 w. 98		

Inventory number	Description	Material	Date	Size in mm	Plate	Figure
EA 74199	Chair leg, lion form, attached to fragment of seat rail	Wood	18th Dynasty	h. 310 w. 62 d. 100		
EA 55073	Chair leg fragment, lion's paw	Wood	N.K.	h. 107 w. 77		
EA 49125	Chair leg, lion form	Wood	N.K.	h. 265 w. 73		
EA 68262	Furniture fragment, part of a joint structure, Saqqara	Wood and gesso		w. 12 l. 56		
EA 26800	Furniture fragment, wooden panel.	Wood, gilded with inlaid glass		l. 420 w. 80		
EA 50984	Chair leg, lion form	Wood	N.K.	l. 154 w. 56		
EA 35813	Chair fragment, open-work representation of Taweret	African blackwood	N.K.	h. 249 t. 11		
EA 68167	Furniture fragment, Saqqara H5-153	Wood	L.P.	w. 33 l. 160		
EA 2504	Chair fragment	Sycomore fig		l. 172 dia. 47		
EA 47567	Model chair leg, lion form.	Wood	M.K.	w. 27 l. 81		
EA 49494	Model table, cylindrical	Wood	M.K.	h. 240 dia. 53		
EA 61610	Bedframe fragment, terminal in form of cow's head	Wood and resin	19th Dynasty	h. 205 w. 250 l. 415		
EA 74106	Bes figure furniture fragment	Wood	N.K.	h. 270 w. 105 d. 70		
EA 58082	Stool, manufactured to resemble turned work	Wood and glazed composite	M.K.	h. 181 l. 114		
EA 90159	Stool leg, bovine form	Wood		l. 235		
EA 90184	Two bovine formed legs	Wood		l. 240		
EA 13513	Chair, bronze frame and feet, wooden legs	Wood and bronze	R.P.	h. 518 l. 556 w. 378		

Inventory number	Description	Material	Date	Size in mm	Plate	Figure
EA 23443	Bedframe fragment	Bronze	L.P.	l. 139 h. 1,031		
EA 71019	Furniture fragment, includes name of Ptolemy V	Wood, plaster, linen, glass	P.P.	l. 332 w. 51		
EA 5907	Box, with shrine shaped lid, dedicated to the sailor Denreg	Wood, painted	N.K.	l. 338 w. 247 h. 250	V.III. 63–67	V.III. 25

UNITED KINGDOM: EGYPT CENTRE, UNIVERSITY OF SWANSEA, SWANSEA

Inventory number	Description	Material	Date	Size in mm	Plate	Figure
EC 8	Lion head, furniture fragment	Wood	N.K.			
EC 11	Furniture leg, lion form	Wood				
EC 609a	Furniture fragment	Wood				
EC 701	Handle	Wood				
EC 781	Pair of lathe turned legs	Wood				
W 355	Chair leg, lion form	Wood	N.K.			

UNITED KINGDOM: IPSWICH MUSEUM, IPSWICH

Inventory number	Description	Material	Date	Size in mm	Plate	Figure
1921.89.47	Box lid fragment	Wood	19th Dynasty Sedment, Cemetery A, Grave 131	l. 150 w. 36 t. 6		
1921.89.46	Box lid fragment with mushroom shaped handle	Wood	19th Dynasty Sedment, Cemetery A, Grave 131	l. 307 w. 102 t. 11		
1932.27.6	Box lid fragment	Wood	N.K.	h. 330 w. 282 t. 11		
1932.27.1	Chair, original legs with modern seat rails	Wood	12th Dynasty	h. 340 d. 330 w. 330		
1944.44.34	Stool leg	Wood.	12th Dynasty	h. 200 w. 40		

UNITED KINGDOM: FITZWILLIAM MUSEUM, CAMBRIDGE

Inventory number	Description	Material	Date	Size in mm	Plate	Figure
E.236.1932	Bedframe footboard slat, embellished with the God Bes	Wood	N.K.	h. 203	V.III. 52	
E.GA. 2681.1943	Bedframe footboard slat, in shape of the god Bes	Wood	N.K.	h. 201	V.III. 53	

UNITED KINGDOM: MUSEUM OF ARCHAEOLOGY AND ANTHROPOLOGY, CAMBRIDGE

Inventory number	Description	Material	Date	Size in mm	Plate	Figure
MAA. 1948.2744	Box rail, from tomb of Rameses IX, found in tomb DB 320, from a box preserved in Egyptian Museum, Cairo, JE 26271, on loan to the Fitzwilliam Museum	Wood and ivory	20th Dynasty	l. 160 w. 24 t. 14		
MAA. Z 45809	Box lid	Wood		l. 123 w. 50 t. 6		

UNITED KINGDOM: VICTORIA AND ALBERT MUSEUM, LONDON

Inventory number	Description	Material	Date	Size in mm	Plate	Figure
475-1908	Stool leg, roughly shaped to a round form with an adze	Wood	N.K.			
751-1907	Stool leg, round form					
510-1891	Stool leg, turned					
534A-1891	Stool leg, turned	Wood	N.K.			
557A-1891	Stool leg, assembled from wooden rings on a metal pillar	Wood	R.P.			
536-1891	Stool leg, turned	Wood	R.P.			
540-1891	Furniture leg, slender leg with lion form foot	Wood	R.P.			
533-1891	Stool leg, turned	Wood	R.P.			
541-1891	Round pole	Wood	R.P.			

Inventory number	Description	Material	Date	Size in mm	Plate	Figure
537-1891	Round pole, furniture element? Wooden spike at one end	Wood	R.P.			
532-1891	Stool leg, turned	Wood	R.P.			

UNITED KINGDOM: WESTON PARK MUSEUM, SHEFFIELD

Inventory number	Description	Material	Date	Size in mm	Plate	Figure
J1939.58	Chair leg, lion form	Wood	N.K.	h. 157 w. 50 d. 38		
J5.5.80. 1–6	Stool fragments, three ancient turned legs and three ancient stretchers	Wood	N.K.	h. 210 w. 295		

UNITED STATES OF AMERICA: AMERICAN MUSEUM OF NATURAL HISTORY, NEW YORK

Inventory number	Description	Material	Date	Size in mm	Plate	Figure
2316 a,b 1804 a,b	Box, with dovetailed corners	Wood	17th Dynasty			
2320/4989	Furniture fragment	Wood	N.K.			
2323/6466	Furniture fragment	Wood	N.K.			
2324 a,b 6479 a,b	Furniture fragment	Wood	N.K.			
2325/6464	Furniture fragment	Wood	N.K.			
2326/5836	Furniture fragment	Wood	N.K.			
2327/6465	Furniture fragment	Wood	N.K.			
2430 a,b/ 7752	Legs and stretchers from two stools	Wood	N.K.			
95/2480B	Stool leg	Wood				
95/2430A	Stool leg and stretcher	Wood				
95/2430B	Stool stretcher	Wood				

UNITED STATES OF AMERICA: BROOKLYN MUSEUM, NEW YORK

Inventory number	Description	Material	Date	Size in mm	Plate	Figure
37.253 LC	*Djed* symbol from a piece of furniture	Wood				
37.253 LA	*Tyet* symbol from a piece of furniture	Wood				
08.4.80.177	*Tyet* symbol from a piece of furniture	Wood				
37.2.66 L	Duck head from folding stool	Wood				
37.2.466 L	Folding stool leg	Wood				
37.444 LA	Stool leg, gazelle form	Wood				
60.1.1	Box, veneered with ivory strips	Wood and ivory				
36.290.1	Stool leg, bovine form	Wood	E.D.P.			

UNITED STATES OF AMERICA: THE FIELD MUSEUM OF NATURAL HISTORY, CHICAGO

Inventory number	Description	Material	Date	Size in mm	Plate	Figure
30071	Bed	Wood	E.D.P.			
30072	Bed	Wood	E.D.P.			
30073	Stool	Wood				
88901	Chair with feline legs	Wood	N.K.			
105205	Box	Wood				

Bibliography

Allam, S. 1973. *Hieratische Ostraka und Papyri aus der Ramessidenzei*. Tübingen: Selbstverlag.

Andreu, G. 1997. *L'Egypte ancienne au Louvre*. Paris: Hachette.

Assmann, J. 1991. *Das Grab des Amenemope, TT 41*. Mainz am Rhein: von Zabern.

Baker, H.S. 1966. *Furniture in the Ancient World: Origins & Evolution, 3100-475 B.C.* London: The Connoisseur.

Baud, M. 1935. *Les Dessins Étauchés de la Nécropole Thébaine*. Cairo: IFAO.

Brunner-Traut, E.1956. *Die Altägyptischen Scherbenbilder der Deutschen Museen und Sammlungen*. Wiesbaden: Franz Steiner.

Bruyère, B. 1924. *Rapport sur les Fouilles de Deir el Médineh (1922–1923)*. Cairo: IFAO.

Bruyère, B. 1925. *Rapport Sur Les Fouilles de Deir el Médineh (1923–1924)*. Cairo: IFAO.

Bruyère, B. 1926. *Rapport Sur Les Fouilles de Deir el Médineh (1924–1925)*. Cairo: IFAO.

Bruyère, B. and Kuentz, C. 1926. *Tombes thébaines: La Nécropole de Deir el-Médineh: La tombe de Nakht-Min et la tombe d'Ari-Nefer*. Cairo: IFAO.

Bruyère, B. 1927. *Rapport Sur Les Fouilles de Deir el Médineh (1926)*. Cairo: IFAO.

Bruyère, B. 1928. *Rapport Sur Les Fouilles de Deir el Médineh (1927)*. Cairo: IFAO.

Bruyère, B. 1929. *Rapport Sur Les Fouilles de Deir el Médineh (1928)*. Cairo: IFAO.

Bruyère, B. 1930. *Rapport Sur Les Fouilles de Deir el Médineh (1929)*. Cairo: IFAO.

Bruyère, B. 1933. *Rapport Sur Les Fouilles de Deir el Médineh (1930)*. Cairo: IFAO.

Bruyère, B. 1937A. *Rapport Sur Les Fouilles de Deir el Médineh (1933–1934)*. Cairo: IFAO.

Bruyère, B. 1937B. *Rapport Sur Les Fouilles de Deir el Médineh (1934–1935)*. Cairo: IFAO.

Bruyère, B. 1939. *Rapport Sur Les Fouilles de Deir el Médineh (1934–1935)*. Cairo: IFAO.

Bruyère, B. 1952. *Tombes Thébaines de Deir el Médineh à decoration monochrome*. Cairo: IFAO.

Bruyère, B. 1959. *La Tombe N° 1 De Sen-nedjem, A Deir el Médineh*. Cairo: IFAO.

BS EN 1729-1: 2006. *Furniture – Chairs and tables for educational institutions, Part 1 : Functional dimensions*. BSI.

Cailliaud, F. 1831. *Recherches sur les et arts métiers ; les usages des anciens peuples de l'Egypte, de Nubie et de l'Ethiopie*. Paris.

Calverley, A.M.; Broom, M.F. and A.H. Gardiner. 1933. *The temple of King Sethos I at Abydos. Vol. 1. The chapels of Osiris, Isis and Horus*. Chicago: EES & Oriental Institute.

Calverley, A.M ; Broom, M.F. and A.H. Gardiner. 1935. *The temple of King Sethos I at Abydos. Vol. 2. The chapels of Amen-Re', Re'-Harakhti, Ptah, and King Sethos*. Chicago: EES & Oriental Institute.

Černý, J. 1973. *A Community of Workmen at Thebes in the Ramesside Period*. Cairo: IFAO.

Cherpion, N. 1999. *Deux tombes de la XVIIIe dynastie à Deir el-Medina: Nos 340 (Amenemhat) et 354 (anonyme)*. Cairo: IFAO.

Cooney, K. M. 2006. T. *An Informal Workshop: Textual Evidence for Private Art Production in the Ramesside Period. In, Living and Writing in Deir el-Medine, Socio-historical Embodiment of Deir el-Medine Texts* (eds. Dorn, A. and Hofmann, T). Basel: Ægyptiaca Helvetica, 19: 43–56.

D'Auria, S.H. 1990. In Lacovara, P. *Deir el-Ballas: Preliminary report on the Deir el-Ballas Expedition, 1980-1986*. American Research Center in Egypt, Volume 12, Winona Lake, Indiana.

D'Auria, S.H. (ed) 2008. *Servant of Mut, Studies in Honor of Richard A. Fazzini*. Leiden and Boston: Brill.

D'Abbadie, V. and Jourdain, G. 1939. *Deux Tombes de Deir el Médineh, II La Tombe du scribe royal Amenempot.* Cairo: IFAO.

Daressy, G. 1902. *Catalogue Général des Antiquités Égyptiennes du Musée du Caire, Fouilles de la Vallée des Rois (1898–1899).* Cairo: IFAO.

Davies, N. de G. 1927. *Two Ramesside Tombs at Thebes.* New York: MMA.

Davies, N. de G. and Gardiner, A.H. (ed.) 1948. *Seven Private Tombs at Kurnah.* London: EES.

Demarée, R.J. 2002. *Ramesside Ostraca.* London: BMP.

Description de l'Egypte, 1821. Volume II. Paris: Imprimerie impériale.

Eaton-Krauss, M. 1997. Three stools from the tomb of Sennedjem, TT1, 179–192. In *Ancient Egypt, the Aegean, and the Near East: Studies in Honour of Martha Rhoads Bell*, I. (ed. Phillips, J). San Antonio: Van Sicklen Books.

Eaton-Krauss, M. 1989. Walter Segal's Documentation of CG 51113, the throne of the Princess Sat-Amun. *JEA* 75: 77-88.

Eaton-Krauss, M. 2008. *The Thrones, Chairs, Stools, and Footstools from the Tomb of Tutankhamun.* Oxford: Griffith Institute.

Emery, W.B. 1949. *Great Tombs of the First Dynasty*, Volume I, Cairo: Government Press.

Emery, W.B. 1954. *Great Tombs of the First Dynasty*, Volume II, London: OUP.

Faulkner, R.O.1985. *The Ancient Egyptian Book of the Dead*; edited by Carol Andrews. London: Published for the Trustees of the British Museum by British Museum Publications.

Fischer, H.G. 1986. Stuhl, in Helck, F.W. and Westendorf, W. LÄ, 6: 91-99.

Garstang, J. 1907. *The Burial Customs of Ancient Egypt as illustrated by tombs of the Middle Kingdom : being a report of excavations made in the necropolis of Beni Hassan during 1902–4.* London: Constable.

Green, C. I. 1987. *The Temple Furniture from the Sacred Animal Necropolis at North Saqqâra. 1964–1976.* London: EES.

Guilmant, F. 1907. *Le tombeau de Ramses IX.* Cairo: IFAO.

Haring, B. 2000. Towards decoding the necropolis workmen's funny signs. *GM*, 178: 45–58.

Helck, W. 2002. *Die datierten und datierbaren Ostraka, Papyri und Graffiti von Deir el-Medineh.* Wiesbaden: Harrassowitz.

Hofmann, E. 1995. *Das Grab des Neferrenpet gen Kenro (TT 178).* Mainz: von Zabern.

James, T.G.H. 1970. *Hieroglyphic texts from Egyptian stelae, etc.* 9. British Museum: BMP.

Janssen, J.J. 1975. *Commodity Prices from the Ramessid Period, An Economic Study of the Village Necropolis Workmen at Thebes.* Leiden: E.J. Brill.

Janssen J.J., Frood, E. and Goecke-Bauer, M. 2003. *Woodcutters, Potters and Doorkeepers, Service Personnel of the Deir el-Medina Workmen.* Leiden: Nederlands Instituut Voor Het Nabije Oosten.

Janssen, J.M.A. 1955. Die Grabstele des Ptahemheb (Theben Nr. 193). In *Ägyptologische Studien, Institut Für Orientiorschung Veröffentlichung*, 29 (ed. Firchow). Berlin: Deutsche Akademie der Wissenschaften zu Berlin.

Kemp, B. 1978. 'The harim-palace at Medinet el-Ghurab', *ZÄS* 105: 122–133.

Killen, G. 1980. *Ancient Egyptian Furniture, 4000–1300 BC, I.* Warminster: Aris and Phillips.

Killen, G. 1994. *Ancient Egyptian Furniture, Boxes, Chests and Footstools, II.* Warminster: Aris and Phillips.

Killen, G. 2002. John Garstang's discovery of wooden furniture at the Middle Kingdom necropolis of Beni Hasan. In *Egyptian Museum Collections around the World* (eds. Eldamaty, M. and Trad, M.). Cairo: Supreme Council of Antiquities.

Killen, G. and Weiss, L. 2009. Markings on Objects of Daily Use from Deir El-Medina, Ownership Marks or Administrative Aids? In *Non-Textual Marking Systems, Writing and Pseudo Script from Prehistory to Modern Times* (eds. Andrássy, P. Budka, J. and Kammerzell. F). Göttingen: Lingua Aegyptia – Studia monographica 8: 137–158.

Killen, G. 2015. Woodworking. In *Egyptology in the Present: Experiential and Experimental Methods in Archaeology* (ed. Graves-Brown). The Classical Press of Wales: 91–111.

Killen, G. 2017A. *Ancient Egyptian Furniture, 4000–1300 BC, I.* Oxford: Oxbow Books. Second Edition.

Killen, G. 2017B. *Ancient Egyptian Furniture, Boxes, Chests and Footstools, II.* Oxford: Oxbow Books. Second Edition.

Killen, G. 2017C. *Ancient Egyptian Furniture, Ramesside Furniture, III.* Oxford: Oxbow Books.

Kitchen, K.A. 1993. *Ramesside Inscriptions/Translated and Annotated: Translations*, I. Oxford: Blackwell.

Lopez, J. 1978. *Ostraca ieratici.* Milano: Cisalpino-La Goliardica.

Lucas, A. 1926. *Ancient Egyptian Materials.* London.

Mahmoud Abd el-Qader, A. 2011. (ed. Sylvie Donnat). *Catalogue of Funerary Objects from the Tomb of the Servant in the Place of Truth Sennedjem (TT1)*. IFAO.

Manniche, L. 1988. *Lost tombs: a study of certain eighteenth dynasty monuments in the Theban Necropolis*. London: KPI.

Martin, G.T. 1985. *The tomb-chapels of Paser and Raia at Saqqara*. London: EES.

Martin, G.T. 1997. *The Tomb of Tia and Tia: A Royal Monument of the Ramesside Period in the Memphite Necropolis*. London: EES.

Martin, G.T. 2001. *The Tombs of Three Memphite Officials: Ramose, Khay and Pabes*. London: EES.

Maystre, C. 1936. *Tombes de Deir El-Médineh, La Tombe de Nebenmât (No 219)*. Cairo: IFAO.

McDowell, A.G. 1993. *Hieratic Ostraca in the Hunterian Museum Glasgow (The Colin Campbell Ostraca)*. Oxford: Griffith Institute.

McDowell, A.G. 1999. *Village Life in Ancient Egypt: Laundry Lists and Love Songs*. Oxford: OUP.

Negm, M. 1997. *The Tomb of Simut called Kyky, Theban Tomb 409 at Qurnah*. Warminster: Aris and Phillips.

OIP 94, 1970: University of Chicago Oriental Institute. *Epigraphic Survey. Medinet Habu*. Volume VIII. Chicago: Oriental Institute Publications.

Peterson, B.E.J. 1973. *Zeichnungen aus einer Totenstadt*: Stockholm: Medelhavsmuseet Bulletin 7-8.

Petrie, W.M.F. 1890. *Kahun, Gurob and Hawara*. London: K. Paul, Trench, Trübner.

Petrie, W.M.F. and Brunton, G. 1924. *Sedment II*. London: BSAE.

Petrie, W.M.F. 1927. *Objects of Daily Use*. London: BSAE.

Piankoff, A. 1954. *The tomb of Ramesses VI*. New York: Pantheon Books.

Porter, B. and Moss, R. 1960. *Topographical Bibliography of Ancient Egyptian Hieroglyphic Texts, Reliefs, and Paintings I, Part 1. The Theban Necropolis, Private Tombs*. Oxford: Griffith Institute.

Prisse d'Avennes, E. 1997. *Atlas of Egyptian Art*. Cairo: American University in Cairo Press.

Quaegebeur, J. 1994. *La table d'offrandes grande et pure d'Amon*. Volume dédié à la mémoire de Charles Maystre, La Société Française d'Égyptologie. Paris: RdE, 45: 155-173.

Raven, M.J. 1991. *The Tomb of Iurudef: A Memphite Official in the Reign of Ramesses II*. Leiden: National Museum of Antiquities, and London: EES.

Reisner, G.A. 1955. *A History of the Giza Necropolis, The Tomb of Hetep-Heres the mother of Cheops*. Volume II. Cambridge, Massachussetts: Harvard University Press.

Ricke, H. Hughes, G.R and Wente, E.F. 1967. *The Beit el-Wali Temple of Ramesses II*. The University of Chicago Oriental Institute Nubian Expedition, Volume I. Chicago.

Robins, G. 1993. *Women in Ancient Egypt*. London: BMP.

Robins, G. 1997. *The Art of Ancient Egypt*. London: BMP.

Rosellini, I. 1832–1844. *Monumenti dell'Egitto e della Nubia: disegnati dalla spedizione scientifico-letteraria toscana in Egitto; distribuiti in ordine di materie*. Pisa: Presso N. Capurro e c.

Schiaparelli, E. 1924 and 1927. R*elazione sui lavori della Missione archeologica italiana in Egitto, anni 1903–1920, La tomba intatta dell'architetto Cha nella necropoli di Tebe*, 2 volumes. Torino: Museo di antichità.

Schneider, H. D. 1997, *Life and Death under the Pharaohs*. Perth.

Seele, K.C. 1959. *The Tomb of Tjanefer at Thebes*. Chicago: The University of Chicago Press.

Seyfried, K-J. 1990. *Das Grab des Amonmose (TT 373)*. Mainz am Rhein: von Zabern.

Seyfried, K-J. 1995. *Das Grab des Djehutiemhab (TT 194)*. Mainz am Rhein: von Zabern.

Silvano, F. 2004. Catalogue of Jaipur, Central Government Museum. In *Egypt in India: Egyptian Antiquities in Indian Museums* (eds. Bresciani, E. and Betró, M.C). Pisa: Pisa University Press.

Smith, H.S. and Stewart H.M. 1984. The Gurob Shrine Papyrus. London: *JEA* 70: 54-64.

Spencer, N. 2009. Cemeteries and Late Ramesside Suburb at Amara West, In *Sudan and Nubia*. London: SARS 13: 47-61.

Spencer, P. 1997. *Amara West, I. The Architectural Report*. London: EES.

Spencer, P. 2002. *Amara West, II. The cemetery and the pottery corpus*. London: EES.

Steindorff, G. 1937. *Aniba, Mission Archéologique de Nubie 1929–1934*. 2 vols, Gluckstadt: SAE.

Strouhal, E. 1992. *Life in Ancient Egypt*. Cambridge: CUP.

Strudwick, N. 1996. *The Tombs of Amenhotep, Khnummose, and Amenmose at Thebes*, 2 vols. Oxford: Griffith Institute.

Thomas, A. 1981. *Gurob: A New Kingdom Town*, Warminster: Aris and Phillips.

Toivari-Viitala. J. 2001. *Women at Deir el-Medina: A study of the status and roles of the female inhabitants in the workmen's community during the Ramesside Period*. Leiden: Nederlands Instituut Voor Het Nabije Oosten.

Valbelle, D. 1975. *La Tombe de Hay, À Deir El-Médineh (No 267).* Cairo: IFAO.

Valbelle, D. 1985, *Les Ouviers de las tombe; Deir-el-Médineh à l'époque Ramesside.* Cairo: IFAO.

Vandier, J. 1935. *Tombes de Deir El-Médineh, La Tombe de Nefer-Abou.* Cairo: IFAO.

Vandier, J. 1954. *Deux Tombes Ramessides À Gournet-Mourraï.* Cairo: IFAO.

Wente, E.F. 1967. *Late Ramesside Letters.* Chicago: University of Chicago Press.

Wild, Henri, 1979. *La Tombe de Néfer.hotep (1) et Neb.néfer à Deir El-Médîna (No 6).* Cairo: IFAO.

Zivie, A-P, 1979. *La tomb de Pached à Deir El-Médîna (No 3).* Cairo: IFAO.